ADMINISTRATION OF SALES TAX

Administration of Sales Tax

By

Dr. Radhey Shyam Sharma

ATLANTIC PUBLISHERS & DISTRIBUTORS
B-2, Vishal Enclave, Najafgarh Road,
NEW DELHI-110027

Published by
Atlantic Publishers & Distributors
B-2, Vishal Enclave, Najafgarh Road,
New Delhi-110027
Phone: 5413460

Printed by
Typographers (India) at Rashtravani Printers,
A-49/1, Mayapuri, Phase I, New Delhi.

Dedicated to
my beloved grand-father
late Shri Chuni lal Pandia

Jaipur
Rajasthan

Heera Lal Indora,
State Minister,
Finance, Mines, Industries &
Social Welfare.

Date 4th November, 1987

FOREWORD

I am glad to write this foreword to Dr. R.S. Sharma's study of the "Administration of Sales Tax." The work was originally prepared as a thesis for the degree of Doctor of Philosophy under the guidance of Professor M.C. Khandelwal, Dean, Faculty of Commerce, University of Rajasthan, Jaipur. In the present form it has been considerably revised in the light of recent developments.

Sales Tax being State's major source of revenue and contributing 66% of the revenue in Rajasthan, plays a very important role in the development of the State. It is an instrument of development finance. Keeping in view the growing importance and controversy about sales tax, Dr. Sharma has analysed the issue in the field of indirect taxation in very lucid and critical manner. The presentation of the study shows a commendable grip on the theoretical aspects as well as practical working of the sales tax administration. His recommendations regarding the reforms of sales tax will go a long way in solving some of the important problems of sales taxation and his suggestions if implemented would yield higher revenue to the state exchequer.

Sd.
Heeralal Indora

PREFACE

In a federal state like India, the financing of developmental plans in public sector depends, to a great extent, on the mobilisation of resources by the State Governments through an effective utilisation of their powers of taxation. In state taxation, the importance of sales tax needs no exaggeration. In modern times, it has come to occupy an important place in the developed as well as the developing countries. Particularly, in India, this tax holds a very important place in the fiscal structure.

At present, sales tax occupies the key position in the budget of the state governments. It is the most elastic and major source of revenue of the states and known as KAMDHENU, but since its inception states are facing manifold problems in the operation of this tax. Moreover, frequent amendments have been made in the name of simplification and to streamline the working of Sales Tax Department but they have yielded no positive results so far. Therefore, sales taxation still needs empirical investigations on many counts, specially with reference to developing countries.

The present study aims to analyse the working of Sales Tax Departments of the states of Rajasthan, Uttar Pradesh, Haryana and Punjab and to identify the problems in operation of sales tax so that the suggestions for the solution of these problems may be put forward accordingly. To make this study more beneficial and to explore the idea of 'Zonal Sales Tax Administration', a comparative study of these four neighbouring states has been made because in operation of the sales tax, the rate structure, administrative organisation and policies of the neighbouring states play an important role.

The book contains seven chapters. The first chapter has been devoted to the introduction of the subject of study including the brief history of the sales taxation. The chapter two deals with the states' dependence on sales tax. It signifies the role of sales tax in states taxes, total taxes, indirect taxes and growth of sales tax during the period 1975-76 to 1983-84. In this chapter it has also been discussed whether sales tax can be abolished.

Chapter three examines inter-state rate structure. It reveals how in the operation of sales tax, rate structure plays an important role. Rate differentiation creates many operational problems and also gives the incentives to tax dodgers. In chapter four and five a study of the organisational structure and other operational aspects of sales tax has been made.

Chapter six analyses the incidence of sales tax with respect to population and states' net domestic products, and also studies the commodity-wise importanee of the sales tax. All the above mentioned issues have been brought together in the last chapter *viz.*, summary of findings and suggestions.

Much of the work in the study is based on the data collected from the Commercial Taxes Department, Rajasthan, Excise and Taxation Department, Haryana and Punjab, Sales Tax Department, Uttar Pradesh and Directorate of Economics and Statistics, Rajasthan. I thank the officials of these bodies for providing me all the help needed from time to time.

I am grateful to Shri Heera Lal Indora, Honourable State Minister of Finance, Mines, Industries and Social Welfare, Government of Rajasthan for his constant advice and encouragement in my academic pursuit and for writing the foreword of this book.

The work has been completed under the able guidance and supervision of Professor M.C. Khandelwal, Dean of Facutly of Commerce, Director, P.G. School of Commerce and Principal, University Studies in Commerce, Jaipur. Words can hardly express my sense of sincere and deep gratitude and indebtedness to him for his large heartedness. Professor Khandelwal's scholarly and valuable advice, encouragement, inspiration, positive attitude and kind cooperation have helped me in completing this book.

It is a matter of great pleasure for me to acknowledge my indebtedness to all faculty members of my Deptt. whose cooperation helped me in completion of this book. I am particularly thankful to Prof. K.S. Mathur; Dr. D.C. Jain; Shri

M.L. Oswal; Dr. Som Doe; Dr. S.G. Sharma; Dr. G.L. Gaur; for rendering their helping hands from time to time.

A special word of appreciation is also due to Mr. K.R. Gupta, Atlantic Publishers and Distributors, NEW DELHI for publishing this work well in time and in delightful get-up.

It will be my moral duty to mention the name of my elder brother Shri H.L. Pandia, Assistant Commercial Taxes Officer, Jaipur for his perennial encouragement in my life.

I am sure that because of the blessings and encouragement of my parents and family members the work could see the light of thc day.

Radhey Shyam Sharma

CONTENTS

1

INTRODUCTION

The modern form of sales taxation in all the States of India, is of recent origin. However, it's imposition can be traced back to very early period in world history. There are proofs to conclude that a tax on sales or purchases of goods had existed and used to be levied and collected in one or the other form in ancient time. Taxes were levied in ancient Egypt, Greece and China. It was found in the Greek City States (404-354 B.C.) that the Athens levied various taxes on the sale of commodities in the market including a transfer tax of the sales of wholesale merchants and a tax on the sales of landed property.[1] References of such a levy are also found in Egypt under Ptolemaic Dynasty (343-335 B.C.) with rates as high as 5 per cent.[2]

Historical Background of Sales Tax in the World

In 6 A D. Roman Emperor Augustus introduced the *Centi sima rerum venalium* which was a one per cent general sales or turnover tax. It was applied only to goods sold at auction which was their customary method of marketing of all commodities except articles of domestic consumption. This tax was continued during the reign of Tiberius with rates reduced temporarily to one half per cent during 17 A.D. Caligula removed it for sometime but it was reimposed by Claudius. The tax was still levied during the reign of Nero (54-68 A.D.) and it further included a levy of 4 per cent on the sale of slaves.[3]

1. August, Boekh: *The Public Economy of the Athenians*, Little, Brown and Co, Boston, 1857, pp. 422-33.
2. Sir John Mahaffy. *History of Egypt Under Ptolemaic Dynasty*, C. Scribner's Sons, New York, 1897, p, 164.
3. Cliton V. Oster: *State Retail Sales Taxation*, The Ohio State University, Ohio, 1957, pp. 8-9.

The Romans brought general sales taxation to Spain and France where it was continued after the Roman lost control of Western Europe.[4] In France a general tax was imposed by king Philip at the rate of 5/12 per cent even before 1292. It was repeated and reimposed many times. In fact the tax was so unpopular in France that no substantial yield could be collected. This general unpopularity of the tax over the years made the tax to be abolished at the outbreak of French Revolution.

There are evidences that in Italy, Naples collected sales tax in fifteenth century. Survival of this tax in the later years has been referred to by Adam Smith also.[5] Prof. Buehler in this regard states that "Spain was the only nation in the medieval period of public finance that collected the general sales tax as a regular source of revenue."[6] Spain introduced *alcavala* as a national tax in 1342. Alcavala, over the years, rose to heavy rates of 10 to 15 per cent and it was levied on every stage of production and distribution process which created a serious burden on industry, trade and commerce as well as on the consumers. It was widely known and hated. It had been charactecrised as the most notorious tax in the history of taxation. Adam Smith had condemned it as a major factor in the decay of Spain.[7] Finally, this tax was repeated in 1819 but its remnants were witnessed in Uruguay up to 1852 and in Mexico in the early 20th century.[8]

Historical Background of Sales Tax in India

The taxes on sales and purchases have a long history in India too. A tax on the sales and purchases of goods was not unknown even during the period when Maharishi Manu compiled his famous book "Manu Samriti."[9] In the early traces of sales taxes were rather obscure, and there is very little informa-

4. Alfred G. Buehler: *General Sales Taxation*: The Business Course, New York, 1932, p. 3.
5. Adam Smith: *The Wealth of Nations*, Random House, New York. 1937, pp. 850-51.
6. A.G. Buehler: *op. cit.*, pp. 4-5.
7. Adam Smith: *op cit.*, pp. 850-51.
8. John F. Due: *Sales Taxation*, Routledge and Kegan Paul, London, 1957, p. 2.
9. Sunil Rajan Sarkar: "Sales Tax Has a History in India," *Indian Journal of Economics*, Vol. 34, October, 1953, p. 93.

tion on how they actually operated. During the times of Maurayan (323-185 B.C.), there have been a positive evidence of the fact that some form of tax on sale of cows, grains and gold was well recognised. Mention of this sort made by Megasthenes, shows that the rate of sales tax was 1/10th of prices of the articles sold.[10]

Arthasastra does provide clear evidence of such a levy. In its section on law and polity, there is found a mass of rules regulating sales taxation. Kautilya states[11] that the superintendent of merchandise (Panyadhyaksa) was required to collect, *inter alia*, compensation fee (Vyaji) on the sale of royal merchandise which was imposed according to the manner of sales to the extent of 1/10th on those sold by weight and 1/11th on those sold by counting.[12] We find that the tax was also charged on the sale of liquor as compensation fee (Vyaji) as well as sulka at the rate of 5 per cent. There are specific references of the tax on the sale of threads, oil, ghee, sugar[13] and on salt as well as on the sale of animals. In regard to sales tax, other than these references, in the Arthasastra there are lot of rules regarding differential rates, operations and administration of the tax including rules and punishment of evasion.

It is believed that in India this tax was also levied during Scythian period as it had been continuing from the earlier periods. Also there are reasons to believe that the tax which existed during Mauryan period was not abolished during the Gupta period.[14] There are reference of the 'grants of exemptions' from payment of Klripta and Upaklripta—the taxes which has been characterised by Mookerji as a sales tax.[15]

10. Dr. Radha Kumud Mookerji: *Chandra Gupta Maurya and His Times*, Moti Lal Banarsi Das, Delhi, 1966, pp. 116-117.
11. *Kautilya Arthasastra*. II p. 16.
12. R.P. Kangle: *The Kautilya Arthasastra—A Study*, University of Bombay, Bombay, 1965, Part III. He refers Vyaji to be a sort of sales taxes on the sales of the produce from the mines, (p. 183) and on the sales of all other produce (p. 188).
13. Balkrishana: "The Hindu Taxation System", *Indian Journal of Economics*, Part I, July 1927, p. 31.
14. Sunil Rajan Sarkar: *op. cit.*, p. 101.
15. Dr. Radha Kumud Mookerji: *Ancient India*, Indian Press Publications Private Ltd., Allahabad, 1956, p. 333.

It was also prevalent during the Rajput period[16] and also in Kashmir during the time of king Uccala (1101-1111 A.D.)[17] The South Indian inscriptions of Tanjavur Temple give sufficient evidence that the tax had also found a place during Cholan Empire.[18] The Anvada inscription also records that during the reign of Sarangadeva, ruling at Anahillapataka in 1291 A.D., the sellers paid this tax. Thus in ancient India, it was well accepted that those who were engaged in trade and commerce must pay some thing to the State exchequer.

Taxes on sales of goods prevalent in India during the Hindu period and continued to be levied during the medieval period. During the period of Firuz Shah, an attempt was made to abolish this tax. It is thought that the abolition work was done only on the paper and in practice it was collected regularly. This practice went on through the reign of Sher Shah up to that of Jehangir in some form or the other.[19] It further continued during the Akbar reign, differential rates of sales tax were imposed according to the religion of the dealers. The rate of sales tax was 5 and 2-1/2 per cent on Hindu and Muslim dealers respectively. Again Jehangir attempted to abolish it but some how the tax existed even during the rule of Shah Jahan and Aurangzeb.[20] During Mugal period although direct taxes like land revenue and capitalisation tax were more important source of revenue yet the sales tax took its place with the custom duties as one of the two important indirect taxes in the Mugal period. In the cities, markets for the sale of goods were fixed, sometimes separate places were set aside for the sale of certain classes of goods. Only first sales of goods was taxable provided an article had remained with its owner for more than one year. Sale below Rs. 53 was exempted from payment of tax. This resulted in many goods sold by importer or manufacturer direct to the consumer going as tax free.

Coming to the seventeenth century the position as it existed

16. Todd: *Annals and Antiquities of Rajasthan*, Routledge and Kegan Paul Ltd., London, Vol. I, 1914, p. 111.
17. Sarkar: *op. cit.*, p. 103.
18. Dr. E. Hultzsch: *South Indian Inscriptions*, Government Press, Madras 1891, Vol. II, Part I, p. 117.
19. H.M, Elliot: *History of India*, Rubner and Company, London, 1875, Vol. VI, p. 284.
20. *Ibid.*, pp. 247-48.

in India, Tavenier, a French traveller, depicted it as under:

. . . . . before exposing any thing for sale, (manufacturers of textiles in Benares) have to go to him who holds the contract for collecting the tax on sales in order to get the King's stamp impressed on the prices of calico or silk, otherwise, they are fined and flogged.[21]

During the 18th and 19th centuries except in India and England sales tax did not find favour among other countries. England used consumption taxes in the 19th century. In India the tax continued to be levied during the East India Company rule. Such taxes were collected on the sale of alcoholic liquors and intoxicating drugs during later period also.[22]

Thus one finds that the sales tax which has its origin in the beginning of human civilization, has been continuing as a revenue measure ever since its inception.

Development of Sales Tax during the 19th Century

Prior to World War I, the sales tax had lost its importance to such an extent that as a measure of any significance it existed only in two countries. The Philippines had a levy on gross sales in 1904, at the rate of 1/3 per cent on the gross value of all goods, wares and merchandise with exemption on food products at retail.[23] The other country was Mexico having a sales tax system as of Spanish alcavala.

Modern form of sales taxation, however, is said to be a product of first world war, when the governments, had to reinforce their exchequers and found difficult to balance their budgets. The growing popularity of sales tax after first world war increased mainly by pressure of circumstances which left most governments with no other acceptable alternative resource while economists were very much against such a type of taxation. Most of the States had included this tax as a normal feature in their budgets but the original intent of these countries was to adopt it as a temporary measure. The second world war and later the depression period had proved to be a boon

21. W.C. Vasisht: *A Chrono-Legal Study of The Punjab General Sales Tax Act*: Neelam Publishers, Jullundur, 1981, p. 4.
22. V.S. Rajan: *Economic History of India 1757-1947*, East and West Book House, Baroda, 1955, pp. 346-375
23. Buehler: *op. cit.*, pp. 143-45.

not only in the spreading of sales tax still further, but in its being firmly established in countries which had been already using it. Thus a tax, which essentially had crept in by the back door entry during the period of crisis and was brought to be justified by the governments as a temporary measure not only stayed on but even gained respectability with the passage of time.

France had to resort this tax soon after the outbreak of world war I. In 1914 Payments Tax[24] was adopted. The rates ranged from 1.2 per cent on the first million francs of annual turnover to 6 per cent on the turnover in excess of 200 million francs. Changes were made in 1916 and 1917 but due to need for larger revenue, in 1920, it simultaneously imposed a broad Commodity Transfer Tax at the rate of 10 per cent on the gross monthly sales of manufacturers and merchants.[25] Exemptions included sales by farmers, independent artisans and members of the liberal professions. Commodities such as bread, newspapers and goods subject to special taxes were not subjected to the new tax. Rates of taxes were increased to 2 per cent of the turnover in 1926. The tax reached all stages of production and distribution but services were exempted from such tax. The tax was complicated in structure and later on became more difficult to be operated. In 1935 a single tax, collected usually at the time and place of production, replaced the turnover tax in case of coal, sugar, foodstuffs, beer and a few other commodities.[26] Nevertheless, the original tax was reintroduced after four years, i.e., in 1939 causing two taxes to exist simultaneously. This development caused multiple taxation. In 1955, however, the manufacturer's tax was replaced by the value added tax, and transaction tax was repealed.

Germany was the major country to impose sales tax. It introduced a tax on commodity transfers in 1916 which had a rate of .1 per cent.[27] The disappointing yield and increased fiscal requirements led to a general turnover tax (Umsatzsteur)

24. National Industrial Conference Board: *General Sales of Turnover Taxation*, NICB, New York, 1929, p. 171.
25. *Ibid*, p. 172.
26. G. Findlay, Shirras: *Science of Public Finance*, MacMillan and Co., 3rd Edition, Vol. II, 1936, p. 167.
27. National Industrial Conference Board: *op. cit.*, p. 166.

in 1918. The adoption of umsatzsteur, according to Moak and Frank, heralded the birth of modern day sales taxes in Europe during the early 1920.[28] This tax applied to the sales of both commodities and services at a general rate of .5 per cent. Exemptions included casual sales, sales by government managed or regulated enterprises, sales by consumer's co-operative and transfer of land.[29] With the increasing necessity of larger revenues, rate of the tax was raised and some of exemptions were withdrawn. During the period of depression, the rate was further raised to 2 per cent in 1931, and the agricultural commodities were taxed at 1.0 per cent. The rate of the tax on the firms, with annual turnover over one million Reichmarks, was, however, 2.5 per cent according to progressiveness introduced.[30] This structure prevailed during 1930 and the world war II period. Thereafter, the general turnover tax has been continued in West Germany and it is believed that East Germany also employed a broad turnover tax, similar to that used in West Germany, but with slightly lower rates.[31]

Like Germany and France many other countries also followed the suit and over a short period of time about thirty national governments had introduced sales taxes. Most of them enacted sales tax laws to meet the costs of post-war reconstruction but others had utilised it to meet some other contingencies.

Italy was the third major European country which adopted sales tax in 1919. This tax was originally imposed as a retail sales tax at a 10 per cent rate on luxuries and a 2 per cent rate on other items. In 1923 and subsequently in 1930 the base was broadened and some changes were introduced to increase the yield. In spite of these efforts finally in 1940 this tax was replaced by a multiple stage tax.

Czechoslovakia levied a general tax at 1 per cent rate of multiple stage sales tax in December 1919. It had a supplementary tax of 10 and 12 per cent on luxuries—which was

28. Moak and Frank: *Manual of Suggested Practice for Administration of Local Sales and Use Taxes*, Municipal Finance Association of the United States and Canada, Illinois, 1961, p. 4.
29. Alfred Buehler: *op. cit.*, pp. 97-102.
30. Clinton V. Oster: *op. cit.*, p. 12.
31. *Ibid.*, p. 13.

collected from either the manufacturers or the retailers. In 1922 the rate was raised to 2 per cent and single stage collection was introduced. This had been extended to many other commodities.[32]

After the repeal of the excess profits tax and sharp reduction in income-tax rates, Canada discovered that post war budget needs would require additional revenue sources. In 1920 this led to a modified turnover tax of 1.0 per cent levied on sales and import made by manufacturers and wholesalers. Provision was also made for a 2 per cent tax on sales by producers direct to retailers or consumers. The structure provided for exemption to necessities, viz., food, fuel and electricity, etc. . .[33] During 1921 and 1922 the rates of the tax were raised but the tax was criticised by many persons including members of Parliament.[34] As a result only after three years of its enactment, in 1923, it was replaced by a manufacturer's sales tax. The rate originally imposed was 6 per cent on sale price of all goods produced or manufactured in Canada. The tax has been characterised by Prof. Buehler as a limited consumption tax upon the sales of certain non-essentials.[35]

Belgium imposed a general sales tax on all sales of tangible personal property except those of retail sales in 1921. The rate of tax was 1 per cent and exemptions included food.[36]

Sales tax in American States was enacted for the first time in 1921 by West Virginia. But the tax did not gather momentum in other States at that time. In fact twenty-four States enacted sales tax during 1933 through 1935. Though many States repealed it after 1937 but later many States re-enacted and presently 33 States impose States sales taxes.[37]

The USSR adopted the turnover tax in July 1921 along with the launching of the New Economic Policy. Hungary, Rumania and Yugoslavia followed more or less the Austrian pattern and adopted turnover tax in the year 1921. Poland also joined them

32. John F. Due: *op. cit.*, p. 347.
33. A. Buehler: *op. cit.*, pp. 116-118.
34. John F. Due: *The General Manufacture's Sales Tax in Canada*, Canadian Tax Foundation, Toronto, 1931, p. 7.
35. A Buehler: *op. cit.*, p. 128.
36. Clinton V. Oster: *op. cit.*, pp. 13-14.
37. *Ibid.*, pp. 23-33.

in 1923. During 1922 Cuba also imposed a general multiple stage sales tax.

During 1925 and 1930 five more countries followed the suit.[38] They were Equador, Puerto Rico, Danzing, Uruguay and Australia. Equador had imposed 1 per cent multiple stage sales tax in 1925. During 1931 and 1940 many other countries imposed sales taxes, viz., Argentina, Netherlands, New Zealand, Norway, India and Great Britain. New Zealand in 1933 adopted a single stage wholesale tax on the pattern of Australia but with a larger list of exemptions. Initially the rate of the tax was 5 per cent on wholeseller but was raised to 10 per cent in June, 1940 and to 20 per cent on some articles in May, 1942.[39]

The Philippines had also, during the post-war period, replaced its turnover tax by a single stage retail sales tax with three basic rates of 50 per cent on luxuries, 30 per cent on cheap cars, clocks, electrical equipments, etc., and 7 per cent on other products. Later some changes were made on the recommendations of U.S. Economic Survey Mission, 1930.[40]

In September 1948, Japan had also enacted a multiple stage turnover tax. It applied to all transactions at all levels including retailing. However, it was replaced after an year only in December, 1949 due to its meagre returns and much administrative difficulties.

Others who joined the line in imposing the tax were Pakistan, Indonesia and Burma. Pakistan imposed a single point tax on the sale of wholesale dealers or licensed manufacturers. In 1930, Indonesia imposed 2-1/2 per cent multiple stage tax on all sales of merchandise at all levels of production and distribution. In 1951 this was replaced by a manufacturer's sales tax and levied at a 5 per cent rate with a 10 per cent rate on various luxury goods. Besides foodstuffs and other necessaries were exempted.[41]

Development of the Sales Tax System in India during 19th Century

In modern time, however, the imposition of sales tax was

38. John F. Due: *op. cit.*, p. 345.
39. *Ibid.*, pp. 195-200.
40. *Ibid.*, pp. 340-341.
41. *Ibid.*, p. 339.

first mooted by Indian Taxation Enquiry Committee 1924 known as Tod Hunter Committee which recommended the levy of retail sales tax as a substitute for octroi and terminal tax levied by municipalities. But the recommendation was not accepted. Government of India Act, 1935 envisaged a federal character with a provision of provincial autonomy. The introduction of provincial autonomy in the eleven provinces of British India brought heavy responsibilities on provincial Governments in the field of developmental activity.[42] The scope of the provincial revenue was, however, more or less inelastic and whatever sources of revenue could be available had to be tapped. It was, thus that sales tax came to be introduced, for the first time in India. The province of Bombay was pioneer to levy a tax on sales of tobacco with certain limited urban and semi-urban areas in 1938.[43] Second in line was Central Province (Madhya Pradesh) which levied a retail sales tax on motor spirit and lubricants in January 1939. However, the first province to resort to general sales tax was Madras which levied multiple point sales tax in 1939. Primarily the purpose was to make up for the loss of revenue as a result of the policy of prohibition. The Central Government, also challenged the legality of this Act, questioning the right of the provinces to tax sales by manufacturers. However, the Federal Court favoured Provincial Government, observing that the sales tax on manufacturers or producers could not be distinguished from a tax on other sales and that the Provincial Government had power to tax sales of every kind, including sales by a manufacturer of producer. During the next decade, sales taxation was introduced by most of the Indian States. In 1941, Bengal adopted a single general sales tax system levied at the retail level. In the same year Punjab introduced a general sales tax modelled on the Madras system. A general sales tax of the type of Bengal was introduced by Bihar in 1944 and by Bombay in 1946. In the next two years general sales taxes were introduced in Assam, Madhya Pradesh, Orissa and Uttar Pradesh. Rajasthan was formed on April 7, 1949 and Rajasthan Sales Tax Act,

42. Sant Ram Verma, Anand Mohan Suri: *East Punjab General Sales Tax Act*, Law Reporter Press, Sherfied, Simla, 1949, p. 1.
43. Government of Bombay: *Report of Sales Tax Enquiry Committee*, Government Central Press, Bombay, 1958, p. 6.

1954 came into existence on April 1, 1955. Punjab General Sales Tax Act, 1948 was enforced in the State of joint Punjab with effect from 1st May, 1949 so as to provide for the levy of general tax on sale or purchase of goods in the State. The State of Punjab was reorganised in the year 1966 and Haryana emerged as a separate State with effect from 1·11·1966. After the reorganisation, the Punjab General Sales Tax Act, 1948 was extended to the State of Haryana which remained in vogue in the State till its repeal and replacement by the Haryana General Sales Tax Act, 1973 with effect from 5th May, 1973.

Table 1.1 gives the year of introduction of sales tax and present nature of sales tax in Indian States.

TABLE 1.1

Introduction of Sales Tax in Indian States

States	*Year*	*Nature of Sales Tax*
Andhra Pradesh	1947-48	(*a*) Multiple point sales tax
		(*b*) Single point sales tax
Assam	1948	Single point sales tax
Bihar	1944	(*a*) Multiple point sales tax
		(*b*) Single point sales tax
Gujarat	1946	Double point sales tax
Punjab/Haryana	1941	Single point sales tax
Haryana	1973	Single point sales tax
Himachal Pradesh	1958	Single point sales tax
Jammu & Kashmir	1945-46	—
Karnataka (Mysore)	1948	(*a*) Multiple point sales tax
		(*b*) Single point sales tax
Kerala	1950	(*a*) Multiple point sales tax
		(*b*) Single point sales tax
Madhya Pradesh	1947	Single point sales tax
Maharashtra	1946	
Orissa	1947	Single point sales tax
Rajasthan	1955	(*a*) Single point sales tax
		(*b*) Multiple point sales tax
Tamil Nadu	1939	(*a*) Single point sales tax
		(*b*) Multiple point sales tax
Uttar Pradesh	1948	Single point sales tax
West Bengal	1941	Single point sales tax

Sources: (1) M.C. Purohit: *Sales Taxation in India*, Sultan Chand and Company Private Ltd., New Delhi, 1975.

(2) G. Thimmaiah: *Perspectives on Tax Design and Tax Reform*, Ashish Publishing House, New Delhi, 1984, pp. 164-71.

It can be observed from Table 1.1 that by 1950, almost all the States, except Rajasthan, Himachal Pradesh and Haryana had introduced sales tax into their tax structure. Though the birth of sales tax is of recent origin, it has developed as one of the most elastic and main source of revenue in all the Indian States. It is yielding adequate and substantial revenue for meeting the expenditure on developmental plans and projects. The system of sales tax is not uniform in all the States. Variations in the system of sales taxation found in different States reflect varying conditions and economic factors of the States. Some States have adopted single point taxation while some other States contain a combination of single point and multiple point taxes. Gujarat is the only State that has double point tax.[44]

The sales tax systems originally introduced have undergone substantial modifications and were occasionally replaced by altogether different systems. Models earlier adopted underwent overhauling and also many States levied taxes on exports and some of the provinces imposed taxes on various raw materials and on goods entering into inter-State trade, more than once. Thus, many problems were being experienced by double taxation, while some of the problems were settled in Finance Ministers Conference held in 1948. Thus the States were restricted from the imposition of tax on newspapers and on the sale or purchase in the course of inter-state trade and commerce and on the sale outside the State and on the export or import of the goods. Moreover, the power of the States to impose taxes on goods declared 'essential' by the Parliament was subjected to the prior approval of Parliament. The period following the adoption of the Constitution up to 1955 was transitional period for sales taxation. It was with the Supreme Court judgment in 1955 that State's power to impose sales tax was clearly demarcated. As a necessity, therefore, the Constitution was amended and the taxes on sales or purchase of goods in the course of inter-State trade and commerce were brought expressly within the purview of legislative jurisdiction of Parliament. As a result Central Sales Tax Act, 1956 was passed. It authorised the States to impose and collect taxes on inter-State trade and commerce

44. M.C. Purohit: "Structure of Sales Taxes in India." *Economic and Political Weekly*, Vol. XVII, No. 34, August 21, 1982, p. 1365.

on behalf of the Union Government. The present sales tax structure in India, therefore, falls under two heads:

(*i*) that which falls under the jurisdiction of the State Government, and

(*ii*) that which is the concern of the Union Government which includes Central Sales Tax and Additional Excise Duties.

Concept of Sales Tax

The sales tax family includes a wide variety of taxes with bases ranging in scope from selective sales tax to broad multiple turnover taxes. Generally speaking, sales tax is a tax on the sales of commodities at the retailing, whole selling or manufacturing stage and it is a wide connotation which includes purchses tax too, but a precise definition which draws a clear-cut demarcation between levies known as sales taxes and closely related taxes such as purchase, excises, octroi, customs, etc., is more difficult. It has been defined by Buehler as a tax imposed upon the sales of numerous commodities and the use of personal services at uniform rates.[45] It has been defined by Plank as "a tax upon the sale or exchange of goods or services which is proportioned to the value or quantity of the things transferred."[46] This definition does not clearly differentiate sales tax from other levies.

Haig has defined sales tax as tax which includes within the scope all business of sales of tangible personal property, either at retailing, wholeselling or manufacturing stage with the exceptions noted in the taxing law.[47] Sales tax is leviable on sales price while purchase tax is leviable on purchase price of goods. Generally commodities which are in purview of taxation but sales tax is not levied on them, purchase tax is leviable under the sales tax laws of the States. Therefore, the sales/purchases tax can be defined as a levy imposed upon sales or purchases or elements incidental to sales purchases of all or wide range of commodities. The tax may be confined to physical commodities

45. Buehler: *op. cit*, p. 1.
46. E.H. Plank: *Public Finance*, Richard D. Irwin, Illinois, 1953, p. 327.
47. Shoup and Haig: *The Sales Tax in the American States*, Columbia University Press, New York, 1934, p. 3.

but may even extend to services rendered by commercial enterprises, professions, etc. Our Constitution, however, permits only for commodity taxation and not for services taxation. In fact, sale or purchase tax is tax on sale and purchase of goods, and is levied on the occasion of sale or purchase.

Different Forms of Sales Taxation

Sales tax being the only productive tax in the State list, all the States have adopted this form of taxation. The nature and scope of sales tax vary greatly. Structural differentiation is prevailing in different States. To analyse the different form of sales taxation, it may be classified into three categories, viz., according to scope, according to legal basis and according to total turnover.[48]

CHART 1.1

Forms of Sales Taxation

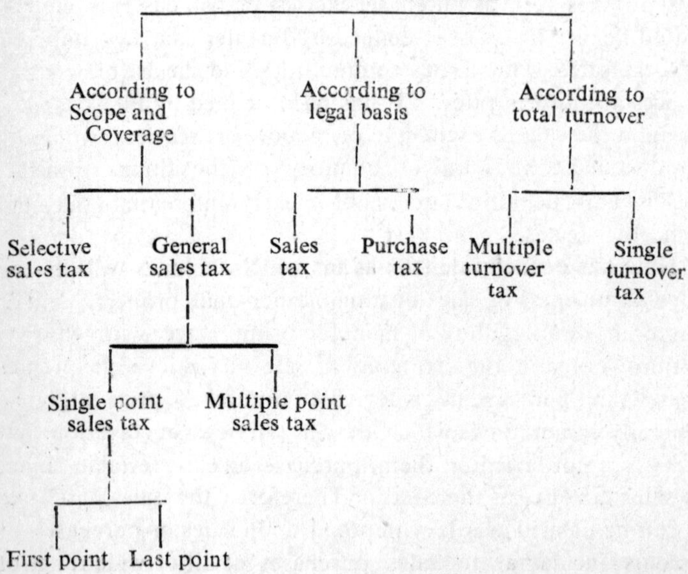

According to Scope and Coverage

As per the scope or coverage the tax may be classified into two parts:

48. A.K. Agarwal: *Commodity Taxes in India*, Chugh Publications, Allahabad, 1981, p. 38.

(*i*) **Selective Sales Tax**

Only selected goods are brought under the purview of sales tax Legislature of a State. All the States have adopted this form of tax for the purpose of levying tax on motor spirit. For this purpose Motor Spirit Taxation Acts have been separately enacted. In Rajasthan Motor Spirit Act, 1954 was replaced and merged in sales tax law and it was felt that there was no justification for having a separate law for sales tax on petrol, etc.

(*ii*) **General Sales Tax**

A general sales tax may be defined briefly as a levy at a uniform rate on the sales of commodities at retail or wholesale. This tax is applied on all sales of the commodities which are not exempted by law. Most of the States have one Sales Tax Act for imposition of general sales tax while in Assam and Bengal the States govern their general sales tax through Sales Tax Act and Finance Act. The general sales tax prevalent in the Indian States is of three types, viz., single point, double point and multiple point tax. The single point tax is a tax which is levied at one point (First and last) from producer to the final stage of consumption. Under the multiple point system the tax is imposed on every point of sales till it reaches the final consumer.[49] When the tax is collected at two point instead of one, i.e., on two different sales of two dealers through whom the articles have passed to the consumer, it is called double point sales tax. It may be termed as a substitute to single point system. In Rajasthan, Uttar Pradesh, Haryana and Punjab single point taxation is in vogue.

According to Legal Basis

The sales tax in India is legally imposed on the dealers and not on the consumers, i.e., the impact of the tax is on the dealers. The tax is imposed either on the dealer who sells the commodities or on the dealer who purchases it. Since the sales and purchases are two aspects of the same transactions, when the tax is imposed on sales, it is termed sales tax and when it is imposed on the purchases, it is called purchase tax.

49. Mathur and Saxena: *Public Economics*, Jai Prakash Nath and Company, Meerut, 1958, p. 176.

According to Turnover

Sales tax is also imposed on the basis of turnover of sales.[50] Tax on turnover means the tax on total sales of the dealer. Multiple turnover taxes are imposed more than once in the production-distribution stage, on account of their cumulative effects these taxes are also referred to as cascade taxes.[51] Single turnover tax is levied only at one stage. The above classification of sales tax serves the purpose of highlighting the main features of sales tax system which are prevalent in India. Different State Governments have adopted different tax systems and levy it at different points in their jurisdiction. The single point sales tax system has been adopted by Delhi, Punjab, Haryana, West Bengal and Maharashtra. Tamil Nadu, Andhra Pradesh, Uttar Pradesh and Rajasthan have adopted a combined system, i.e., single point and multiple point system of taxation. In Rajasthan 1 per cent multiple point tax on gems, precious stones etc., was in vogue. The most recent version of sales tax is the value added tax as employed in France and Britain which is levied at all points on the value of goods, it is added in production and distribution process. Value added tax is now talked of too much in India but it has not been introduced by any State in sales taxation, so far.

Sales Tax and Other Related Taxes

The definition of sales tax may be confused with other related taxes, in so far as all are shifted finally to the consumers. Therefore, it is necessary to make a distinction between sales tax, purchase tax, excise duty, octroi and customs duties.

Sales Tax vs. Purchase tax

The sales and purchase taxes are taxes on the sales and purchases of goods.[52] Sales tax is a tax on a sale whereas the purchase tax is a tax on the purchase. In other words, sales and

50. While the customary classification according to turnover imposition of sales tax according to frequency of imposition in production distribution process. Our classification implies total turnover of the dealer. Clinton V, Oster: *op. cit.*, pp. 3-7.
51. Sijbren Cnossen: "The Role and Structure of Sales Tax and Excise System", *Finance and Development*, March, 1975, p. 30.
52. Government of India: *Report of the Taxation Enquiry* Commission, 1953-54, Vol. 3, p. 3.

purchase are merely different ways of looking at the same transaction. Every act of sale is an act of purchase as well. When the tax is levied on an act of sale-*cum*-purchase and collected from the seller, it may be called sales tax when the State collects from the buyer it is called a purchase tax. In this connection, it is important to note that the dealer may enter the picture either as seller or buyer, whereas the non-dealer (consumer) enters it only as buyer.

Sales Tax vs. Excise Duties

The main differences between sales tax and excise duties are[53] (*i*) Sales tax has a wide coverage in the sense that exemptions from it are very few, whereas excise tax is selective and confined to few commodities in most of the cases, (*ii*) Sales tax is a levy imposed on the sale of a commodity in the process of production or distribution, whereas an excise tax is essentially a tax imposed on the production of a commodity and collected at the factory, (*iii*) In a federal form of government, sales tax is invariably imposed by the States while major excise duties are levied by the Centre, and (*iv*) Both sales and excise taxes drive a wedge between price and factor payments, but they differ as to base. The former is assessed on gross receipts, and is a function of price, while the latter is assessed on the unit of output, and constitutes a constant addition to variable costs.[54]

Sales Tax and Customs Duty

Customs duties are taxed on the movement of goods between countries and are unrelated to sales or consumption. Sales tax implies change of ownership while customs duty change of location. For example a person while taking his own goods across the border of a particular territory or bringing in may be liable to pay customs duty, on the other hand, sales tax is paid when particular taxable goods are purchased and its ownership is changed. Therefore, one may have to pay sales tax as well as customs duty when one after purchasing the goods takes them across border, either in the form of an export duty to the

53. Shiv Kumar Singh: *Central Excise Duties and Economic Development of India*, S. Chand and Co. Ltd., New Delhi, 1977, pp, 16-17.
54. R.A. Musgrave: *The Theory of Public Finance*, International Student Edition, Kegakusha Co. Ltd., Tokyo, 1959, p. 287.

government of the territory from which it is intended to be taken out or as an import duty to the government of the territory in which he brings.

Conclusion

Thus, it may be concluded that in the most of the countries sales tax was first imposed as an *ad hoc* measure to collect revenue in the times of special financial stringencies. Now this tax has become an important part of the tax structure of many countries. In India, all the States have adopted sales tax to fulfil their financial requirement for their plans and projects.

2

FINANCIAL DEPENDENCE OF STATES ON SALES TAX

Introduction

India is a federal State where there prevails diversity in uniformity. In the words of R.N. Bhargava "a federal structure is a marriage of unity and 'diversity".[1] The federal structure had its birth with the introduction of Montagu-Chemsford reforms of 1920. Since then there has been greater devolution of power and responsibility from the Centre to the States. With the inauguration of provincial autonomy on April 1, 1937 and the adoption of the Indian Constitution on January 26, 1950, the progress towards federalism was completed. Since the federal government was born as a result of devolution of power and responsibility from the Centre to the States, the Central Government is relatively stronger. Wheare has described the Indian Constitution as "quasi-federal"[2] mainly because the president retains some of the reserve powers formerly vested in the British Viceroys.

An important characteristic of federal type of government is the division of powers and functions between the Centre and federating units. India is an example of unique federation in the world where legislative, administrative and financial powers are distributed between the Centre and the States. The division of functions and resources is based on scientific principles and on efficiency consideration, so that what belongs to one government is placed in its sphere. The jurisdiction and authority of

1. R.N. Bhargava: "The Theory of Federal Finance,", *The Economic Journal*, March 1953, p. 84.
2. K.C. Wheare: *Federal Government*, Oxford University Press, London, 1968, p. 28.

the Centre and States is separately defined in the Union and State lists. In addition to this the concurrent list gives subjects, in which the Union and State Governments have a concurrent authority and responsibility. The division of resources is also based on efficiency consideration. There is a clear bifurcation of tax jurisdiction between the two governments. In this manner an attempt has been made to avoid duplication in tax administration or competitive exploitation of the same tax and to provide sufficient resources to the States.

In any federation, for proper functioning of the federal principle, the fiscal autonomy rests on adequacy and elasticity of the revenue resources of the governments. 'Adequacy' means that the government command sufficient resources to perform its function as also to maintain a certain standard of administration efficiency. 'Elasticity' implies that resources should have the capacity to expand with the growing needs of States. But in India the Centre is more powerful. Rao has observed that "The Indian Constitution gives specific recognition to the fact that the power of Centre to levy taxes or raise loan is much larger in fiscal term than that of States and, therefore, provides for distribution to the States of the whole or part of many of the taxes that can be levied only by the Central Government and of central loan to the States".[3] Because of this corollary system of levying and collecting jurisdiction for two layers of the governments, problems in inter-governmental fiscal and financial relation arise. But in any federation "it is impossible to effect a clean separation of finances of the several layers of government".[4] While it is scarcely possible to have an absolute equilibrium and independence for each layer of government in federal set up, the very concept of federalism would get frustrated and thrown into a jeopardy if the federating entities are obliged to depend on the federal apex to an extent of subservience. Wheare asserts that "The essential point in a federal principle is that neither of the two tiers of government would be subordinate to the other, both the general and regional governments must have under its own independent control and financial resources suffi-

3. V.K.R.V. Rao: "Centre-State Financial Relations in India", Institute for Social and Economic Changes, *Staff Paper* No. 7, 1953, p. 3.
K.V.S. Sastri: *Federal State Fiscal Relation in India*, Oxford University
4. Press, 1966, p. 5.

cient to perform its exclusive functions".[5] Even otherwise dependence is a curse and no unit government should agree to an arrangement whereby it has to submit and look to the apex government as a "giver". Financial autonomy of the unit government is essential and vital to the preservation of the federal principle.

Constitutional Provisions

The Seventh Schedule of the Constitution of India lays down the functions and resources of the Centre and States. It contains three lists, viz., the Union list, the State list and the concurrent list. The union list consists of 97 entries according to which some important tax revenue resources of the Central Government are the following[6]:

1. Taxes on income other than agricultural income (Entry 82).
2. Duties of customs including export duties (Entry 83).
3. Duties of excise on tobacco and other goods manufactured or produced in India except—
   (*a*) alcoholic liquors for human consumption,
   (*b*) opium, Indian hemp and other narcotic drugs and narcotics, but including medicinal and toilet preparations containing alcohol or any substance included in sub-paragraph (*b*) of this entry (Entry 84).
4. Corporation tax (Entry 85).
5. Taxes on the capital value of the assets, exclusive of agricultural land, of individuals and companies; taxes on the capital of companies (Entry 86).
6. Estate duty in respect of property other than agricultural land (Entry 87).[7]
7. Duties in respect of succession to property other than agricultural land (Entry 88).
8. Terminal taxes on goods or passengers, carried by railway, sea or air; taxes on railway fares and freights

5. K.C. Wheare: *Federal Government*, *op. cit.*, p. 12.
6. *The Constitution of India*, Eastern Book Company, Lucknow, 1977, pp. 196-97.
7. Budgetary provisions for 1985-86 provides for the abolition of estate duty, *Financial Express*, New Delhi, 17th March, 1985, p. 1,

(Entry 89).

9. Taxes other than stamp duties on transactions in stock exchanges (Entry 90).
10. Rates of stamp duty in respect of bills of exchange, cheques, promissory notes, bills of lading, letter of credit, policies of insurance, transfer of shares, debentures, proxies and receipts (Entry 91).
11. Taxes on the sale or purchase of newspapers and on advertisements published therein (Entry 92).
12. Taxes on the sale or purchase of goods other than newspapers, where such sale or purchase takes place in the course of inter-State trade or commerce (Entry 92A).
13. Taxes on inter-State consignments of goods (Entry 92B).[8]

The non-tax sources of revenue for the Government of India include the following;

1. Internal and external borrowings,
2. Income from government undertakings,
3. Income occurring the government on account of exercise of its sovereign rights.

The List II, i.e., State list of the Seventh Schedule covers functions and financial resources of the States. The list contains 66 entries. Some important entries of tax revenue are as under.[9]

1. Land revenue (Entry 45).
2. Taxes on agricultural income (Entry 46).
3. Duties in respect of succession to agricultural land (Entry 47).
4. Estate duty in respect of agricultural land (Entry 49).
5. Taxes on land and buildings (Entry 49).
6. Taxes on mineral rights subject to any limitations imposed by Parliament by law relating to mineral development (Entry 50).
7. Duties of excise on the following goods manufactured or produced in the State and countervailing duties at the same or lower rates on similar goods manufactured or

8 This entry was made in February, 1983 by virtue of 46th Constitutional Amendment. Quoted from M.L. Bhatia: *Public Finance*, Vikas Publishing House (P) Ltd., 1983, New Delhi, p. 341.

9. *Constitution of India, op. cit.*, pp. 200-1.

produced elsewhere in India:

(*a*) alcoholic liquors for human consumption,

(*b*) opium, Indian hemp and other narcotic drugs and narcotics; but not including medicinal and toilet preparations containing alcohol or any substance included in sub-paragraph (*b*) of this entry (Entry 51).

8. Taxes on the entry of goods into a local area for consumption, use or sale therein (Entry 52).
9. Taxes on the consumption or sale of electricity (Entry 53).
10. Taxes on the sale or purchase of goods other than newspapers, subject to the provision of entry 92A of Union list (Entry 54).
11. Taxes on advertisements other than advertisements published in the newspaper (and advertisements broadcast by radio or television) (Entry 55).[10]
12. Taxes on goods and passengers carried by road or on inland waterways (Entry 56).
13. Taxes on vehicles (Entry 57).
14. Taxes on animals and boats (Entry 58).
15. Tolls (Entry 59).
16. Taxes on professions, trades, callings and employments (Entry 60).
17. Capitation taxes (Entry 61).
18. Taxes on luxuries, including taxes on entertainment, amusements, betting and gambling (Entry 62).
19. Rates of stamp duty in respect of documents other than those specified in the provisions of Union list with regard to rates of stamp duty (Entry 63).
20. Fees in respect of any of the matters in this list, but not including fees taken in any court (Entry 66).

The non-tax sources of State revenues include:

(*i*) Borrowings subject to limits imposed by State Legislatures or the Government of India.

(*ii*) Profit from State Government owned undertakings.

(*iii*) Income from public property owned by the State

10. Inserted by the Constitution (Forty-second Amendment) Act, 1976, Section. 57.

Government.

(*iv*) Royalty from mines, forests, treasures and bones etc.

(*v*) Grant-in-aid from the Centre.

(*vi*) Share in specified Union taxes.

(*vii*) Other grants.

The constitutional provisions not merely identify the sources of revenue but also lay down provisions regarding levying, collection and appropriation of revenue. Administrative and financial efficiency are the factors that determine the basis on which these powers are divided between the Centre and the States.

Distribution of Fiscal Powers

The distribution of fiscal powers between the Centre and the States are as under:

Firstly, there are taxes which are levied, collected and retained by the Union Government. All taxes of the Union list except income-tax and excise duty are in this category.

Secondly, these are taxes which are levied and collected by the Central Government but are wholly assigned to the States. Estate duty, succession tax, terminal taxes on goods and passengers carried by railways, sea or air, taxes on railways freight and fares and taxes on newspapers and newspaper advertisements, are in this category.

The third category consists of those taxes which are levied and collected by Union Government but which are shared with the States either on mandatory or permissive basis. Income-tax and Union excise duty belong to this category. The surcharge on income-tax is not shared with the States.[11]

Taxes in the fourth category are levied by the Centre but collected and retained by the States. This is to ensure uniformity. Stamp duty and excise duty on medical and toilet preparations are in this category.

In the fifth category all taxes are levied, collected and retained by the States.

All residuary powers of taxation vest in the Union authority.

11. Budgetary provision for 1985-86 provides for abolition of the surcharge on Income-tax, *Financial Express*, 17 March, 1985, p. 5.

However, some restrictions have been placed in regard to levy of taxes on the sale and purchase of newspapers and advertisement therein.

States' Dependence on Centre

When the functions and resources are allocated in the manner described above, the Centre comes to possess an elastic and productive source of revenue while the expanding social and developmental services fall in the sphere of States. This gives rise to the problem of non-correspondence between functions and resources of the two layers of government.[12] Hicks, while analysing the Centre-State financial relations, has emphasised that "The national government will tend to have more than it needs, while the States will not be able to perform their duties without considerable amount of help. This imbalance is in fact typical of almost al l federations; it is naturally more serious for the poorer States who have less opportunity of raising revenue, and for this reason it tends to be more acute problem in developing federation than in an advanced one."[13]

The revenue allocation between the Centre and the States as provided in the Constitution is such that though the States have jurisdiction over a wide field of direct taxation in the form of land revenue, agriculture income-tax and estate duty in respect of agriculture land, etc., but the levels of implementation are administratively very inconvenient, and in terms of yield are very inadequate and inelastic. On the other hand, the Centre has exclusive jurisdiction over some very lucrative and indirect levies such as corporation tax. Although the federal fiscal provisions also provide for sharing of Central taxes, the States shall have to look to the Centre for the sharing of taxes which fall in the permissive category and not in obligatory category. No doubt, so far the Central Government has accepted the awards of the finance commissions *in toto*, but constitutionally the States have to depend on the Centre and the Centre plays the role of "Donor".

State Governments are responsible for providing various

12. Scott Authony: The Economic Goals of Federal Finance, *Public Finance*: London, Vol. XX, 1969, p. 241.
13. Ursula K. Hicks: *Development Finance—Planning and Control*, Cambridge University Press, London, 1965, p. 124.

social and developmental services. In view of this fact the expenditure of the State Governments on nation building activities such as education, medical and public health has increased rapidly due to increased population. R.N. Bhargava has further emphasised that the fiscal needs of the States have tended to increase on account of their expanding functions.[14] Obviously, the States have been put under pressure from both sides, they have less money and more responsibilities. The expenditure of State Government on non-developmental items such as civil administration, debt servicing, cost of collection of taxes also require huge funds. The result is that the States find it very difficult to discharge their functions adequately without financial assistance from the Centre.

Taxing power of the States in comparison to Centre is very meagre and the imbalance in division of tax revenue functions assigned to the two layers of the government are sought to be corrected through the mechanism of sharing grants-in-aids and loan from the Centre to the States. This mechanism of transfer of resources from the Centre to the States increase dependence of the States on the Centre. Moreover, development needs of the States are increasing at faster rate than increase in the source of revenue. To keep pace with the increased needs it is essential for the States to depend more and more on the Centre. The position of transfer of resources from the Centre to the States is presented in Table 2.1 as given on next page.

Table 2.1 reveals that the total resources transferred from the Centre to the States increased from Rs. 1,431 crores in the First Plan to Rs. 2,868 crores in the Second Plan, Rs. 5,600 crores in the Third Plan, Rs. 15,312 crores in the Fourth Plan, Rs. 27,728 crores in the Fifth Plan and finally to Rs. 34,090 crores in the Sixth Plan. The total transfers have increased more than 19 times between 1951 to 1979. The growth rate during the planning period is 2 times (approx.) in each successive plan over the previous plan. The position of Finance Commission as a mechanism for Centre-State fiscal resources has been weakened over the years because of the increasing importance of transfer through the Planning Commission. But during the Fourth, Fifth and Sixth Plans the position of Finance

14. R.N. Bhargava: "Recent Trend in Federalism", *Public Finance*, George Allen and Unwin Ltd., London, 1954, p. 261.

TABLE 2.1
Transfer of Resources from the Centre to the States from 1951 to 1985

(*Rs. in crores*)

Plan	*On recommendation of Finance Commission* (*Rs.*)	*Through Planning Commission* (*Rs.*)	*Other* (*Rs.*)	*Total (2+3+4)* (*Rs.*)	*Growth-rate plan-wise*	*Expenditure of the States Revenue Account Capital Account* (*Rs.*)	*Percentage of total amount transferred to total Expenditure*
	1	2	3	4	5	6	7
First Plan (1951-56)	447 (31.24)	880 (61.49)	104 (7.27)	1431	—	3,352	42.69
Second Plan (1956-61)	918 (32.01)	1344 (46.86)	606 (21.13)	2868	2.0	5,846	49.06
Third Plan (1961-66)	1590 (28.39)	2738 (48.89)	1272 (22.72)	5600	1.95	10,720	52.24
Three Annual Plan (1966-69)	1782 (25.05)	1917 (26.95)	3415 (48.00)	7114	1.27	9,912	71.77
Fourth Plan (1969-74)	5420 (35.40)	4900 (32.00)	4992 (32.60)	15312	2.15	27,549	55.58
Fifth Plan (1974-79)	13079 (47.17)	10595 (38.21)	4054 (14.62)	27728	1.81	49,029.2	56.55
Sixth Plan (1989-85)	20845	13245	NA	34090	—	—	—

Note : Figures in parenthesis are percentage to total transfer.

Source: (*i*) D.T. Lakdawala—"Plan Finance in Federal Economy", *Yojana*, 16th May, 1979, p. 7.

(*ii*) B.L. Pahariya —"Inter-State Finance Relations and Dependence in India", *Manthan*, April, 1980, p. 33.

(*iii*) H.L. Bhatia —*Centre-State Financial Relations in India*, Abhinav Publications, New Delhi, 1979, p. 126.

Commission has improved and more resources have been transferred through this channel. These data amply demonstrate that States fiscal dependence on the Centre has been increasing rapidly in past three decades. And the State Governments have found it difficult to raise adequate funds for meeting their continuously increasing expenditure. During 1951-56, 42.69 per cent of the States expenditure was met by resources transferred by the Centre and in the Second Plan 49.06 per cent, in the Third Plan 52.24 per cent and in the Fourth Plan 55.58 per cent of the resources transferred from the Centre to the States. Finally in the Fifth Plan resources transferred by the Centre were to pay 56.55 per cent of total expenditure of the States. The States could not cover the remaining expenditure from their own revenues. So the overall budgetary deficits of the State Governments kept increasing rapidly. The result is that presentation of deficit budgets seem to have become a permanent feature for a number of the State Governments in recent years, which is not a healthy trend for the developing economies.

Tax Structure of States

The tax system and tax policy of the government have a great importance for planned economic development. Taxes are an important tool of raising revenue and to achieving certain other objectives. Undoubtedly, the objective of a tax is to raise revenue but "no clear line can be drawn between the legislation that is non-fiscal and that which is fiscal in character."[15] Therefore, many taxes may be justified on social and political grounds and may not meet the primary objective of raising revenue, e.g., a tax on liquor, the primary objective of which may be to discourage the consumption of liquor.[16] However, in the early stages of economic development greater weightage may be given to revenue consideration in order to raise adequate tax revenue to finance economic development.[17]

Taxes which are levied and collected by the States form the most important source of revenue of the States. This is so

15. Harold M. Groves; *Financing Government*, Henry Holt and Rinhert Company, New York, 1968, p. 43.
16. R.N. Bhargava: Taxation Policy, *Public Finance*, *op. cit.*, p. 324.
17. P.K. Bhargava: Article on "Tax Policy in a Developing Economy—Need for Greater Incentives", *Capital*, Sept., 1968, pp. 543-45.

because States have the privilege of utilising the receipts therefrom in the manner they like. Moreover, in the States revenue structure, their place and contribution is certain together with the element of flexibility therein. On the other hand, the share of every State in the Union taxes, such as Income-tax, Estate duty, Union excise and Grants-in-aid depend on the recommendations of the finance commissions. But the States cannot be sure of their share in the shared taxes. As a consequence, the significance of taxes is being growingly felt in the revenue structure of the States. It has been gradually realised that the States by their own efforts can increase their revenue receipts from their own taxes which they have the power to levy and collect, because other sources of revenue appear to be relatively less elastic.[18]

In India, the main sources of revenue of the States are four, viz., their own taxes, non-tax revenue, share of central taxes and central grant-in-aid.[19] In each State its own taxes are by and large, the most important single source of revenue. Table 2.2 substantiates this fact.

In is evident from Table 2.2 that the States taxes constituted 45 per cent of total revenue in 1955-56, 43 per cent in 1960-61, 45 per cent in 1970-71, 44 per cent in 1980-81 and 46 per cent in 1983-84 (Budget estimates). The share of central taxes ranged between 18 to 25 per cent during 1955-56 to 1983-84. The share of grants-in-aid and other contributions from the Centre was little more than 6 per cent in 1955-56, though during the course of time it increased and was 17 per cent in 1970-71 but finally in 1983-84 it dropped to 14 per cent.

Thus, the major source of revenue for the State Governments is their own taxes. But in the States like Manipur, Meghalaya, Nagaland, Sikkim, Tripura, their own taxes and non-taxes revenue are not productive and they rely heavily on grants from the Centre. In the year 1982-83 their share in grants was 75 to 85 per cent of total revenue,[20] which is too high.

18. Rajendra Jain: *State Taxation in India*, Progress Publishers, Bhopal, 1972, p. 148.
19. Baljit Singh: "An Approach to State Taxes" in M.D. Joshi (Ed.) *Mobilisation of State Resources*, Impex India, New Delhi, 1968, p. 9
20. *Reserve Bank of India Bulletin*, October 1983, p. 643.

TABLE 2.2

Revenue Receipts of States from 1955-56 to 1983-84

(Rs in crores)

	1955-56 (*Rs.*)	*1960-61* (*Rs.*)	*1965-66* (*Rs.*)	*1970-71* (*Rs.*)	*1975-76* (*Rs.*)	*1980-81* (*Rs.*)	*1981-82* (*Rs.*)	*1982-83* (*R.E.*) (*Rs.*)	*1983-84* (*B.E.*) (*Rs.*)
A. State Tax Revenue	180 (45.46)	442 (43.72)	842 (45.51)	1528 (45.33)	3546 (44.67)	6505 (41.60)	8234 (44.62)	9475 (44.44)	10706 (45.97)
B. Share in Central Taxes	101 (25.50)	182 (18.00)	276 (14 92)	756 (22 42)	1599 (20.14)	3706 (23.70)	4260 (23.08)	4738 (22.22)	5209 (22.37)
C. State Non-Tax revenue	90 (22.73)	226 (26.31)	403 (21.78)	521 (15.46)	1574 (19.83)	2737 (17.50)	3234 (17.52)	3529 (16.55)	3929 (16 87)
D. Grants in-aid and contribution	25 (6.31)	121 (11.97)	329 (17 78)	556 (16.79)	1219 (15.36)	2691 (17.20)	2726 (14.78)	3579 (16.79)	3445 (14 79)
Total	396	1011	1850	3371	7938	15639	18454	21321	23289

Note : R.E. = Revised Estimates. B.E. = Budget Estimates.
Figures in brackets are percentage to total.

Source : *Reserve Bank of India Bulletins.*

Major Components of tax Revenue of States

State Governments have three different sources of tax revenue. These are revenue from taxes on income, (Agricultural income-tax, Profession tax) revenue from taxes on property and capital transactions (Stamps and registration fees, Land revenue Urban immovable property tax) and revenue from commodity taxes, i.e., Sales tax, State excise, Motor vehicle tax, Taxes on passengers and goods, Electricity duty, Entertainment tax, etc. Commodity taxes are the most important sources of revenue to the States.

The chief source of revenue from which the States derive their tax revenue are Sales tax, state excise duties, motor vehicle tax and stamp and registration fees, etc. Table 2.3 on the next page gives the comparative importance of revenue sources of State Governments.

Table 2.3 reveals that the share of agriculture income-tax and profession tax have been very meagre. The urban immovable property tax has contributed (only Rs. 5.9 crores in 1983-84) (.06 per cent) in the total tax revenue of all the States taken together. The land revenue and stamps and registration fees were important sources of revenue in 1955-56, and contributed 27.63 per cent and 10.27 per cent respectively. But after that share from these taxes declined to 12.86 per cent and 8.52 per cent in 1965-66. A sharp decline was also noticed in the relative importance of land revenue which accounted for 6.48 per cent in the total State tax revenue in 1975-76, 2.21 per cent in 1980-81 and finally 1.9 per cent in 1983-84. Stamp and registration fees contributed 7.98 per cent in 1970-71, 6.45 per cent in 1980-81, but only 5.76 per cent in 1983-84. It reveals that contribution of stamps and registration fees in the total revenue of State is also declining gradually. Table 2.3 further reveals that there are substantial increases in the revenue from motor vehicle tax. Such revenue increased from Rs. 15.9 crores in 1955-56, to Rs. 64.2 crores in 1965-66, Rs. 203.3 crores in 1975-76, Rs 421.7 crores in 1980-81 and finally it shot up to Rs. 663 crores in 1983-84. The percentage of motor vehicle tax to total State taxes revenue has been steadily increasing. The entertainment tax contributed to State taxes revenue Rs. 7.3 crores in 1955-56, Rs. 29.4 crores in 1965-66, Rs. 149.9 crores in 1970-71, Rs 253.9 crores in 1980-81 and finally as high as Rs. 392.9 crores in

TABLE 2.3

State's Own Tax Revenue from 1955-56 to 1983-84

(*Rs. in crores*)

Year	*Land Revenue*	*Agriculture income tax*	*State excise*	*Sales tax +*	*Motor vehicle tax*	*Goods and passengers tax*	*Entertainment tax*	*Electricity duty*	*Stamp and Registration fee*	*Profession tax*	*Urban immovable property tax*	*Other*	*Total*
	Rs.	*Rs.*	*Rs.*	*Rs.*	*Rs.*	*Rs.*	*Rs.*	*Rs.*	*Rs.*	*Rs.*	*Rs.*	*Rs.*	*Rs.*
1955-56	78.00	7.70	45.10	81.60	15.90	—	7.30	5.80	29.00	0.10	2.10	9.70	282.30
	(27.63)	(2.73)	(15.98)	(28.91)	(5.63)	—	(2.59)	(2.05)	(10.27)	(0.03)	(0.74)	(3.44)	
1960-61	97.20	9.50	53.10	158.80	34.10	5.80	13.10	12.50	43.30	0.40	1.00	19.40	448.20
	(21.69)	(2.12)	(11.85)	(35.43)	(7.61)	(1.29)	(2.92)	(2.79)	(9.66)	(0.09)	(0.22)	(4.33)	
1965-66	111.90	9.90	96.40	367.80	64.20	27.80	29.40	35.40	74 10	0.80	3.90	48.20	869.80
	(12.86)	(1.14)	(11.08)	(42.29)	(7.38)	(3.20)	(3.38)	(4.07)	(8.52)	(0.09)	(0.45)	(5.54)	
1970-71	112.61	10.50	193.92	766.20	104.70	67.80	57.52	67.20	121.90	3.10	4.10	18.30	1527.85
	(7.37)	(0.69)	(12.69)	(50.15)	(6.85)	(4.44)	(3.76)	(4.40)	(7.98)	(0 20)	(0.27)	(1.20)	
1975-76	229.70	28.49	435.50	1943.67	203.30	166.90	149.90	111.40	216.90	17.20	7 80	35.30	3546.60
	(6.48)	(0.80)	(12.28)	(54.80)	(5.73)	(4.71)	(4.23)	(3.14)	(6.12)	(0.48)	(0.22)	(1.00)	
1976-77	183.04	34.55	504.80	2270.39	238.80	189.75	175.16	132.51	231.79	27.50	7.10	38.06	4033.45
	(4.54)	(0.86)	(12 52)	(56.29)	(5.92)	(4.70)	(4.34)	(3.29)	(5.75)	(0 68)	(0.18)	(0.92)	
1977-78	166.11	61.98	569.87	2414.29	258.46	204.43	180.56	136.35	286.50	29.87	4.20	36.62	4349.24
	(3.82)	(1.42)	(13.10)	(55.51)	(5.94)	(4.70)	(4.15)	(3.14)	(6.59)	(0.69)	(0.09)	(0.88)	
1978-79	188.27	80.36	583.00	2773.31	292.52	234.55	204 88	190.87	333.33	35.57	4.51	48.13	4970.35
	(3.79)	(1.62)	(11.73)	(55.80)	(5.89)	(4.72)	(4.12)	(3.84)	(6 70)	(0.74)	(0.09)	(0.96)	
1979-80	151.90	58.35	698.48	3211.09	373.00	266.53	230.64	209.36	367.94	50.56	4.49	46 80	5669.14
	(2.68)	(1.03)	(12.32)	(56.64)	(6.58)	(4.70)	(4.07)	(3.69)	(6.49)	(0.89)	(0.08)	(0.83)	

1980-81	144.00	50.10	781.40	3794.50	421.70	269.90	253.90	248.20	419.30	67.00	5 50	49.60	6505.10
	(2.21)	(0.77)	(12.01)	(58.33)	(6.48)	(4.15)	(3.90)	(3.82)	(6.45)	(1.03)	(0.08)	(0.76)	
1981-82	204.50	37.62	1115.30	4893.40	453.90	312.80	304.00	250.00	514.90	75.68	5.50	66.70	8234.30
	(2.48)	(0.46)	(13.54)	(59.43)	(5.51)	(3.80)	(3.69)	(3 04)	(6.25)	(0.92)	(0.06)	(0 82)	
1982-83	170.70	38.36	1330.50	5563.50	537.40	445.80	346.00	328.80	559.60	83.53	5.80	64.70	9474.69
(R.E.)	(1.80)	(0.40)	(14.04)	(58.72)	(5.67)	(4.71)	(3.65)	(3.47)	(5.81)	(0.88)	(0.06)	(0.68)	
1983-84	206.00	39.31	1496.20	6309.90	663.00	445.80	392.70	356.60	616.40	90.30	5.90	84.40	10706.51
(B.E.)	(1 92)	(0.37)	(13 97)	(58.94)	(6.19)	(4.16)	(3.67)	(3.33)	(5.76)	(0.84)	(0.06)	(0.79)	

Source : *Reserve Bank of India Bulletins.*

Note : + = Sales Tax Revenue includes Sales Tax, Central Sales Tax, Motor Spirit Tax and Purchase Tax on Sugarcane. Figures in brackets are percentages to total

1983-84. The revenue from electricity duty is also mounting. It contributed Rs. 5.8 crores in 1955-56, Rs. 35.4 crores in 1965-66, Rs. 111.4 crores in 1975-76 and Rs. 356.6 crores in 1983-84. The percentage of these two taxes in the total State taxes is not major but these taxes are of progressive nature. The revenue from goods and passengers taxes is steadily increasing. It contributed 3 to 4 per cent to the total tax revenue of the States during 1960-61 to 1983-84. Table 2.3 shows that revenue from excise duties amounted to Rs. 45.1 crores in 1955-56, Rs. 96.4 crores in 1965-66, Rs. 435.5 crores in 1975-76, Rs 781.4 crores in 1980-81 and finally Rs. 1496.2 crores in 1983-84. The Table reveals that although revenue from State excise duties is increasing but its percentage to total States tax revenue has declined slightly during the period covered by this Table. This decline is mainly due to the emergence of some new sources of taxes revenue, particularly the sales tax, and also due to adoption of complete or partial prohibition by many States. However, still it is the second important source of revenue in the States.

In 1955-56, sales tax brought the largest revenue to the States followed closely by the land tax and State excises. Even now, the sales tax is the single largest tax for the States. In the words of R.C. Tress "it is an efficient engine of finance."[21] The contribution of sales tax revenue to State taxes revenue was only 28.91 per cent in 1955-56, 35.43 per cent in 1960-61, 50.15 per cent in 1970-71, and 59.43 per cent in 1981-82. After that the percentage of sales tax slightly fell down to 58.72 per cent in 1982-83 and 58.94 per cent in 1983-84. Conclusively, sales tax is the most important source of revenue in the States tax structure.

Role of Sales Tax in Resource Mobilisation of States

John F. Due defines sales tax as "a levy imposed upon the sales or elements incidental to the sales such as receipt from them, of all or wide range of commodities."[22] Tripathy observes that "In recent years sales tax have come to be very widely

21. R.C. Tress: Trend in Public Finance, *Lloyds Bank Review*, July 1953, No. 29, p. 37.
22. John F. Due: *Sales Taxation*, Routledge and Kegan Paul, London, 1957, p. 3.

used in almost all the countries for mobilisation of resources, for regulation of demand and for achieving in a large measure, the objectives of a general expenditure tax without the disadvantages of latter."[23] In India sales tax has gradually come to occupy an important place in the financial structure of States. The financial requirements of States have been continuously increasing and sales tax has come to be recognised as 'KAMDHENU' to meet the increasing requirements of the States because of its elasticity and productivity.

The sales tax has become popular as a source of revenue for the States on account of the following reasons:

(A) Sales tax is based on expenditure. In the words of B.N. Gupta, "Expenditure basis of taxation is regarded superior to income basis of taxation due to its incentive effects on savings, economic growth and inflation control."[24] Moreover, sales tax has greater coverage than taxes like excise, etc.

(B) Sales tax is superior from administrative point of view also because it is easy to collect from small number of firms instead of large number of individuals.

(C) Sales tax fulfils the need for autonomous revenue source for the States in a federal system. In federal countries income taxation is dominated by the federal government. As a consequence, the States turn to sales taxation in order to obtain sufficient autonomous source or tax revenue.

Not only India but other developed and developing countries are also dependent on sales tax due to various reasons. Its administrative simplicity and feasibility make it better suited for taxing persons on the basis of their consumption. Imposition of sales tax reduces the dependence of governments on progressive income-taxes for augmenting their resources for development. In those underdeveloped countries where an effective system of taxing income has not been evolved sales tax constitutes a good substitute. In a developing economy marked by inflationary pressures, these taxes not only help in

23. R.N. Tripathy: *Public Finance in Underdeveloped Countries*, Sterling Publishers Pvt. Ltd., New Delhi, 1985, p. 215.
24. B.N. Gupta: *Indian Federal Finance and Budgetary Policy*, Chaitanya Publishing House, Allahabad, 1970, p. 284.

ploughing back a portion of the increasing income into public saving but also in keeping the inflationary forces under check. Even in socialist economy like U.S.S.R. "The turnover tax is one of the major instruments of Soviet planning and it is not merely an important source of revenue but a means by which price policies appropriate to the investment programme are enforced."[25]

Share in Direct and Indirect Tax Revenue

The most productive direct taxes in India are the subject of Union Government, the States get only a certain portion out of total collection, according to principles formulated by Union Legislation. The direct taxes of States are Land revenue, Taxes on agricultural income, Profession tax, Stamps and registration fees and Urban immovable property tax. These taxes are not much more productive, as the State Governments hesitate due to fear of losing votes. Non-levying of taxes on agricultural income, which may bring adequate tax revenue to meet the fast increasing financial requirements of the States, is a glaring example. Moreover, the tax administrative machinery in federating States is not efficient in administering the direct tax laws. Consequently, there is no way except to impose indirect taxes to fulfil financial requirements. In the words of K.K. Andley and K.P.M. Sundharam "Indirect taxation is good way of mopping-up surplus purchasing power of general public, for it affects a larger part of the population than direct taxation."[26] Further John F. Due has observed that "The most significant merit of indirect taxation is its ability to raise much more revenue than would be politically, economically and administratively feasible with direct taxes."[27]

In India, indirect taxation has emerged, as one of the most handy and effective devices for resource mobilisation in post-independence era. Not only the Union Government but also the State Governments have designed these devices in their own way for the imposition of indirect taxes on goods and services with

25. A.B. Ghosh: *Sales Tax in India*, Ranjit Printers, Delhi, 1954, p. 5.
26. K.K. Andley and K.P.M. Sundharam : *Public Economic and Public Finance*, Ratan Prakashan, Agra, 1979, p. 300.
27. John F. Due : *Indirect Taxation in Developing Economies*. The John Hopkins Press, Baltimore and London, 1970, p. 15.

low elasticities of demand and supply. One of the main reasons for bringing in a large number of goods and services within the ambit of indirect taxes has been that such a wide coverage would result in a constantly increasing flow of revenue to the States. The basic objective of indirect taxation has been to mobilise maximum resources for carrying out developmental programmes. Table 2.4 gives the details of the growth of the share in various direct and indirect taxes of the States under study during 1975-76 to 1983-84.

Table 2.4 gives the comparative analysis of direct and indirect taxes which are assigned to the States. It reveals that direct taxes in Rajasthan contributed only Rs. 21.62 crores in 1975-76. It decreased to Rs. 19.41 crores in 1976-77 to Rs. 18.07 crores in 1977-78 but increased to Rs. 22.64 crores in 1978-79. It again declined to Rs. 19.77 crores in 1979-80, but again rose to Rs. 21.66 crores in 1980-81, Rs. 41.34 crores in 1981-82 and further to Rs. 43.77 crores in 1982-83. Finally it dropped down to Rs. 41.08 crores in 1983-84. The direct taxes have contributed in the range of 9.12 per cent to 16.53 per cent to the State total taxes revenue. Revenue from indirect taxes has been continuously increasing since 1975-76. It was Rs. 109.18 crores in 1975-76. After that it showed a continuous increase thoughout the period of study. It contributed Rs. 132.26 crores in 1976-77, Rs 197.02 crores in 1979-80, Rs. 202.83 crores in 1980-81 and Rs. 345.7 crores in 1982-83. Finally it spurted to Rs. 388.94 crores in 1983-84. Indirect taxes contributed to the State's total tax revenue in the range of 83.47 per cent to 90.88 per cent. The Index number on the base of 1975-76 shows that direct taxes index are not increasing continuously, it has dropped down to 89.78 per cent in 1976-77 to 83.58 per cent in 1977-78, while in 1978-79 it increased to 104.72 per cent. After that it again declined to 91.44 per cent in 1979-80. In the succeeding three years it again increased and reached 202.45 per cent in 1982-83 but finally, dropped down to 190 per cent in 1983-84. The index number of indirect taxes has shown much stable growth and after making a continuous increase it reached 356.24 per cent in 1983-84.

In Uttar Pradesh, a similar trend as in Rajasthan has been witnessed in direct and indirect taxes. The State direct taxes contributed Rs. 67.13 crores in 1975-76 in State total taxes. It

TABLE 2.4
Comparative Analysis of Direct and Indirect Taxes Revenue

(*Rs. in crores*)

Year	*RAJASTHAN*					*UTTAR PRADESH*				
	Direct taxes	*Indirect taxes*	*Total taxes*	*Index No. of direct taxes revenue 1975-76 as base*	*Index No. of indirect taxes revenue 1975-76 as base*	*Direct taxes*	*Indirect taxes*	*Total taxes*	*Index No. of direct taxes revenue 1975-76 as base*	*Index No. of indirect taxes revenue 1975-76 as base*
	Rs.	*Rs.*	*Rs.*			*Rs.*	*Rs.*	*Rs.*		
1975-76	21.62 (16.53)	109.18 (83.47)	130 80	100 00	100 00	67.13 (17.07)	326.08 (82.93)	393.21	100.00	100.00
1976-77	19.41 (12.80)	132.26 (87.20)	151.67	89.78	121.14	77.50 (17.05)	377.16 (82.95)	454.66	115 45	115.66
1977-78	18.07 (10.46)	154.64 (89.54)	172.71	83.58	141.64	76.24 (16.31)	391.37 (83.69)	467 31	113.57	119 93
1978-79	22.64 (11.46)	174.87 (88.54)	197.51	104.72	160.17	103.78 (20.42)	404.37 (79.58)	508 15	154.60	124.01
1979-80	19.77 (9.12)	197.02 (90.88)	216.79	91.44	180.45	90.60 (16.11)	471.67 (83.89)	562.27	134.96	144.65
1980-81	21.66 (9.67)	202.33 (90.33)	223.99	100 19	185.32	88.31 (15.18)	493.35 (84.82)	581.66	131.55	151.30
1981-82	41.34 (13.25)	270 64 (86.75)	311 98	191.21	247.88	122.66 (14.91)	700.17 (85.09)	822.83	182.72	214.72

1982-83	43.77	345.70	389.47	202.45	316.63	138.85	790.45	929.30	206.83	242.41
	(11.24)	(88.76)				(14.94)	(85.06)			
1983-84	41.08	388.94	430.02	190.00	356.24	140.70	849.60	990.30	209.59	260.55
(R.E.)	(9.55)	(90.45)				(14.21)	(85.79)			
			HARYANA					*PUNJAB*		
1975-76	17.35	99.60	116.95	100.00	100.00	21.44	151.36	172.80	100.00	100.00
	(14.84)	(85.16)				(12.40)	(87.60)			
1976-77	15.64	122.43	138.07	90.14	122.92	19.58	182.40	201.98	91.32	120.50
	(11.33)	(88.67)				(9.70)	(90.30)			
1977-78	15.68	132.00	147.68	90.37	132.53	23.98	211.14	235.12	111.84	139.49
	(10.62)	(89.38)				(10.20)	(89.80)			
1978-79	17.98	152.59	170.57	103.63	153.20	30.28	236.80	267.08	141.23	156.44
	(10.54)	(89.46)				(11.34)	(88.66)			
1979-80	18.45	178.65	197.10	106.34	179.36	32.83	276.23	309.06	153.12	182.49
	(9.36)	(90.64)				(10.62)	(89.38)			
1980-81	21.09	213.97	235.06	121.55	214.83	38.05	310.00	348.05	177.47	204.80
	(8.97)	(91.03)				(10.93)	(89.07)			
1981-82	29.02	260.75	289.77	167.26	261.79	49.94	382.24	432 18	232.92	252.53
	(10.01)	(89.99)				(11.56)	(88.44)			
1982-83	28.56	308.12	336.68	164.61	309.35	53.49	436.98	490.47	249.48	288.70
	(8.48)	(91.52)				(10.91)	(89.09)			
1983-84	41.84	361.20	403.04	241.15	362.65	58.55	484.55	543.10	273.08	320.13
(R.E.)	(10.38)	(89.62)				(10.78)	(89.22)			

Source: *Reserve Bank of India Bulletins*

Note : Figures in parenthesis are percentage to total tax.

Direct taxes include Land Revenue, Stamps and Registration Fee, Urban Immovable Property Tax and Profession Tax.

Indirect taxes include Sales Tax, States Excise, Motor Vehicle Tax, Entertainment Tax, Electricity Duties, etc.

increased to Rs. 77.50 crores in 1976-77. While in 1977-78 it declined to Rs. 76.24 crores. It again increased to Rs. 103.78 crores in 1978-79. However, it again fell to Rs. 90.6 crores in 1979-80 and further to Rs. 88.31 crores in 1980-81. After that in the three successive years it increased and finally reached Rs. 140.7 crores in 1983-84. The percentage of the State's total tax revenue has been fluctuating. It was 17.07 per cent in 1975-76 and dropped down to 17.05 per cent in 1976-77 and to 16.31 per cent in 1977-78. While in 1978-79 it increased to 20.42 per cent. It again declined in the three succeeding years and finally reached 14.21 per cent in 1983-84. The indirect taxes contributed Rs. 326.08 crores in the Uttar Pradesh State total tax revenue in 1975-76. Which increased to Rs. 377.16 crores in 1976-77 to Rs. 404.37 crores in 1978-79 and to Rs. 493.35 crores in 1980-81. The revenue from indirect taxes shot up to Rs. 700.17 crores in 1981-82, to Rs. 790.45 crores in 1982-83 and finally to Rs. 849.6 crores in 1983-84. Its contribution in the State's total tax revenue varied between 79.58 per cent to 85.79 per cent throughout the period of study. The Index number of direct taxes increased to 115.45 per cent in 1976-77 over the base year 1975-76. In next year it dropped down to 113.57 per cent but again increased to 154.60 per cent in 1977-78. It again dropped to 134.96 per cent in 1979-80 and to 131.55 per cent in 1980-81. After that it increased in the three successive years and finally reached 209.59 per cent in 1983-84. The index number of indirect taxes are not fluctuating like those of direct taxes. They have shown a continuous increase and reached 260.55 per cent in 1983-84.

In Haryana, State direct taxes contributed Rs. 17.35 crores to State total taxes revenue in 1975-76. It declined to Rs. 15.64 crores in 1976-77, while in the further five succeeding years its revenue increased to previous year, which was to Rs. 15.68 crores in 1977-78 to Rs. 17.98 crores in 1978-79, to Rs. 18.45 crores in 1979-80, to Rs. 21.09 crores in 1980-81, and to Rs. 29.02 crores in 1981-82. It dropped to Rs. 28.56 crores in 1982-83 and finally reached Rs. 41.84 crores in 1983-84. Indirect taxes contributed Rs. 99.60 crores in 1975-76. It increased to Rs. 122.43 crores in 1976-77 to Rs. 132.00 crores in 1977-78, to Rs. 213.97 crores in 1980-81 and to Rs. 308.12 crores in 1982-83, and finally increased to Rs. 361.20 crores in 1983-84.

The direct taxes index number declined to 90.14 per cent in 1976-77 over the base year 1975-76 to 90.37 per cent in 1977-78 It increased continuously and reached 167.26 per cent in 1981-82, while it declined to 164.61 per cent in 1982-83, it again increased to 241.15 per cent in 1983-84. The indirect taxes index number are increasing continuously and finally it reached 362.65 per cent in 1983-84.

In Punjab, State direct taxes contributed Rs. 21.44 crores in 1975-76. It declined to Rs. 19.58 crores in 1976-77. It increased to Rs. 23.98 crores in 1977-78, to Rs. 30.28 crores in 1978-79, to Rs. 32.83 crores in 1979-80 to Rs. 38.05 crores in 1980-81 and to Rs. 49.94 crores in 1981-82. Finally, it rose to Rs. 58.55 crores in 1983-84. The revenue from direct taxes has been increasing since 1977-78 but the percentage to total State taxes has not increased. It contributed 12.40 per cent in 1975-76 and declined to 9.70 per cent in 1976-77. It increased to 10.20 per cent in 1977-78 and to 11.34 per cent in 1978-79. It again declined to 10 62 per cent in 1979-80. In the further two succeeding years its contribution again increased to previous year and reached 11.56 per cent in 1981-82. Finally its contribution in State total taxes declined 10.78 per cent in 1983-84. Revenue from indirect taxes increased continuously. It contributed to Rs. 151.36 crores in 1975-76, to Rs. 182.40 crores in 1976-77, to Rs. 211.14 crores in 1977-78, to Rs. 236.80 crores in 1978-79 to Rs. 276.23 crores in 1979-80, to Rs. 310 crores in 1980-81, to Rs. 382.24 crores in 1981-82 and Rs. 436.98 crores in 1982-83 and finally reached Rs. 484.55 crores in 1983-84. The percentage of indirect taxes to total State taxes varied between 87.60 to 90.30 throughout the period of study. The index number of direct taxes has declined to 91.32 per cent in 1976-77 over the base year 1975-76, after that making a steady growth it reached 273.08 per cent in 1983-84. While the indirect taxes index increased continuously and reached 320.13 per cent in 1983-84.

Conclusively, the direct taxes are not much productive, they contributed only 9.12 per cent to 16.53 per cent in Rajasthan, 14.21 per cent to 20.42 per cent in Uttar Pradesh, 8.48 per cent to 14.84 per cent in Haryana, 9.70 per cent to 12.40 per cent in Punjab. The direct taxes have increased only 1.90 times in Rajasthan, 2.10 times in Uttar Pradesh, 2.41 times in

Haryana and 2.73 times in Punjab since 1975-76, while the indirect taxes have increased to 3.56 times in Rajasthan, 2.60 times in Uttar Pradesh, 3.62 times in Haryana and 3.20 times in Punjab. It shows that the direct taxes are not much productive, and the increasing trend of indirect taxes has motivated the State Governments to lean more and more on indirect taxes. Table 2.4 reveals that the States have heavily relied upon indirect taxes. The share of indirect taxes increased regularly while the share of direct taxes revenue has shown many fluctuations throughout the period of study. The ratio of direct and indirect tax in the combined sources of revenue indicates that indirect taxes are playing a major role in the State's total tax revenue. In 1975-76 the ratio between direct and indirect taxes was 16.5 : 83.5 in Rajasthan, 17.1 : 82.9 in Uttar Pradesh, 14.9 : 85.1 in Haryana, 12.4 : 87.6 in Punjab, while in the 1983-84 it was 9.5 : 90.5 in Rajasthan, 14.2 : 85.8 in Uttar Pradesh 10.4 : 89.6 in Haryana, 10.8 : 89.2 in Punjab. It shows that indirect taxes contributed 85 to 90 per cent in the States' total taxes revenue. The index number of indirect taxes has also shown continuously increasing trend throughout the period of study. Thus it can be inferred that in the recent few years in the tax structure of northern States, the direct taxes have been regressive, while the indirect taxes have tended to be progressive.

Contribution of Sales Tax in the Indirect Taxation

The importance of sales tax as a source of revenue to the State Governments is undoubted. It is the most expanding source of revenue for all the State Governments in the country. It is the largest source of revenue in every State. Whenever the Union Government has expected the States to raise additional resources for the fulfilment of plan targets, the States in their turn have looked towards the sales taxes to yield the requisite revenue.[28]

Table 2.5 presents the contribution of sales tax in indirect

28. The Planning Commission is responsible in India to frame Five Year Plans as well as annual plans. While formulating the plans and examining the availability of resources with the States, the Planning Commission recommends mobilisation of additional resources.

taxes and State's own taxes in the four States under study for the period from 1975-76 to 1983-84. The study of correlation between sales tax and indirect taxes and State's own taxes has also been presented in the Table, given on the next page.

Table 2.5 reveals that the yield from indirect taxes is highly affected by sales tax. In fact, out of total receipts from indirect taxes, sales tax alone contributed more than half of the indirect taxes. In Rajasthan sales tax contributed Rs. 67.60 crores in 1975-76. It increased to Rs. 84.29 crores in 1976-77, to Rs. 100.25 crores in 1977-78, to Rs. 145.00 crores in 1980-81 to Rs. 186. 21 crores in 1981-82, to Rs. 222.23 crores in 1982-83 and finally reached Rs. 248.00 crores in 1983-84. Sales tax contributed in the range of 61.9 to 71.66 per cent in the indirect taxes. It, however, contributed in the State's own taxes revenue in the range of 51.68 to 64.74 per cent during the period of study.

In Uttar Pradesh, sales tax contributed Rs. 208.26 crores in 1975-76. It increased to Rs. 243.17 crores in 1976-77, to Rs. 246.03 crores in 1977-78, to Rs. 272.25 crores in 1978-79, to Rs. 313.97 crores in 1980-81, to Rs. 486.98 crores in 1982-83 and finally it shot up to Rs. 530.38 crores in 1983-84. The percentage of sales tax to State's own taxes and indirect taxes is in the range of 52.40 to 55.10 and 61.61 to 67.33 respectively, during the period of study.

In Haryana, the sales tax contributed Rs. 49.50 crores in 1975-76. It registered a steady growth and reached Rs. 63.95 crores in 1976-77, Rs. 69.62 crores in 1977-78, Rs. 90.05 crores in 1979-80, Rs. 138.37 crores in 1981-82, Rs. 160.48 crores in 1982-83 and finally Rs. 189.70 crores in 1983-84. The sale tax has contributed in the State's indirect taxes in the range of 49.7 to 53.06 per cent, while in the States own taxes revenue, it has contributed in the range of 42.34 per cent to 47.67 per cent during 1975-76 to 1983-84.

In Punjab, the sales tax contributed Rs. 73.16 crores in 1975-76 and increased to Rs. 96.12 crores in 1976-77, to Rs. 107.51 crores in 1977-78, to Rs. 119.31 crores in 1978-79, to Rs. 160 crores in 1980-81, to Rs. 191.82 crores in 1981-82, to Rs. 219.93 crores in 1982-83 and finally reached Rs. 249.95 crores in 1983-84. In the State's indirect taxes, it contributed in

TABLE 2.5

Contribution of Sales Tax in Indirect Taxes and States Own Taxes Revenue

(*Rs. in crores*)

Year	RAJASTHAN			UTTAR PRADESH			HARYANA			PUNJAB		
	Sales tax Rs.	Indirect taxes Rs.	States own taxes Rs.	Sales tax Rs.	Indirect taxes Rs.	States own taxes Rs.	Sales tax Rs.	Indirect taxes Rs.	States own taxes Rs.	Sales tax Rs.	Indirect taxes Rs.	States own taxes Rs.
1975-76	67.60	109.18	130.80	208.26	326.08	393.66	49.50	99.60	116.95	73.16	151.36	172.80
	(61.90)			(63.86)			(49.70)			(48.33)		
	[51.68]			[52.90]			[42.34]			[42.34]		
1976-77	84.29	132.26	151.67	243.17	377.16	454.66	63.95	122.43	138.07	96.12	182.40	201.98
	(63.73)			(64.47)			(52.23)			(52.70)		
	[55.77]			[53.48]			[46.32]			[47.59]		
1977-78	100.25	154.64	172.71	246.03	391.07	467.31	69.62	132.00	147.68	107.51	211.14	235.12
	(64.82)			(62.90)			(52.74)			(50.92)		
	[58.04]			[52.64]			[47.15]			[45.72]		
1978-79	113.68	174.87	197.51	272.25	404.37	508.15	79.68	152.59	170.57	119.31	236.80	267.08
	(65.00)			(67.33)			(52.22)			(50.38)		
	[57.56]			[53.58]			[46.72]			[44.67]		
1979-80	135.86	197.02	216.79	302.52	471.67	562.27	90.05	178.65	197.30	129.79	267.23	309.06
	(68.95)			(64.13)			(50.40)			(46.99)		
	[62.67]			[53.80]			[45.64]			[42.00]		
1980-81	145.00	202.33	223.99	313.97	493.35	581.66	108.00	213.97	235.06	160.00	310.00	348.05
	(71.66)			(63.64)			(50.47)			(51.61)		
	[64.74]			[53.98]			[45.95]			[45.97]		

1981-82	186.21 (68.80) [59.69]	270.64	311.98	453.35 (64.75) [55.10]	700.17	822.83	138.37 (53.06) [47.61]	260.75	290.62	191.82 (50.18) [44.39]	382.24	432.18
1982-83	222.23 (64.28) [57.06]	345.70	389.47	486.98 (61.61) [52.40]	790.45	929.30	160.48 (52.09) [47.67]	308.12	336.68	219.93 (50.32) [44.84]	436.98	490.47
1983-84 (R.E.)	248.00 (63.76) [57.67]	388.94	430 02	530.38 (62.42) [53.55]	849.60	990.30	189.70 (52.52) [47.06]	361.20	403.04	249.95 (51.58) [46.02]	484.55	543.11
Correlation of sales tax to indirect tax.			+.994			+.998			+.999			+.997
Correlation among sales tax and State own taxes.			+.993			+.783			+.999			+.997

Source: *Reserve Bank of India Bulletins*.

Sales Tax Revenue includes Revenue from General Sales Tax, Central Sales Tax, Purchase Tax on Sugarcane, Motor Spirit Tax.

Figures in parenthesis ( ) are percentage of sales tax to indirect taxes.

Figures in brackets [ ] are percentage to States own taxes.

the range of 46.99 per cent to 52.70 per cent, while in the State's own taxes it contributed in the range of 42.00 per cent to 47.59 per cent throughout the period of study.

Conclusively it may be stated that the sales tax is an important source of revenue among indirect taxes and also in the State's own taxes revenue. In Rajasthan it contributed in the range of 61 9 to 71.66 per cent in the indirect taxes revenue and in State's own taxes its contribution varied in the range of 51.68 to 64.74 per cent. In Uttar Pradesh, it contributed in the range of 61.61 to 67.33 per cent in indirect taxes and 52.40 to 55.10 per cent in the State's own taxes revenue. While in Haryana the contribution is in the range of 49.7 to 53.06 per cent in indirect taxes revenue, and 42.34 to 47.67 per cent in State's own taxes revenue, in Punjab its contribution was in the range of 46.99 to 52.70 per cent in indirect taxes and 42.00 to 47.59 per cent in the State's own taxes revenue. It reveals that sales tax is a highly productive source of revenue for the States. Rajasthan occupies the first rank followed by Uttar Pradesh, Haryana and Punjab. It is crystal clear that every second paisa in State taxes revenue has sprung from sales tax. The growth of indirect taxes revenue is highly affected by sales tax. This is the main reason why the States are not interested in the abolition of sales tax.

Relationship Between Sales Tax and Indirect Taxes and States' Own Taxes Revenue

The correlation between sales tax and indirect taxes as also between sales tax and State's taxes revenue has been studied by applying the following formula as propounded by Karl Pearson.

$$r = \frac{N \, . \, \Sigma XY - (\Sigma X)\,(\Sigma Y)}{\sqrt{[N \, . \, \Sigma X^2 - (\Sigma X)^2]\,[N. \, \Sigma Y^2 - (\Sigma Y)^2]}}$$

The correlation (r) as also between sales tax and indirect taxes comes to +.994 in Rajasthan, +.998 in Uttar Pradesh, +.999 in Haryana, +.997 in Punjab. It shows a high degree of positive correlation between revenues from sales tax and the State indirect taxes. Correlation between sales tax and State's own revenue is +.993 in Rajasthan, +.783 in Uttar Pradesh, +.999 in Haryana, +.997 in Punjab. It also shows a high degree of positive correlation. It puts Haryana on the first position, followed by Punjab, Uttar Pradesh, and Rajasthan in regard to State's indirect taxes while in the own tax revenue the first rank again goes to Haryana followed by Punjab, Rajasthan and Uttar Pradesh. Such high degree of positive correlation between sales tax and indirect taxes and State's own taxes revenue signifies that State revenues are highly affected by sales tax and major share is derived from sales tax in State sources. The State of Uttar Pradesh is the only exception which has diversified its revenue base indicating the lowest correlation (+.783) among all the States.

Role of Sales Tax in Total Revenue and Total Tax Revenue

Over the years, the taxes have come to occupy a very important place in Indian fiscal structure. Sales tax occupies a key position in the revenue system of the States. P.K. Bhargava has observed that, sales tax is the most elastic source of revenue and called State's milch cow.[29] All the sources of State revenue can be grouped under two major heads : (*i*) tax revenue (*ii*) non-tax revenue. The tax revenue includes all the receipts from the Centre (share in Income-tax, Estate duty, Union excise duties) and Land revenue, Stamps and registration fees, Sales tax, State excise, Taxes on Vehicles, Entertainment tax, Electricity duties, etc. Under non-tax revenue, all the receipts from public undertakings and economic services (Forests, Agriculture, Irrigation, Power projects, Dairy development, Multi purpose river schemes, Royalty on minerals, Animals husbandry, etc.) general services (State lotteries) interest and dividend receipts, social and community services and plan and non-plan grants-in-aid from the Centre are included.

The share of sales tax in total revenue and total tax revenue in the States under study is depicted in Table 2.6 (as given on next page).

It is evident from Table 2.6 that sales tax contributes the lion's share to the total revenue and total taxes revenue of the States, where about third or fourth of the tax pie springs from this source. In Rajasthan, sales tax contributed 17.12 per cent to total revenues in 1975-76. It increased to 20.60 per cent in

29. P.K. Bhargava : "Sales Tax : The States Milch Cow" *Eastern Economist*, October 20, 1967, p. 724.

TABLE 2.6

Contribution of Sales Tax in Total Revenue and Total Tax Revenue from 1975-76 to 1983-84

(*Rs. in crores*)

Year	*RAJASTHAN*			*UTTAR PRADESH*			*HARYANA*			*PUNJAB*		
	Total Revenue	*Total Tax Revenue*	*Sales Tax Revenue*	*Total Revenue*	*Total Tax Revenue*	*Sales Tax Revenue*	*Total Revenue*	*Total Tax Revenue*	*Sales Tax Revenue*	*Total Revenue*	*Total Tax Revenue*	*Sales Tax Revenue*
1975-76	394.92	205.29	67.60	951.06	650.21	208.26	228.53	144.09	49.50	304.41	210.98	73.16
			(17.12)			(21.90)			(21.66)			(24 03)
			[32.93]			[32.03]			[34.35]			[34.68]
1976-77	452.59	230.71	84.29	1105.31	728.11	243.17	257.79	157.65	63.95	376.41	241.51	96.12
			(18.62)			(22.00)			(24.81)			(25.54)
			[36.54]			[33.40]			[40.56]			[39.80
1977-78	486.54	256.70	100.25	1164.66	758.55	246.03	295.84	185.26	69.62	406.12	277.33	107.51
			(20.60)			(21.12)			(23.53)			(26.47)
			[39.05]			[32.43]			[37.58]			[38.77]
1978-79	595.88	289.25	113.68	1361.81	825.78	272.25	334.83	203.63	79.68	481.01	312.76	119.31
			(19.08)			(19.99)			(23.80)			(24.80)
			[39.30]			[33.33]			[39.13]			[38.15]
1979-80	653.37	374.02	135.86	1684.47	1131.39	302.52	402.12	251.36	90.05	519.35	382.41	129.79
			(20.79)			(17.96)			(22.39)			(24.99)
			[36.32]			[26.74]			[35.83]			[33.94]
1980-81	730.30	392.28	145.00	1827.24	1193.30	313.97	459.07	295.41	108.00	563.61	425.12	160.00
			(19.85)			(17.18)			(23.53)			(28.39)
			[36.96]			[26.31]			[36.56]			[37.54]

1981-82	857.08	508.34	186.21 (21.72) [36.63]	2259.67	1534.70	453.35 (20.06) [29.54]	536.07	358.65	138.37 (25.81) [38.58]	682.61	524.42	191.82 (28.10) [36.58]
1982-83	1009.06	603.08	222.23 (22.02) [36.85]	2556.08	1704.63	486.98 (19.05) [28.57]	611.62	409.29	160.43 (26.24) [39.21]	786.04	589.70	219.93 (27.98) [37.30]
1983-84 (R.E.)	1148.83	672.03	248.00 (29.59) [36.90]	2796.82	1859.57	530.38 (18.96) [28.52]	733.27	485.71	189.70 (25.87) [39.06]	905.56	654.77	249.95 (27 60) [38.17]

Source: *Reserve Bank of India Bulletins.*

Note : Figures in parenthesis ( ) percentage of Sales Tax to Total Revenue and
Figures in bracket [ ] are percentage of Sales Tax to Total Tax Revenue.

1977-78. After making short fluctuations it reached 22.02 per cent in 1982-83 and finally it contributed 21.59 per cent to States total revenue during 1983-84. Sales tax contributed 32.93 per cent to total tax revenue in 1975-76. After making a steady growth in the three succeeding years it reached 39.30 per cent in 1978-79, but in the four successive years its contribution dropped down slightly and finally reached 36.90 per cent in total tax revenue in 1983-84.

In Uttar Pradesh, sales tax contributed 21.90 per cent to total revenue in 1975-76. It contributed 22.00 per cent in 1976-77. After that it has shown a downward trend and reached 17.18 per cent in 1980-81. However, it again increased to 20.06 per cent in 1981-82 but declined to 19.05 per cent in 1982-83 and further to 18.96 per cent in 1983-84. Sales tax contributed 32.03 per cent in 1975-76 to total tax revenue. It increased to 33.40 per cent in 1976-77. The percentage dropped, in comparison to the previous year and touched the level of 32.43 per cent in 1977-78. In 1978-79 its contribution increased to 33.33 per cent. It again declined, in the two succeeding years and reached 26.31 per cent in 1980-81 and finally in 1983-84 it contributed 28.52 per cent.

In Haryana, sales tax contributed 21.66 per cent to the total revenue in 1975-76. Its contribution increased to 24.81 per cent in 1976-77. But the percentage dropped to 23.53 in 1977-78. It again increased in 1978-79 to 23.80 but declined to 22.39 in 1979-80. After making a steady growth in the three succeeding years the contribution of sales tax to the States total revenue reached 26.24 per cent in 1982-83 but finally dropped down to 25.87 per cent in 1983-84. The sales tax contributed 34.35 per cent to the State's total tax revenue in 1975-76. It rose to 40.56 per cent in 1976-77 but declined to 37.58 per cent in 1977-78. It again increased to 39.13 per cent in 1978-79, fell to 35.83 per cent in 1979-80. After that it made a steady growth in the three succeeding years and the contribution reached 39.21 per cent in 1982-83. However, it marginally declined to 39.06 per cent in 1983-84.

In Punjab, sales tax contributed 24.03 per cent to the total revenue in 1975-76. In the further two years, its contribution increased to 25.54 per cent and to 26.47 per cent respectively. After making short fluctuations in the two succeeding years it reached 28.39 per cent in 1980-81. After that it showed a declining trend in the succeeding three years and finally contributed 27.60 per cent in 1983-84. The sales tax contributed 34.68 per cent to the total tax revenue in 1975-76. Its contribution increased to 39.80 per cent in 1976-77. In further three succeeding years, its percentage registered a fall and reached 33.94 in 1979-80. Its contribution increased to 37.54 per cent in 1980-81 but again declined to 36.58 per cent in 1981-82. After that it made a steady growth, and contributed 38.17 per cent in 1983-84.

Conclusively, the revenue from sales tax, total tax and total revenue has been increasing. The sales tax revenue has increased 3.67 times in Rajasthan, 2.55 times in Uttar Pradesh, 3.83 times in Haryana, and 3.42 times in Punjab during the period of study. It shows that growth of sales tax is the highest in Punjab followed by Haryana, Rajasthan and Uttar Pradesh. The total revenue has increased 2.91 times in Rajasthan, 2.94 times in Uttar Pradesh, 3.20 times in Haryana and 2.97 times in Punjab. The total tax revenue has increased 3.27 times in Rajasthan, 2.86 times in Uttar Pradesh, 3.37 times in Haryana and 3.10 times in Punjab. It reveals that the total tax revenue and the total revenue are increasing but it could not keep pace with the increasing trend of sales tax revenue except in Uttar Pradesh, where the growth of sales tax is lower that of the total revenue and total tax revenue. The revenue receipts from sales tax in the States under study has been increasing since the last decade. But the percentage to total tax has been fluctuating in the range of 32.93 to 39.30 in Rajasthan, 26.31 to 33.40 in Uttar Pradesh, 34.35 to 40.56 in Haryana and 33.94 to 39.80 in Punjab. Punjab is the State, where sales tax contributed higher percentage to total revenue and total tax revenue, followed by Haryana, Rajasthan and Uttar Pradesh.

Replacement of Sales Tax

A strong plea has been made by representatives of trade and industry as well as others for abolishing sales tax as separate levy and incorporating it in the Union Excise Duties. The Election manifesto of the Janata Party in 1977 had promised the abolition of sales tax in India. The All India Congress Committee (I) session of 1984, too stressed replacement of sales tax on key commodities by Union Excise Duty. Tripathi Committee also suggested to levy excise duty in lieu of sales tax on cement and cement products, petrol and petroleum products, paper and paper board, medicines and hydrogenated oils.[30] Sales tax has grown into an independent as well as very elastic and lucrative source of revenue for the State Governments, the question of its abolition has not been decided as yet. 'If sales tax is abolished then what alternative approaches can be searched to secure States share, is a very crucial question. In this regard two approaches have been suggested from time to time by different parties. There are, firstly replacement of sales tax by Additional Excise Duties and, secondly, the introduction of Value Added Tax (VAT).

Replacement of Sales Tax by Additional Excise Duties

Sales tax is a very important source of revenue of the States but it has given birth to several problems in the fiscal structure of India. Rate differentiation from State to State on the same commodity, difference in exemption limits of turnover of dealers, procedural variation in realisation create the problems especially for the trading community because free movement of goods across the boundaries of the State leads to widespread evasion of sales tax. It has compelled the State Governments to restore to certain inconvenient methods such as the creation of check posts on the borders of the States. A high rate of inter-State sales tax has also induced big producers of one State to establish warehouses in other States where the products are to be sold and to transfer them from the point of production to warehouses without payment of inter-State sales tax, and discrimination between local producer and outside producer regarding rate of local sales tax has also motivated out side dealers to get them-self registered in the local State and to issue sales tax exemption sale vouchers showing it as indigenous produce. Furthermore, "the inflationary situation in the country, which has been partly due to frequent hiking of the rates of sales tax which are mostly *ad valorem*, has created a negative reaction of the public in the form of resistance to rate hikes because sales tax pushes up the

30. *Tripathi Committee Report* : Ministry of Finance, New Delhi, 1983 Quoted in *Hindustan Times*. "Formulae to Allay Fear Over ST Replacement" May 24, 1983, p. 4.

prices."[31] Such reaction makes tax evasion easy for dealers in collusion with the consumers.

Thus, sales tax system today needs reforms and it is demanded from the Central Government to take over the power of levy of sales tax and replace it by additional excise duties. Business community viewed that replacement will eliminate the difficulties of compliance with sales tax laws and relieve many traders of liability to submit returns, assessment, etc. Secondly, it is much harder for manufacturers to evade excise duties than small traders to evade sales tax. Thirdly, unnecessary movement of goods due to rate differentiation will wither away.

It is in this context that the feasibility and desirability of extending additional duties in lieu of sales tax on few more essential commodities has been examined.

In fact, the history of arguments for abolishing sales tax and replacing it by additional excise duty dates back to 1956. Following the recommendations of National Development Council in 1966, and after considering the Second Finance Commission's view, the States sales tax levy on sugar, textiles and tobacco was replaced by additional excise duties. It did not cover the inputs required in the manufacture of these commodities. As a result the States continued to levy a sales or purchase tax on the inputs like sugarcane and cotton yarn. It was also decided that the net proceed would be distributed among the States, subject to the condition that the previous revenue of the States from the sales tax on these goods was assured to them, the States agreed to this arrangement. The principle of distribution had to be determined by the various Finance Commissions. Rao has observed that "this arrangement has been treated by all the Finance Commissions essentially as a tax rental agreement between Central Government and State Government."[32]

Analysis of Present Working System and Problems

India is a federal country where States have their own fiscal autonomy. Any step which proposes to take the existing fiscal power of the State Governments is opposed vehemently by the

31. G. Thimmaiah : *Perspectives on Tax Design and Tax Reform*, Ashish Publishing House, New Delhi, 1984, pp. 161-63.
32. Hemalata Rao : *Centre-State Financial Relations*, Allied Publishers (P) Ltd., New Delhi, 1981, p. 19.

States. Moreover, the sales tax being an *ad valorem* levy, all the State Governments are benefited automatically through changing price levels. On the other hand the additional excise duties are specific, as such the State share is not likely to increase automatically with the increase of prices of the commodity. All the State Governments have raised the rates of sales tax since 1956-57 and increased the revenue, but the rates of additional excise duties have not kept pace. Rather the Central Government has time and again increased its own basic excise duty rates on similar commodities. This policy was unjust and obviously backed by illogical reasons. State Governments feel that they would have got more revenue from the three commodities if these had remained under their jurisdiction. They have bitter experiences of the way in which, after having agreed to replace the sales tax on textiles, tobacco and sugar by additional excise duty, their revenue from these items remained virtually frozen and no fair treatment was given by the Finance Commission. Sales tax has its strong points and serve some objective which the excise duties do not provide.

A major drawback of levying additional excise duty is that several commodities would get freed from taxation without any justifiable economic reason. Though excise taxation is levied at the point of production, in actual practice, it covers mostly industrial production. While, legally speaking, excise duty can be imposed on agricultural production, too, it would be simply impracticable and uneconomic to try to tax millions of small agricultural producers. Even within the sphere of industry, the production that takes place in numerous units in the unorganised sector is left out of the excise ambit for administrative reasons. Here sales tax plays useful role because through this tax it becomes possible to cover agricultural commodities and other goods which could not be taxed at the stage of production.

Views of Different Authorities

The question of levying additional excise duties was brought before the Taxation Enquiry Commission (1953-54). The Commission rejected the idea and emphasised that sales tax must continue to be a tax of the State as a source of revenue and each State should be free to evolve the system of sales tax best suited to its economic conditions.[33]

Bhoothalingam Committee viewed that in the larger interest of the country and on strict economic consideration it would be desirable not only to continue the current system of excise duties in lieu of sales taxes but to extend its scope to other commodities of mass consumptions which are manufactured widely in the country.[34]

However, the Committee maintained that the Central Government should adopt a more liberal or generous policy regarding the making up of the potential loss of revenue to the States.

Lakdawala[35] observed that the States can only be reconciled to the surrender of this power if they can be assured of an adequate share in the tax proceeds which will more than compensate them for not only their immediate revenue loss but also for the potential loss. However, he cautioned that the past experience of sharing additional excise proceeds in India should be taken note of while introducing changes in the federal tax structure.

The question of abolition of sales tax has been re-examined in detail by the Jha Committee[36] and Raja J. Chelliah.[37] The Jha Committee did not recommend the replacement of sales tax by additional excise duties. However, the Jha Committee brought out ways in which the major indirect taxes in the country, viz., import duties, central excise duties, sales tax and the octroi interacted with one another and exerted an impact on prices and allocation of resources. The committee stressed the need for harmonisation of the indirect tax structure.

The National Development Council (N.D.C.) on 28th December, 1970 discussed the complaints of the States regarding

33. Government of India : *Report of Taxation Enquiry Commission, 1953-54* Vol. III, pp. 55-6.
34. Bhoothalingam, S. : *Review of Sales Tax in Andhra Pradesh*, NCAER, New Delhi, 1971, p. 26.
35. D.T. Lakdawala : "Value Added Tax", *The Indian Economic Journal*, October—December 1976, No. 2, pp. 183-207.
36. Government of India : Ministry of Finance, *Report of the Indirect Taxation Enquiry Committee*, New Delhi, January, 1978, Vol. II, p. 228.
37. Raja J. Chelliah : "Reform of Sales Tax" *The Economic Times*, September 11, 12, 1980.

the lower rates of additional duties of excise and other issues relating to their financial autonomy. The council decided to continue the existing scheme subject to the rates of additional excise duties stopped at 10.8 per cent of the value clearances in a period of two to three years and to maintain in future the ratio between basic and additional excise duties at 2.1. It further decided that the specific duties be converted into *ad valorem* duties exept in regard to unmanufactured tobacco. In pursuance of these decisions, the additional excise duties were raised substantially in three successive Central Budgets from 1971 to 1973.

The Union Finance Minister convened meeting of Chief Ministers in September 1980 in which it was decided to levy additional excise duty on vanaspati, cement, drugs and medicines, petroleum products, paper and paper products.[38] Actually original proposal was to include vanaspati and life saving drugs in the list of items in respect of which sales tax can be replaced by additional excise duties. The proposals were opposed by States like Kerala, Tamil Nadu, West Bengal and Tripura. These States were of the opinion that it would increase the dependence of the States on the Centre for funds needed for essential developmental activities.

A committee was constituted to go into this issue and make recommendations. From the recommendations of this committee[39] it appears as though the sales tax is going to be gradually replaced by union excise duties. If this ever happens, it will have serious financial implications for the State Governments. However, the committee has recommended replacement of sales tax on vanaspati, drugs and medicines, cement, paper and paper board and petroleum products by additional excise duty.

The suggestion of complete centralization of both levy and administration of sales taxation has been strongly condemned. It would create problems for the States and would virtually lead to an eclipse of the federal system in the country.[40]

38. A.K. Agarwal : "Replacement of Sales Tax by Additional Duties of Excise", *Southern Economist*, May 15, 1982, p. 20.
39. *Tripathi Committee Report*, Ministry of Finance, New Delhi, 1983.
40. R.N. Tripathy : *Fiscal Policy and Economic Development in India*, The World Press Private Ltd., Calcutta, 1958, p. 153.

In the light of the above analysis, if the revenue from additional excise duties is distributed on a rational, fair and equitable basis, than the States may agree for the extension of such scheme on more commodities, of course, it would be very difficult to make all the States agree at one point. It is also necessary that the rates of additional duties of excise should be changed proportionately to the changes in the rates of basic excise dutes, otherwise States would think that they are losing revenue.

Value Added Tax (VAT)

In order to evolve a more rational and broad based system of sales taxation, there has been a world wide interest in the potentialities of value added tax as a source of revenue in place of sales tax. France was the first country to adopt value added tax at the wholesale level in 1954. This system of taxation has been adopted in twelve countries of Europe and also in a few countries of Latin America and Africa. Countries such as Australia, Canada, Finland, New Zealand, Switzerland and United States have discussed the scope for introduction of such a tax.[41]

Definition of VAT

VAT is defined as a tax on the value that is added to goods and services by enterprises at each stage of production and distribution process.[42] Thus, where an industry is horizontally integrated with firms specialising in single process, the tax would be based only as the work done by each firm. It is more broadly based and falls less heavily on particular goods and services than purchase tax. Goods and services not liable to value added tax may be zero-rated or exempted and no tax on inputs may be reclaimed.[43]

41. *O.E C D. Studies in Taxation* ; The Impact of Consumption Taxes at Different Income Levels, Paris, 1981, p. 54.
42. E. Lent George, Caranegra Milk and Guerard. Michela : "The VAT in Developing Countries". *IMF Staff Papers*, Vol. XX, 1973, p. 319.
43. J.L. Hanson : *A Dictionary of Economics and Commerce*, The English Language Book Society and Macdonald and Evans Ltd., London, 1977, pp. 458-59.

Advantages of the VAT

An important merit of VAT is its neutrality with respect to the allocation of resources in the economy. As a substitute for turnover tax of various types (single stage, multi-stage, etc.) VAT would help to avoid the cascading effects in the production. Turnover tax is applied repeatedly to the full value of a production and distribution and thereby distorts the relative prices in the economy. For instance, if there are three firms *A*, *B* and *C* in an economy if firm *B* uses firm *A*'s output as its input and similarly if firm *C* uses the output of other firms as its input in the absence of refund provisions, the tax is levied at each stage and is mixed up with the price of a commodity. However, the VAT assessed at each stage on only the incremental value acquired by the product since the last taxable transaction. This means that at the end of the chain, the total amount of tax paid on a given commodity is only a fraction of the rate of tax and of the final price of the commodity, independently of the number of stages through which it has passed. In particular tax credit method under VAT facilities easy and accurate refund of tax levied on inputs and raw materials used in the process of production.

The intermediate purchases such as inputs and raw materials are subject to tax under a turnover tax. Therefore, there is a scope for vertical integration of firms to avoid liability for taxation, on the other hand, under VAT, since the tax is levied on value added by each firm at each stage, the total tax burden on a product is independent of the number of stages which it would pass through. As such, solely for the purpose of tax evasion, there is no scope for vertical integration of firms under VAT.

In developing countries a value added tax of an universal character has much to commend itself on administrative ground because in these countries the problem of tax evasion exists on considerable scale. It has been argued that in value added tax, under the tax credit method the evasion is more difficult because the system provides for a cross checking process of assessees. The invoice price is important factor to determine tax liability of both the purchaser and the seller. It is in the interest of an assessee to insist the supplier to furnish invoice otherwise he would not be able to claim tax credit scheme benefit.

Adoptability of VAT in Place of Sales Tax

To adopt value added tax, it is essential to examine the basic features of sales tax structure of India. The sales tax is within the jurisdiction of States and each State has planned their own structure according to its needs which differ from State to State. In recent years, there has been a trend to use single point levy imposed at first stage as against last point in the chain transaction to check the evasion of sales tax.

The Jha Committee has pointed out[44] that in practice, the sales tax systems in different States have led to the following problems:

(*i*) the problem of cascading the distortions in the factor prices;

(*ii*) sales taxes imposed by one State affect other States; and

(*iii*) legal, administration and procedural complexities which affect the trade and industry.

Therefore, there are manifold difficulties facing present sales tax system; Multiplicity and discriminatory rates would hinder the free flow of goods between different States. Due to the taxation of inputs and raw materials tax may have cascading effects in production, while differences in turnover limits may affect the very mode inter-State business organisation and vertical integration may also cause inefficiencies in production. In the multiple point of taxation, it is very difficult to ascertain the incidence of tax. Even though the rates may be the same, its ultimate impact may vary from commodity to commodity depending upon the number of stages which the commodity passes through to reach ultimate consumer. Hence, the varying system foster problem to tax management. And this tax may lead to a structure of relative commodity prices which can be far removed from the intended price structure, that is, the differential tax rates structure may not ultimately be reflected in relative prices and may, as a result, distort the consumption pattern.[45]

44. Jha Committee : *Report of Indirect Taxation Enquiry Committee*, Part I, 1977, p. 218.

45. M. Sarvane : "Tax on Value Added for India : Issues and Alternatives" *Reserve Bank of India Bulletin*, March 1976, p. 212.

Now the question is that whether VAT can be adopted at the State level or at the national level in India to replace sales tax. If it is adopted at State level a great number of substantial VAT systems would be in vogue in place of the present sales tax system. The replacement of States sales taxes by a VAT presents no great advantage at the State level[46] and create problems in respect of inter-State trade and commerce.

If the value added tax adopted at national level with a single rate and operated by the centralised authority in the place of existing States sales tax it poses the following problems:

(*i*) Amendment of the Constitution to shift the power of levying sales tax from States to Centre.

(*ii*) The administrative and compliance problem regarding introduction of new tax.

It is very difficult to solve the first problem because it is the question of States finance and Centre-States financial relation which are already crucial at present. States do not want to do away with sales tax because for States development programmes, sales tax yields considerable revenue. The Jha Committee has recognised the role played by the sales tax and did not recommend its replacement by value added tax. Further the committee opined that the loss of power to levy sales taxes would seriously erode the financial autonomy of the State Governments and weaken the federal principal that each subordinate level of government should have discretion to raise more or less revenue as the poeple of State concerned desire.[47]

Value added tax covers large number of scattered or small traders which create problems because it is quite difficult to reach that point and majority of traders are not well educated and not well acquainted with law. It is hoped that they maintain adequate records of purchases of inputs to matched outputs which is not possible in every case. The administration also cannot reach at grassroot level because India is based on agricultural economy. This system is useful in industrially developed countries where the number of traders are small in the economy.

Finally, in Indian context, the power to levy sales tax should

46. D.T. Lakdawala : *op. cit.*, pp. 183-207.
47. L.K. Jha : *op. cit.*, p. 306.

be retained within the subject of States in view of their increasing responsibilities in developmental programming. However, it is necessary that sales tax system of the States should be modified. The regionalisation of sales tax should be performed by dividing India into 5 zones.

Conclusion

The revenue from sales taxes have grown enormously during the lest decade. It has occupied a predominant place in States on taxes revenue, indirect taxes revenue and total taxes revenue. The importance of sales tax has, however, grown comparatively much more than that of any other single tax, and in the States under study, it now yields more than half of the State's own tax revenue except in Punjab, where it contributes 46 per cent to State's own taxes. Sales tax revenue increased 3.67 times in Rajasthan, 3.83 times in Haryana, and 3.42 times in Punjab during 1975-76 to 1983-84. Its growth is much higher than the total taxes growth and States own taxes growth. It shows the significance of the role of sales tax in States exchequer. Uttar Pradesh is the only State, where sales tax growth has not kept pace with the total taxes revenue and State's own resources. The State should do the needful to improve this situation.

The complete replacement of sales tax by additional excise duties is not possible. If the States agree, coal, iron and steel, vanaspati, cement, medicines, petrol and petroleum products, paper and paper board may be kept under the net of additional excise duties in lieu of sales tax.

The introduction of value added tax as a substitute of sales tax is neither feasible nor desirable at present. It is needed to regionalise sales tax and prepare a common model of sales tax structure which will be helpful to reduce diversity and evasion of sales tax.

3

RATE STRUCTURE OF SALES TAX

Introduction

While examining the rate structure certain economic and administrative considerations as well as the consumer's capacity to bear the burden of sales tax have to be kept in view. Rate differentiation on commodities entering consumption budgets of different income-groups is necessary on equity considerations. Rates of sales tax vary from State to State because there is a diversity in the economic conditions of the States and the capacity of consumers to bear the burden of tax also differs.

Fixing the rates of sales tax is a very technical and delicate task. The rate structure is the main factor to operate any tax system efficiently and effectively and it plays an important role in the administration of tax structure. Rate structure specifies the various rates at which different types of commodities are taxed and collected from different types of dealers. Rate is in fact a standard of reckoning, a degree of measure of this charge[1] and in absence of such standard the mechanism of charging and collecting taxes may lead to innumerable difficulties and inconveniences, specially in sales tax where multiplicity and diversity of rates is a common feature. It is very difficult to administer the imposing rate structure effectively, because of the multiplicity and diversity of rates. Therefore, the rates of taxes are systematically determined so that the mechanism of tax collection could operate automatically effectively. In the absence of effective rate structure the mechanism of collection of tax for State exchequer will collapse or it will also give birth to many problems, it implies that systematic rates of taxes hold the key of any tax system. In a democratic country like ours,

1. Hornby, Gatenby, and Wakefield . *The Advance Learners' Dictionary of Current English*, Oxford University Press, 1974, p. 807.

where consumers' sovereignty is nothing but a myth, the rate structure of sales tax needs special attention. In this Chapter an attempt has been made to discuss a comparative position of rates of sales tax in Rajasthan, Uttar Pradesh, Haryana and Punjab.

Liability to Pay Sales Tax

Before discussing the rate structure in detail it is essential to see as to who is liable to pay tax? Only registered dealers are liable to pay sales tax and the same are entitled to collect sales tax. As section 3 of Rajasthan Sales Tax Act, 1954 provides that "No dealer, shall while being liable to pay tax under section 3 of this Act, carry on business as a dealer unless he has been registered and possesses a registration certificate".[2] The registration of the dealers depend upon the liability to pay sales tax, once a dealer is liable to pay sales tax he has to get registration certificate from 'sales tax department'.[3] Total sale proceeds during an accounting year is the criterion for fixing the liability to pay sales tax.

There is a general rule in all the States that dealers should get themselves registered, whenever a minimum prescribed turnover is reached. Liability to pay sales tax differs from dealer to dealer and State to State as different minimum turnover limits have been fixed under local sales tax law in each State.

Under the Central Sales Tax Act, 1956 the liability to pay tax arises when any inter-State transaction in goods takes place. This means that the central sales tax is not linked to the limits of the turnover as prescribed under sales tax law but it is compulsory for every dealer to get himself registered if he is engaged in inter-State trade and commerce.

Taxable Quantum in Different Northern States under Study

For the purpose of prescribed limits the dealers have been classified into the following four categories:

2. Similar definition are given by the Uttar Pradesh Sales Tax Act, Section 3 and Punjab Sales Tax Act, Section 4 and Haryana Sales Tax Act, Section 6.
3. In Rajasthan it is known as Commercial Taxes Department. In Haryana and Punjab there is no separate Sales Tax Department. The Excise and Taxation Department deals with the sales tax matters.

(*i*) Importers (*ii*) Manufacturers (*iii*) Co-operative societies (*iv*) Other dealers. The taxable quantum for liability to pay sales tax in different States is different. The different limits of taxable quantum are prescribed for different types of dealers. Generally, there are two distinct limits, one is for the importers and manufacturers and the other for all other categories of dealers. Any dealer whose turnover does not exceed the prescribed limits is not liable to pay sales tax. Thus, small dealers have been exempted in every State from the burden of sales tax. Dr. A. Venkata Rayudu viewed that "When the minimum turnover limit for taxation is low, sales tax administration faces a number of problems such as that of coverage and the problem of coping up with increased work load, etc."[4] Moreover, in case of "Casual traders"[5] there is no limit of turnover for liability to pay sales tax. He is to pay sales tax on every transaction of sale and purchase irrespective of turnover limits. The liability of payment of sales tax is determined by gross turnover for each type of dealer, but it is the taxable turnover which is taxed at the prescribed rates. Table 3.1 reveals the minimum limits of gross turnover which have been prescribed for fixing the liability to pay sales tax for different classes of dealers in the selected northern States of India.

Table 3.1 indicates that except in Rajasthan there is no limit for co-operative societies in northern States. And further except in Rajasthan there is no minimum turnover limit for importers, while in Rajasthan the limit is only Rs. 10,000. This is a very low limit in comparison to other categories of dealers. In Haryana, Punjab and Uttar Pradesh the other dealers minimum limit is Rs. 1,00,000, while in Rajasthan the limit is Rs. 75,000. In case of Rajasthan, if the sales of a dealer exceed Rs. 75,000 but the taxable turnover does not exceed Rs. 5000 then he is not bound to get himself registered. Rajasthan is the only State where the dealers who are dealing in tax paid goods

4. Dr. A Venkata Rayudu ; *Taxation and Economic Development in India*, Chugh Publications, Allahabad, 1985, pp. 145-46.
5. A casual trader means a person who has whether as principal a gent or in any capacity, occasional transaction of business nature, involving the buying, selling, supplying or distributing of such goods as may be specified by the State Government.

are not liable to pay tax irrespective of any quantum of turnover. For liability to pay sales tax in Rajasthan both the conditions of gross turnover of Rs. 75,000 and taxable turnover of Rs. 5,000, in previous accounting year must be fulfilled simultaneously. This is a unique provision in Rajasthan Sales Tax Act, which provides a heaven for tax evaders by issuing forged tax paid vouchers. In case of manufacturers there is no uniformity in States under study. In Rajasthan and Haryana the limit of sale proceeds is Rs. 25,000 as minimum turnover limit while in case of Uttar Pradesh and Punjab the minimum turnover limit is Rs. 50,000 and Rs. 40,000 respectively.

TABLE 3.1

Minimum Limits of Dealers to Pay Sales Tax in Selected Northern States

States	*Manufacturers* (*Rs.*)	*Importers* (*Rs*)	*Co-operative societies* (*Rs.*)	*Other dealers* (*Rs.*)
Rajasthan	25,000	10,000	50,000	75,000+ 5,000 T.T.O
Uttar Pradesh	50,000	Nil	—	1,00,000
Haryana	25,000	Nil	—	1,00,000
Punjab	40,000	Nil	—	1,00,000

Sources: (*i*) *Sales Tax Rate List*—Government of Uttar Pradesh Publication, 1983.
(*ii*) *Annual Administration Report, Excise and Taxation Department*, Haryana, 1979-80, p. 12.
(*iii*) *Statistical Abstract*, Government of Rajasthan, 1983.
(*iv*) *Rate of Sales Tax in Northern States*, All India Manufacturing Organisation, 1983.

Point of Taxation

Generally, two types of systems have been adopted by all the States, viz., multiple stage sales tax and single stage sales tax. These are discussed below:

Multiple Stage Sales Tax

The multiple stage sales tax in its pure form applies at a uniform rate to all stages of the production and distribution process. In the words of R. Walter and Jr. Mahler "The tax is placed on all transactions through which commodities pass on the way to the consumer".[6] Generally, the rate of tax in multiple point of sales tax is fixed low in comparison to the first and last point taxation. The lower rate of tax is intended to raise revenue and simplify tax structure but it gives birth to evasion of sales tax. In the words of John F. Due "the inequities of the multiple stage taxes as among various business firms are so great as to cause greater pressure toward evasion than is offered by the higher rates of single stage taxes."[7]

The important disadvantage of multiple stage sales taxation is non-uniformity of consumer burden. For example, *A* (producer) sells a fan to *B* (Wholeseller) at the sale price of Rs. 200 and charges sales tax at the rate of 5 per cent in the form of multiple stage taxation. The burden of sales tax fallen on *B* is Rs. 10 and further *B* sells it to *C* (Retailer) then *B* will charge sales tax on Rs. 210 at the same rate and the tax burden fallen on *C* is Rs. 10.50. Finally, *C* sells the fan to *D* (Consumer) charging sales tax on 222.50 at same rate amounting to Rs. 11.02. This type of cumulative burden on various goods will result in varying retail selling price of the goods depending on the series of transactions through which the goods pass on their way to the consumer. This type of tax encourages integration in both production and distribution. Result is that evasion of sales tax will increase and the administration will not be in a position to check it.

Single Stage Sales Tax

Generally the two types of single stage form of sales tax is in practice, viz., first point tax and last point tax.

Under first point tax system, the tax is collected by manufacturers or importers on goods and later on it is passed on to the consumers. In this system, the first sale is taxable and subsequent sales are treated as tax paid. Subsequent dealers are not liable to collect tax because of the first point of collection of tax. The liability of the collection of tax rests with the first dealer. Legally, the first dealer cannot shift the point of taxation, but there are exceptions to it. Manufacturers can shift

6. R. Walter, Jr. Mahler ; *Sales and Excise Taxes in India*, Orient Longman Ltd., New Delhi, 1970, p. 141.
7. John F. Due : *Sales Taxation*, Routledge and Kegan Paul Ltd., London, 1957, p. 353.

their point of tax to the purchasing dealers whenever the concerned State Government issue notification to this effect provided they obtain declaration form from the registered dealers that the goods are purchased for the purpose of resale within the State or in course of inter-State trade and commerce. In such case the liability of sales tax is shifted from the manufacturer to such registered purchaser who gives the declaration. In case of Rajasthan a separate notification has been issued for shifting liability from the manufacturers to the registered dealers.[8]

In case of last point tax system, the sales tax is collected on the last sales, i.e., from the consumer who finally purchases the goods for consumption and not for sale. Prior to the last sale such dealers make a declaration in the prescribed form that they are purchasing goods for resale within the State.

Thus, under single point taxation system each commodity is taxed only once as it passes through production and distribution to the consumer. It avoids the complication and unnecessary burden created by the multiple stage form. This system is considered good for controlling the incidence by ensuring that only a specified amount of tax is added to the price of commodity. Another advantage is that a single point tax ensures administrative simplicity and easy tax compliance. It is true if the tax is levied at the first point, the number of assessees will be small, well organised and can be expected to keep better records to meet the requirement of the law. It is the best system to suit Indian States. Further in the words of A.R. Prest, "First point sales tax is the most satisfactory form for the underdeveloped countries."[9] But the problem arises when production is in small scale and unorganised sector with the result that large part of the turnover would go out side the ambit of tax, leading to a loss in tax revenue. Moreover, regular watch by authorities is a must to check the sales tax paid vouchers.

In many respects, the most satisfactory form of sales tax is the last point taxation under which the tax is collected only at the time of final sales to consumers. In the words of Ann F.

8. Notification No. F.5. (40) FD/RT-63 II, dated 23-3-63 N.L. Pokharana *Current Rajasthan Taxation Manual*, Asha Publishers, Ajmer, 1982, p. 205.
9. A.R. Prest: *Public Finance in Underdeveloped Countries*, Weidenfeld and Nicolson, London. 1962, p. 75,

Friedlaender, this form ensures complete uniformity of rates of tax to consumption expenditure on various goods (assuming complete shifting) since the tax is directly upon the final sales price.[10] The last point tax can easily be made clearly evident to the consumers, through quotation of sales tax separately from the price of the product. On the other hand, a single point levy at the last point obviates the deficiency of inadequate coverage. A single point tax at the last stage would bring a very large number of dealers, most of them small and petty with insufficient education and expertise to maintain accounts in a way satisfactory to the tax authorities. Administration of last point tax is extremely difficult and relatively costly. In such circumstances widespread evasion would be inevitable.

Conclusively, it may be stated that a single point tax at the first point would have the defect of inadequate coverage resulting in loss of revenue though having the advantage of administrative simplicity. A single point tax at the last stage, while giving a fuller coverage, would not be preferable because of administrative complexity and difficulties of the dealers in complying with the requirements of the law. Single point levies may be confined to items which are produced or imported in large scale and also where the trade is well organised, where production and trade are such that they cannot be adequately taxed at one stage in the process of production or distribution they could be brought under multi-point levy. Theoretically, it is true but in practice the goods having multiple point of taxation are vouched arbitrarily at low prices, causing a big loss to the revenue. So a combined system of single point (first, last) levy according to the suitability of the item would, in a large measure, minimise the shortcomings of either system adopted exclusively.

Point of Taxation in the Northern States

The single stage first point/last point taxation system is generally prevalent in all the States at present. In Rajasthan most of the commodities are taxed at first point and last

10. Ann. F. Friendlaender: "Indirect Taxes and Relative Prices", *Quarterly Journal of Economics*, Vol. 31, February 1967, pp. 344-45.

point.[11] However, exceptionally multiple point taxation is also in vogue. In Rajasthan this type of tax system has been adopted in case of gems, stones and pearls.

In Uttar Pradesh, Sales Tax Act provides for the single stage first point and last point sales tax. Previously the multiple point of taxation was in practice on a number of commodities. Only a few commodities are taxed at the last point (sale to consumer), while the remaining commodities are taxed at first point.

In Haryana and Punjab most of the commodities are taxed at the last point, the rates of tax are high for luxuries and low for necessaries. Only life saving goods are taxable at the first point.

Appendix I gives the names of commodities which were taxable at the last point in Rajasthan, Uttar Pradesh, Haryana and Punjab during 1983-84. In Rajasthan, only 30 items are taxable at the last point and rates of tax vary in the range of 4 to 8 per cent. Only the poppy head was taxable at a high rate of 20 per cent in 1983-84. In Uttar Pradesh, the rates of sales tax at the last point also varied in the range of 4 to 8 per cent, but bhang, ganja and charas are taxable at the rate of 14 per cent and motor vehicles are taxable at the rate of 10 per cent. In Haryana, the commodities which are used by higher income groups are taxable at the rate of 12 per cent at the last point of taxation and other commodities are levied at lower rates, which vary in the range of 1/2 to 4 per cent. Indian made foreign liquor are taxable at the rate of 20 per cent during 1983-84. Similar policy is also in vogue in Punjab, where most of the commodities are taxable at the last point of taxation and luxuries are taxable at the rate of 10 per cent, and other commodities are taxable in the range of 1/2 to 4 per cent during 1983-84.

Rate Structure

Sales tax being a State subject, different rates of taxes are fixed on sales or purchases of commodities in different States. The rates at which the State sales taxes are levied depend on whether it is a single point tax or a multi-point tax and on the

11. Notifications of last point taxable goods have been withdrawn w.e.f. 24-12-85.

nature of goods sold. Rates of sales tax vary from State to State and it is generally prescribed in the sales tax law itself with the liberty to the State Government to vary the rates either way. The rate which is fixed on selected commodities under State Governments notifications is called selective rate of tax, the general rate of tax is levied on aggregate sales of all commodities except such specific commodities which are exempted from tax.

Rates of Sales Tax in Rajasthan

Sales tax in Rajasthan was introduced in 1955. It came into operation with effect from 1st April, 1955. Initially, "The rates were fixed on a slab system and there were four slabs, viz., 3-1/8 per cent, 4-11/16 per cent, 6-1/4 and 12-1/2 per cent."[12] After that many changes have been made in the slabs to increase revenue receipts from the sales tax. More and more commodities have been included in this ambit. General rate had been increased from 3-1/8 per cent to 8 per cent. Specific rates have also been increased from time to time. Presently rates of tax on different commodities vary from 1 to 20 per cent. The State Government also allows exemptions from local sales tax on some transactions and commodities. Table 3.2 reveals the progression of general rate in Rajasthan since its inception.

Table 3.2 indicates that the general rate of sales tax is

TABLE 3.2

Progress of General Rate of Sales Tax since 1955 in Rajasthan

S. No.	*From*	*To*	*Rate of tax (Per cent)*
1.	1.4.1955	8.3.1960	3-1/8
2.	9.3.1960	8.3.1961	4
3.	9.8.1971	1.3.1963	5
4.	2.3.1963	7.8.1969	6
5.	8.8.1969	6,2.1979	7
6.	7.2.1979	On ward	8

Source: N.L. Pokharna; *Manual of Sales Tax in Rajasthan*, Asha Publishers, Ajmer, 1982, p. 553.

12. R.S. Sharma: "Rate Structure and its Execution under Rajasthan Sales Tax Act", Tax Guide, Ganganagar, August 1981, p, 29.

increasing continuously after introduction of sales tax in Rajasthan. It has increased to 2.4 times since its inception.

Rates of Sales Tax in Uttar Pradesh

Sales tax was introduced in Uttar Pradesh with effect from April 1, 1948, and a multi-point sales tax system was adopted. The tax was payable by all dealers whose annual turnover exceeded Rs. 15,000. It was levied at the rate of three pies in the rupee on specified goods. Certain articles were taxed at a single point at the rate of three pies, six pies and one anna per rupee while some others were taxed at nine pies per rupee. In 1956 all goods subject to single point were taxed at the uniform rate of one anna per rupee. Foodgrains, which were untaxed, were also taxed at a single point system. However, the fear was expressed that "It will appreciably raise the cost of foodgrains throughout the State, while the loopholes for evasion will be many."[13] Presently, Uttar Pradesh Sales Tax Act, provides a single point of taxation. Most of the commodities which were under multiple point of taxation, now are subject to single point, first and last point taxation. Only few commodities are taxable at the last point. Single point purchase tax is also in practice. Rates of tax varies from 1 to 20 per cent in Uttar Pradesh.

Rates of Sales Tax in Punjab

The Punjab Sales Tax Act came into force with effect from 15th November, 1948. It provides for levy of tax on the first/last point of sale. Only 26 commodities are taxable at first point. The general sales tax rate was 6 per cent, now it is 7 per cent. Some specified items are taxed at the lower rate, ranging between 1/2 to 6 per cent, while luxury goods are taxed at 10 per cent. In lieu of general sales tax, purchases tax is levied on cotton, oilseeds, rice and paddy. The rates of sales tax on specified commodities vary from 2 to 10 per cent.

Rates of Sales Tax in Haryana

The Haryana Sales Tax Act came into force with effect from 7th May, 1973. It was passed along the line of the Punjab

13. "Tr aders protest against sales tax ordinance", *Capital*, April, 12, 1956, p. 532.

Sales Tax Act. General sales tax is mostly levied at single point last stage in Haryana. The goods are not subjected to the last stage single point but are taxed on the single point first stage. Some commodities are taxable at lower rate ranging between 1/2 to 7 per cent. The general rate of tax is 8 per cent except in case of exempted and specified commodities.

General Rate of Sales Tax

The State sales tax law provides some specified commodities which are taxable at specific rates of tax and commodities which are exempted from tax. But some commodities which do not come in the ambit of specified tax rate and exemptions, are taxable at a residuary rate of tax called "general rate of tax."

Table 3.3 reveals the comparative position of general rates of tax in the States under study.

Table 3.3 shows that general rate of sales tax is equal at 8 per cent in Rajasthan, Uttar Pradesh and Haryana, while it is slightly lower in the case of Punjab.

TABLE 3.3
Comparative Position of General Rates of Sales Tax in Selected Northern States

S. No.	*Name of States*	*Rate of tax prevailing in 1983-84 (per cent)*
1.	Rajasthan	8
2.	Uttar Pradesh	8
3.	Haryana	8
4.	Punjab	7

Source: *Rate of Sales Tax in Northern States:* All India Manufacturers Organisation, Regional Board, New Delhi.

Analysis of Rates of Sales Tax

Different types of commodities are taxable at different rates in northern States, of course, some attempts now and then have been made to minimise the rate differentiation between neighbouring States. These rates are determined by economic as well as administrative considerations. The sales tax rates for various commodities have been revised from time to time. Appendix II given at the end, gives a complete exhaustive list of items which are taxable at different rates of sales tax in the States under study during 1983-84. On the perusal of the rate structure of sales tax in the States under study the following picture would emerge :

1. The fixing of the rates of sales tax is based on certain economic considerations. Food and other conventional necessaries are kept at low rates of tax while items of luxuries are kept at higher rates. The following luxury goods are taxable at high rates of tax :—

(*i*) Electrical goods.

(*ii*) Binoculars, Telescope, operaglasses, computers of analogue and digital varieties.

(*iii*) Motor vehicles as defined in the Motor Vehicles Act, 1939.

(*iv*) Perfumery cosmetics and picnic sets.

(*v*) Refrigerators, air conditioners and other cooling plants, apparatus, components and parts thereof.

(*vi*) Closed circuit, television sets, video, video cassettes and components.

(*vii*) Articles and wares made of stainless steels.

(*viii*) Photographic and linematographic and other cameras projection and enlargers lenes, films and plates.

(*ix*) All arms including rifles, revolvers, pistols and ammunition for the same.

(*x*) Cigarette cases and lighters.

(*xi*) Wireless reception instruments and apparatus, radio, and gramophone and dictaphone.

(*xii*) Sound transmitting equipments.

(*xiii*) All kinds of clocks, time pieces, electric time switches.

(*xv*) Sheets, cushions pillows, mattresses and others made from foam rubber and plastic foam.

More or less every State has agreed that these goods are luxury goods and be taxed at uniform rates to reduce the diversity in tax rates among the States, and eliminate the incentive for consumers to purchase such items from other States, to save sales tax payments. Initially, the rate levied on these items was 7 per cent which was subsequently raised to 10 per cent. Again, after some time the States raised their rates of sales tax on these commodities further higher. Thus, in Rajasthan these commodities are taxable at the rate of 10 to 12 per cent while in Uttar Pradesh and Haryana most of these commodities are taxable at the rate of 12 per cent. In Punjab these commodities are taxable at the rate of 10 per cent. It indicates that in the luxury items there is not major diversity of rates. However, rates for these items have reached their peak point and it is hoped that any further increase in these rates would not produce additional revenue and administratively it will create difficulties as it will provide greater incentive to evade taxes.

2. Narcotic goods are being charged at high rates of tax. Because these are regarded as the items of luxuries and higher rates are considered prudent to discourage formation of addiction habits. According to this policy in Rajasthan bhang, denatured spirit, poppy heads and opium are taxable at the rate of 20 per cent. Indian made foreign liquors and beer are taxable at the rate of 10 per cent, previously it was 60 per cent. In Uttar Pradesh bhang and opium are taxable at the rate of 14 and 20 per cent respectively. While in Punjab and Haryana these commodities are taxable under Excise Duties Act. No separate sales tax is levied on them.

3. Mineral oils and products are taxable at the rate of 12 per cent in Rajasthan. Petrol is taxable at the rate of 15 per cent, while in Punjab and Haryana these are taxable at the rate of 8 per cent and 7 per cent respectively. Therefore, in Rajasthan, petroleum products are costlier in comparison to Punjab and Haryana resulting in smuggling of these goods in Rajasthan from these States.

4. Foodgrains and other essential commodities are taxable at the lower rate of tax. According to some authors increase in tax on food items react regressivity. J.W. Mcgrew has suggested that "possible regressivity can be removed or moderated by exemption of food purchase, household utilities, etc."[14] Food items and life saving drugs are used by every class of income groups. These commodities are taxable at the rate varying between 1 to 4 per cent in Rajasthan, while in Uttar Pradesh, Punjab and Haryana these commodities are taxable at the rate of 4 per cent and in the Union territory of Delhi these goods are exempted from tax.[15]

5. All edible oils (except solvent, hydrogenated, palm) are

14. J.W. Mcgrew: "Effect of a Food Exemption on the Incidence of Retail Sales Tax", *National Tax Journal*, II 1949, pp. 362-67.

15. *Sales Tax Facts and Figures*, Government of India Press, New Delhi, 1982-33, p. 12.

taxable at high rates in Punjab and Haryana (7 and 8 per cent), while in Rajasthan and Uttar Pradesh the rate of tax is 5 and 4 per cent. The hydrogenated vegetable oils, palm oil, solvent oil are taxable at 10, 8 and 8 per cent in Rajasthan. In Uttar Pradesh, the rate for palm oil is 12 per cent and for hydrogenated oil 10 per cent, which is very high as compared to Haryana (7 per cent) and Punjab (8 per cent). If one compares it with the rates of sales tax on deshi ghee, which is levied at the rate of 3 per cent in Rajasthan, 6 per cent in Uttar Pradesh and 4 per cent in Punjab, it would appear that hydrogenated oil which is used by the lower income groups is taxable at high rates while deshi ghee which is used by higher income groups is taxable at low rate of sales tax.[16] These types of anomalies in the rate structure should be removed.

6. Bullion (gold and silver) is taxed at a very low rate, due to two reasons, firstly, it is a costliest metal and if tax is charged on it at higher rate, its cost would naturally go up and its trade would be adversely affected. Secondly, there is every possibility of tax evasion in the case of bullion. It is taxable at the rate of 1 per cent in Rajasthan and Uttar Pradesh, 1/2 per cent in Haryana and 2 per cent in Punjab.

7. Ornaments made of silver (except jewellery studded with stones) are taxable at the rate of 2 per cent in Rajasthan, Haryana and Punjab, while in Uttar Pradesh it is taxable at the rate of 4 per cent. Ornament and gotakinari made of gold are taxable at the rate of 5 per cent in Rajasthan, 8 per cent in Uttar Pradesh and Haryana and at 7 per cent in Punjab. The Jewellery studded with wholly or partly with gems and stones or pearls are taxable at higher rate of tax, which is 10 per cent in Rajasthan and Uttar Pradesh and 7 per cent in Punjab while in Haryana it is taxable at a lower rate of 2 per cent only.

8. All kinds of eatable non-alcoholic liquid such as fruit juice, soup, ark, chatni and murbbas are taxable at the rate of 10 per cent in Rajasthan, 12 per cent in Uttar Pradesh, 8 per cent in Haryana and 7 per cent in Punjab. Other eatable commodities (cornflakes, custard powder, dry fruits and margarine) are taxable at the rate of 10 per cent in Rajasthan, 8 per cent in Uttar Pradesh except margarine which is taxable at the rate

16. R.S. Sharma: "Rajasthan ST—A. Case Study", *Financial Express*, September 13, 1984, p. 7.

of 10 per cent. Higher rates on these commodities are justified on the ground that these are used by higher income group people.

9. Cotton and cotton products are taxable at rates in the range of 1 to 4 per cent in Rajasthan, Uttar Pradesh, Haryana and Punjab. But the tyre cord fabrics are taxable at 7 per cent in Punjab and Haryana and at 4 per cent in Rajasthan. The ready made garments which cost up to Rs. 10 are taxable at the rate of 3 per cent in Rajasthan and at 2 per cent in Haryana and Punjab. Hosiery products are taxable at higher rate, i.e., 8 per cent in Haryana and 7 per cent in Punjab while in Uttar Pradesh and Rajasthan these are taxable at lower rate, i.e., 4 per cent and 3.5 per cent respectively.

10. Office furniture and equipments are taxable at higher rates of tax. In Rajasthan and Punjab these commodities are taxable at the rate of 10 per cent but metal furniture and pile carpets are taxable at the rate of 12 per cent in Rajasthan, while in Uttar Pradesh and Haryana office furniture and equipments are taxable at the rate of 12 per cent. Pile carpets are taxable at the rate of 10 per cent in Uttar Pradesh.

11. The rate for packing material is 8 per cent in Uttar Pradesh and Haryana and 7 per cent in Punjab which is very high as compared to Rajasthan (4 per cent).

12. Power energy sources (coke and coal) are taxable at a uniform rate (4 per cent) in the States under study but fire work show some diversity. It is taxable at the rate of 12 per cent in Rajasthan and Uttar Pradesh which is very high as compared to Punjab (8 per cent) and Haryana (6 per cent).

13. There is considerable diversity in the rates of sales tax on building materials. Rates of sales tax vary from 9 to 12 per cent in Rajasthan, 8 to 12 per cent in Haryana, 6 to 10 per cent in Punjab and 6 to 12 per cent in Uttar Pradesh.

14. Chemical fertilizers (except bone meal and crushed bone) are taxabale at the rate of 5 per cent in Rajasthan and Uttar Pradesh while in Punjab and Haryana it is exempted from tax because of the promotional attitude of States towards fast agricultural advancement.

From the above analysis of rates of sales tax it has been confirmed that the rate differentiation is the most distinguishing characteristic of sales taxation systems in the northern States of

Punjab, Haryana, Rajasthan and Uttar Pradesh. This difference in single rate may be justified only in terms of the export prospects of certain commodities, creation of propitious climate for new manufacturing units and attraction of capital from the neighbouring States, but any tax concession shown to luxury and consumable items may not be justified.[17] Rate differentiation is also found within the States, e.g., in Rajasthan at present thirteen rates of tax are levied on different commodities. But most of sales tax systems in other countries have a single rate irrespective of multiple point or any variety of single point system. In North American States and the Canadian Provinces, sales tax is generally levied at a single rate on all commodities, the same is true in case of Pakistan, New Zealand and Philippines.[18] In northern States, Punjab is the only State where 6 or 7 rates of sales tax are in practice on different types of commodities. This excessive rate differentiation is the most significant defect of sales tax system. Thus, there is a clear need to reduce the number of rates, to adjust the rates to be more in harmony with those prevailing in the neighbouring States, and to revise some of them to make the structure more progressive and economically more beneficial. In this regard, Purohit suggests that all States should follow pattern adopted by Orissa where the rates are limited to four only."[19] So it is recommended that only three or four different rates of taxation should be kept for all commodities. Goods which are declared of special importance by Central Sales Tax Act, may be subjected to 4 per cent, luxurious items may be taxed at higher rate (say 10 per cent), lower rate of tax, i.e., 2 to 3 per cent may be levied on food items and other necessaries and finally narcotic goods may be taxed at higher rate (say 15 per cent) in order to check drinking habits in society. The extensive rate differentiation withholds the achievement of progressive sales tax system, and also there is no other justification for it. When such rate differentiation occurs in sales tax, administrative and compliance

17. S. Chandrasekhar: "Sales Tax in Andhra Pradesh", *Southern Economic Review:* Vol. III, 1974, p. 230.
18. John F. Due: *Sales Taxation* (study of sales tax system in these countries).
19. M.C. Purohit: "Structure of Sales Taxes in India", *Economic and Political Weekly*, August 21, 1982, p. 1371.

costs are increased considerably and a dealer selling commodities, if taxed at five and six different rates will be greatly inconvenienced in keeping records and filing sales tax returns. Similarly, consumers will not be sure that dealers have applied the correct rate of sales tax to each commodity, they purchase. Multiplicity of rates creates confusion among both the traders as well as consumers and the resultant evasion of tax too is likely to be widespread.

Rate differentiation according to commodity price basis is even more complex. In hosiery items, such system prevails which should be avoided. Because it has caused widespread tax evasion through under invoicing. Besides this, it also necessarily increases administrative and compliance costs.

The diversity in sales tax rates among the States gives incentive to the consumers to purchase such items from other States merely to save sales tax payments. For example, in 1983 the State Government of Gujarat claimed that it was losing Rs. 3 crores of revenue from sales tax because of the diversion of sales to Silvassa where there is no sales tax. Most of the truck and tyre companies shifted to Silvassa and the State Government had to loose sales tax revenue. Gujarat State co-operation bought 200 truck chassis and saved Rs. 40 lakhs in sales tax by purchasing such trucks from Silvassa.[20] In recent few years there has been a tendency towards increased rate differentiation among the States. Every State is free to raise or lower down the rates on any or all the commodities at any time. Recently, Rajasthan has given a special relief in the sales tax rate for the purchase of "Maruti Cars". Previously the sales tax rate was 10 per cent, but there was no collection of sales tax on it because of shifting of sales at Haryana. The Government of Rajasthan reduced the tax rate to 6 per cent[21] which resulted in more revenue, although the competition between Haryana and Rajasthan increased. So the diversity in tax rates among neighbouring States should be removed. Rate structure too needs rationalisation and a common rate structure may be developed by a consensus among the States. If it is not possible the policy

20. Ramesh Menon: "Sales Tax, The New Haven", *India Today*, October 31, 1983, p. 100.
21. *Rajasthan Patrika:* Jaipur, April 5, 1985, p. 7.

of common rate structure may be followed by regions by dividing the whole nation into five zones.

Levy of Purchase Tax and Its Rate

The General Sales Tax Laws of the States specially provide for the levy of purchase tax in lieu of sales tax. The reasons for levying purchase tax are to check evasion and to cover those transactions of sale which took place outside the State. But it should be kept in mind that it is restricted to the sales and purchases made within the States and not on the purchases which are made outside the State or in course of inter-State trade or commerce.

Section 5A and 5B of Rajasthan Sales Tax Act, deals with the levy of purchase tax. Section 5A is applicable to purchases made within the State which requires to fulfil the following conditions :—

(*i*) There should be a dealer;

(*ii*) The purchase of goods should be in course of business and should be of such goods which are not exempted and are taxable;

(*iii*) The goods so purchases are (*a*) consumed for manufacturing of other goods or otherwise; (*b*) they are disposed of in any manner other than by way of sales in the State; or (*c*) if the goods are specified goods[22] despatched to places outside the State and in case of other goods despatched to a place outside the State except as a direct result of sale, of purchase in the course of inter-State trade or commerce, shall be liable to pay tax on the purchase price of such goods at the same rate at which it would have been leviable on the sale price of such goods.[23]

Thus, it is clear that every manufacturer is liable to pay purchase tax on the purchase price of the goods purchased from unregistered dealers and consumed in the manufacture of other goods. If the manufactured goods are sold within the State or in the course of inter-State trade or commerce then the

22. Specified goods comprise cereals and pulses including gowar.
23. K.R. Chaturvedi; *The Principles of States Tax Law*, Eastern Law House (P.) Ltd., Calcutta, 1967, p. 1224.

liability under this section is limited by 2 per cent[24] only (read section 5A with section 5C of Rajasthan Sales Tax Act). If such manufactured goods are not sold by him as aforesaid, he would be liable to pay penalty under section 5C (2) for not utilising raw material for the purpose declared by him while purchasing the same. Similarly if he purchases any goods from unregistered dealer/registered dealer on strength of the declaration form in Rajasthan and such goods are disposed of in any manner or sold in the course of inter-State trade or commerce then the purchase tax is levied at the full rate of sales tax applicable on purchase price of such goods. Hence, it is evident that the rates of purchase and sales tax are the same for practical purposes. Section 5B of Rajasthan Sales Tax Act deals with the purchase tax on livestock. Rajasthan is the pioneer State in introducing such type of tax. Every person who intends to export livestock becomes liable to pay purchase tax at the rate of 6 per cent. The person need not be a dealer. All the provisions of returns, assessments, etc., are not applicable to such dealers. Cow is exempted from purchase tax.

Section 3AAA and 3D of Uttar Pradesh deals with liability to pay purchase tax on certain transactions. Any goods liable to tax at the point of sale to the consumer is sold to a dealer but he does not pay sales tax and does not resell such goods within the State or in course of inter-State trade in the same form and conditions in which he had purchased those goods. The purchasing dealer shall be liable to pay tax on such purchases at the rate, which is leviable on sale of such goods to the consumer within the State. Under section 4B, opium is taxable at the rate of 20 per cent at first purchase. Babul bark, gur, shakar, liquid gold, resin and rab are taxable at the rate of 8 per cent and oil seeds, rice bran and husk, oil cake, jute and cereals and pulses are taxable at the rate of 4 per cent at the first purchase.

Section 4B of the Punjab Sales Tax Act deals with the provisions of purchase tax. If a registered dealer purchases any goods other than exempted goods from any source and uses them for manufacture of tax free goods or taxable goods, but sends such manufactured goods out of State or resells in Punjab

24. Previously it was 1 per cent but with effect from 30-3-82 the rate is increased 2 per cent, Substituted by Act 8 of 1982 Section 2.

and there is no tax payable on such goods under any other provision of the Act, then he shall be liable to pay purchase tax on the purchase of such goods. Rate of purchase tax on cotton is 2 per cent while milk, (when purchased for use in the manufacture of taxable goods) rice, and paddy are taxable at the rate of 4 per cent and chillies at 6 per cent).

Section 9 of the Haryana Sales Tax Act has similar provisions like that of Punjab. Cotton, oil seeds, paddy and resin are taxable at the rate of 4 per cent at the last purchase. Livestock are taxable on per head basis. Table 3.4 below gives the rates of tax of livestock in Haryana.

TABLE 3.4

Rates of Tax on Livestock in Haryana

Category of livestock	*Tax per head Rs.*
Buffalo (female)	40
Cow (female)	25
Buffalo bull	30
Cow bull (Ox)	45
Cow calf (male)	15
Cow calf (female)	10
Buffalo calf (male)	10
Buffalo calf (female)	15
Horse	30
Mule and pony	25
Donkey	15
Goat, sheep and pig	3
Camel calf (male or female)	10
Camel	40

Source: Administrative Report of Haryana Excise and Taxation Department, 1982-83, p. 7.

Table 3.4 reveals that buffalo (female) and camel are taxable at the rate of Rs. 40 per head while cow calf (female) buffalo calf (male), camel calf are taxable at Rs. 10 per head. Cow (female) mule and pony at Rs. 25 per head. Pig, sheep and goats are taxable at lower rate of Rs. 3 per head. Cow calf (male), buffalo calf (female) and donkey are taxed at Rs. 15 per head.

It is clear from the above analysis of provisions of purchase tax that all the States under study have almost the same provisions regarding the levy of purchase tax on sale out side the

State in case of last point goods purchases on the strength of declaration forms. Moreover, in case of manufacturers, all the States under review have provided for purchase tax at concessional rate but no standard formula for arriving the purchase price has been made so far, resulting in conflicting views on computing the purchase price. In Haryana the manufacturing of the scientific goods and guar gum have been fully exempted from purchase tax, while in Rajasthan specific provisions have been made for levy of purchase tax in case of manufacturing of goods exempted under section 4(1) and 4(3). Rajasthan and Haryana are also having unique provisions for levy of purchase tax on livestock. In conclusion it may be observed that the States have not provided for set-off of the excess tax paid on purchases of goods which are used in manufacturing process which should be done to encourage industrial development.

Rates of Sales Tax During Inter-State Trade and Commerce

The Central sales tax is levied on the sale or purchase of goods which takes place in the course of inter-State trade. Every State is an exporter of many goods which are produced in the State and an importer of those goods which are in short supply in that State. Section 3(A) and 3(B) of Central Sales Tax Act, 1956 deals with inter-State sales. According to this section, only those sales which occasion the movement of goods from one State to another or are affected by a transfer of documents of title to the goods during their movement from one State to another are regarded as inter-State. If the movement of goods commences and terminates in the same State but passes through the territory of any other State, it shall not be deemed to be a movement of goods from one State to another. However, it will be an inter-State transaction if the buyer comes into the exporting State and takes delivery of the goods there with the intention of exporting goods outside the State.[25] The Taxation Enquiry Commission recommended that inter-State sales tax should be the concern of the union which would charge a tax at a reasonable rate in the interest of the country as a whole. The exporting State should levy this tax on the

25. Indian Law Institute: *Inter-State Trade Barriers and Sales Tax Law in India*, H. M. Tripathi (P.) Ltd., 1962, pp. 32-33.

authorisation and as an agent of the Union.[26] The government adopted the recommendation of the Taxation Enquiry Commission and on the basis of recommendations, the Constitution of India was amended by the Sixth Amendment in the year 1956, which led to the enactment of Central Sales Tax Act, 1956.

The Central sales tax is levied on all sales made by a dealer during inter-State transactions of commodity under section 3 of the Central Sales Tax Act, 1956. There is no minimum turnover limit for a dealer to get exemption from payment of tax. Therefore, all dealers are liable to pay tax at the prescribed rate of tax to the exporting State. The Central sales tax is administered by the State sales tax department. It is collected and retained by the exporting State on behalf of the Central Government.[27]

The Government of India has declared certain goods to be of special importance during inter-State trade and commerce under section 14 of the Central Sales Tax Act, 1956. They are coal, cotton, hides and skins, iron and steel, jute, oilseeds, rayon, silk and woollen fabrics, sugar and tobacco. Section 15 of the Act directs the States to levy sales tax on these specified goods at one stage and the maximum rate of tax is 4 per cent. If these goods have already been taxed by the exporting State and these goods being sold during the course of inter-State trade then the realised tax is to be refunded to the dealer by the exporting State.

Section 8 of the Central Sales Tax Act, 1956 gives the power to the exporting States to grant exemption from tax or impose lower rate than the specified rate of 4 per cent, but this power suffers from the limitation that States cannot increase tax rate without the permission of Union Government. The rate of 4 per cent is applicable only on the sale of goods to government and to registered dealers during inter-State trade. Consumers and unregistered dealers of the importing State are taxed at the rate applicable in the exporting State. The goods exempted from sales tax do not carry any tax during inter-State transactions. If any commodity is taxed at a lower rate than 4 per cent in the exporting State, that commodity will be taxed at the same lower rate during inter-State trade also. Cotton yarn is taxable

26. *Taxation and Enqulry Commission Report*, 1953-54, Vol. III, pp. 45-62
27. Entry 92A list I, Seventh Schedule of the Indian Constitution.

at the rate of 2 per cent, and other commodities which are declared of special importance are taxable at the rate of 4 per cent in Rajasthan, Haryana, Punjab and Uttar Pradesh. For the purpose of availing themselves of these concessions, dealers are required to furnish a declaration Form (C) duly filled and signed by the concerned authorities otherwise concession cannot be availed of. Table 3.5 presents the rate of sales tax under Central Sales Tax Act, 1956.

TABLE 3.5

Rates of Sales Tax Under Central Sales Tax Act

S. No.	*Particular*	*Rate of tax (per cent)*
1.	**Non-declared goods**	
	I When commodities are taxable less than 4% in the State (State rate will be Central sales tax rate)	State rate
	II When commodities are taxable more than 4 per cent in the State	
	A. If purchaser submits C/D form	4
	B. Otherwise 10 per cent or State rate whichever is higher	10 or State rate
2.	**Declared goods**	
	I Rate of tax is 4 per cent or more in the State	
	A. Purchaser submits C/D form	4
	B. Otherwise	8
	II Rate of tax is less than 4 per cent in State	
	A. If purchaser submits C/D form	State rate
	B. Otherwise	Twice the State rate

Source: M.L. Jain: *Rajasthan Sales Tax Act*, P.K. Prakashan, Jaipur, 1981, p. 503.

Table 3.5 reveals that in the case of declared goods of special importance if the rate of State sales tax is less than four per cent then the commodities are taxed at the State rate. In the condition when State rate is more than 4 per cent and dealers do not submit "C" or "D" Forms the rate of tax is 10 per cent or the State rate whichever is higher. In the case of declared goods of special importance if the State rate of sales tax is more than 4 per cent, it is taxed at 4 per cent if the dealer submits the "C" or "D" Form to the authorities, otherwise the rate is 8 per cent. If the rate of sales tax on declared goods does not exceed 4 per cent in the State and dealer files "C" or "D" Form, it is taxed at the State rate otherwise double rate of tax is charged from the dealer.

Under the existing arrangement of Central Sales Tax Act, the tax is assessed and collected by the exporting State. Thus, the incidence of tax is borne by consumers of the importing or consuming State. However, the residents of the importing State do not get any benefit from the revenues derived by the exporting State. P.K. Bhargava has observed that it creates inter-State jealousies and a fiscal inequity. The major beneficiaries are the main producing States and about 55 per cent of total revenue from Central sales tax is derived by the four States of Maharashtra, West Bengal, Tamil Nadu and Gujarat."[28] Therefore, it is suggested that such a provision should be revised and assessment and collection power be given to the importing States. This will increase the revenue of relatively financially backward States like Uttar Pradesh, Bihar and Rajasthan.

The exporting States face the problem of branch/depot transfers under the existing law, no sale outside the State can be taxed in the hands of the local State from which consignment are being sent for sale to other States as per provisions of Entry No. 92B in the Seventh Schedule to the Constitution of India, resulting in big evasion through such transactions, as the dealers practically make inter-State sales in the name of depot transfers. The 46th Amendment to the Indian Constitution has rightly given the powers of levy of consignment tax to the States. It has been discussed in the Chief Ministers conference also,[29] but no solution has been found so far. Therefore, it is suggested that consignment tax should be levied by the States immediately. Regarding rate of such tax, common consensus among States may be evolved.

Sales Tax Exemptions

In order to reduce the regressive nature of sales tax, certain exemptions are provided in the Act. Exemption from tax means

28. P.K. Bhargava: "*Raising Additional Resources for Development of Uttar Pradesh*" Quoted—R.K. Sinha and Jagnath Mishra, *Financing of State Plans*, Sterling Publishers (P) Ltd., New Delhi, 1984, pp. 108-9.
29. *Rajasthan Patrika*: Jaipur, dated 31st May, 1984, p. 4.

being free from tax. This implies that when a commodity or article is not subject to sales tax it is totally exempt from sales tax and consumers of such commodities or article do not bear its incidence.

Whenever a law imposes a liability it also grants exemptions in certain matters, so in case of sales tax laws, every State sales tax law has exempted certain classes of goods and certain classes of persons and institutions from sales tax liability. However, an exemption from liability to tax is not a substantive right. It is only a concession granted under the law and hence if a person claims any exemption, he is under the obligation to follow or fulfil the condition laid down, if any. The person claiming exemption must prove that he is entitled to it.

Before engaging in a detailed "evaluation" of sales tax exemption in the States under study, it would be useful to mention the criteria for sales tax exemptions, which may be justifiable.

Most authorities on taxation have advocated exemptions from tax for basic necessaries of life. N.H. Jacoby recommends a limited number of well defined exemptions,[30] John F. Due has suggested exemption for food and medicines.[31] Frampton and Smith have classified sales tax exemptions on the basis of their purpose or motivation. According to them, "there are exemptions which (*i*) simplify administration, (*ii*) mitigate regressive feature of the tax, and (*iii*) obviate multiple taxation.[32]

Exemption of Food and Other Necessities

The goods generally exempted from sales tax are those which are essential for the life saving of an average man. Foodgrains are essential for every person. The primary purpose of exemptions for food item is to relieve the tax burden on lower income group, and this is justified on grounds of equity in the distribution of tax incidence. But in India, the coverage of

30. N.H. Jacoby; *Retail Sales Taxation*, Commerce Clearing House, Chicago, 1938, p. 277.
31. John F. Due: *Provincial Sales Taxes*, Canadian Tax Foundation, Toronto, 1953, pp. 90-91.
32. T. George, Frampton and Numa R. Smith: *Commodities and Transactions Exempt from Consumption Tax*, "*Law and Contemporary Problems*" Vol. VIII, Duke University School of Law, Summer, 1941, p. 579.

direct taxes is extremely limited and a very large section of population can be reached only through indirect taxes. Exemption is necessary, particularly in food items, but a large part of consumption expenditure would be left out untaxed. Another aspect related to the exemption is that it relieves tax burden of the lower income groups. But a fair and equitable distribution of the tax burden does not necessitate total exemption of lower income groups from all taxes rather the tax burden is distributed over the income groups in accordance with their paying capacity.[33] Therefore, it is neither warranted on equity basis nor desirable on revenue considerations to exempt food and other necessary items from sales tax altogether. Another question is regarding rural and urban disparity in distribution of tax burden. Differences in the expenditure pattern and the nature of coverage of most taxes make the distribution of incidence unequal between the two sectors, with the rural sector incidence being lighter. In this context, if sales tax on food items is charged it assumed that all commodity taxes are generally shifted to the consumer in full, the question of rural urban unequal burden would not be solved because in rural sector food items are largely acquired through non-taxable channels whereas in the urban sector these purchases are taxed. Dr. Lokanathan[34] studied the pattern of trade in agricultural products particularly paddy and rice and came to the conclusion that sales tax on them is generally shifted backwards to the producers. That being so, sales tax on food items would in fact help reduce the disparity in the distribution of tax burden between the urban and rural sectors.

Conclusively, it is not essential to exempt food and other necessary articles totally from sales tax. Certain items such as vegetables, fruits, milk, fish, eggs, meat, etc., may have to be exempted, not because these are necessaries but that these are perishable in nature and that it would make the administration difficult, if taxed.

Producer's Purchases

It is economically desirable to exempt producer's purchases

33. L.S. Sharp: *Federal Finance in Coming Decade*, New York, 1941, p. 58.
34. Dr. P.S. Lokanathan; *Sales Tax System in Andhra Pradesh, A Review*, NCAER, New Delhi, 1963, p. 6.

such as raw materials, intermediates and machinery from sales tax. If sale tax is regarded as tax on consumption expenditure then articles used in further production should not be taxed, if done so it will result in multiple and unequal burdens on the final consumption of various products. Another problem is regarding exportable producers commodities. If tax is levied on final product, its competitiveness in world markets could be maintained by giving tax rebate wherever necessary.

There is also the contrary view, i.e., to allow any one to make tax free purchases for business would pave the way for widespread evasion of tax and vendors would face problems in maintaining records for distinguishing taxable and non-taxable sales. Administratively, it could be impossible to check and control. However, there are very strong arguments for exemption of important producer's purchases, i.e., industrial machinery and equipment and industrial fuel and goods directly consumed in manufacturing process. However, it is not feasible to exempt all goods purchased by business concern, because many items are also purchased for consumption purpose. But the sales tax system should adopt the policy provided in the Central Budget for 1986-87[35] on the pattern of 'MODVAT' in respect of such goods which are purchased by the producers within the State.

Agricuttural Machinery and Others

To develop agriculture based economy it is recommended to exempt agricultural machinery and other agricultural inputs.

Economic or Social Institutions

Sales tax exemptions are also given to promote certain economic, social and other activities. Purchases/sales by institutions engaged in specified activities are exempted from sales tax. These institutions are run on non-profit basis. To promote village cottage industries their products should also be exempted. The States under study are following this policy in case of certain items such as hand made clothes, hand spun yarn, khadi are exempted in a number of States. But such exemptions lead

35. "MODVAT will benefit consumers", *The Economic Times*, New Delhi, March 2, 1986, p. 1.

to administrative complexity and throw open the doors for tax evasion. Exemptions to individual institutions on an *ad hoc* basis are, perhaps the least desirable of all exemptions in the sales tax systems. The existence of such exemptions, almost inevitably results in political pressures for additional exemptions of a similar nature: thus, creating significant administrative difficulties. It would be more effective to promote these activities in a direct and forthright manner such as an out right grant or subsidy for loan. The Taxation Enquiry Committee commented that sales tax concessions are hardly a suitable method of encouraging particular industries and trade activities, etc.[36] It would be preferable to grant subsidies instead of exemption to promote such industries.

Exemptions and Concessions on Sales to Government

The exemption of sales to government can be defended on the ground that to tax governments would merely take money out of one pocket and put it into another. But in certain conditions, when sales are made to federal government and other State Governments it is not necessary that taxes are taken from one pocket and returned to the same source.

Comparative Analysis of Exemptions

Appendix III reveals that there is not a considerable diversity in exemptions in States under study. The items which come closest to the universalities in appendix are salt, vegetables, meat, milk, books and periodicals, etc. However, even when exemption is allowed on the same item in almost all the States, it is frequently the case that some States allow unconditional exemption while others exempt the item under certain conditions, e g., certain fee which is charged on goods from certain class of people and dealers for selling are exempted from sales tax.

Tax policy on food items varies from State to State. Foodgrains are tax free in Delhi while in Rajasthan, Uttar Pradesh, Punjab and Haryana, these are taxable at the rate of 2 to 4 per cent. Only items of perishable nature, i.e., meat, eggs, fish, vegetables, milk are exembted. If these goods are sold in sealed

36. *Taxatiton and Enquiry Commission Report, op. cit.*, p. 41.

containers then no exemption is allowed. It is assumed that these items are consumed only by the rich when sold in sealed containers.

A number of non-food items are also considered necessaries and are exempted in some States. Examples of such goods are footwear made by hand, fire wood, cheap clothes, handlooms, etc. To promote cottage industries khadi, handlooms, charkha, hand made cotton yarn have been made tax free. If tax is levied on these goods their cost would increase and demand of these goods in question would decrease causing adverse effect on the small and cottage industries in rural areas.

Non-mechanized agriculture implements are exempted in all northern States. Tractors, pumping sets and other equipments are taxable in northern States. Parts of agricultural equipments are tax free in the States under study. In Uttar Pradesh these items were taxable previously. But now these are tax free.[37] Rajasthan is the only State where water pumping sets are exempt from levy of tax[38]. Fertilizers (excluding chemical and crushed bone) bullock carts, poultry feeds are exempted. But the livestock is taxable in Rajasthan and Haryana. In Haryana livestock is taxable on per head base. Different amounts are levied on different types of animals. In Indian context where increased agricultural production is urgently required, agricultural machinery should be exempted to develop agricultural based economy.

Books, periodicals, pencils, slates used by students are also exempted. But scientific instruments used by students are not exempted in northern States.

States are not empowered to impose taxes on newspapers and newsprints. The taxes on the sale of newspapers and advertisements have been placed in the Union list, hence exempted.

Some goods already taxed by States under separate law are free from sales tax. Goods which are subjected to additional excise duties are exempted from paying sales tax. Cotton fabrics, woollen fabrics, sugar, tobacco are free from sales tax in northern States. All the northern States except Rajasthan have a separate law providing for sales taxation on motor spirit.

37. "U.P. Tax Relief on Farm Equipment", *Hindustan Times*, Jan. 9, 1985, p. 7.

38. During budgetary provision in 1987, it has been taxed at 4 per cent.

Haryana, Punjab and Uttar Pradesh make a specific exemption for motor spirit from sales tax laws.

To promote cottage industries, small units which are operated by manual labour are exempted from paying sales tax. This policy has been adopted in all northern States. Appendix III reveals that, products of village or cottage industries, i.e., handlooms cloth, hand made papers, hand spun yarn, khadi, hand made soap, chikan work, handicrafts are exempted from levy of sales tax. Sales to certain economic institutions which are of non-profitable nature such as sale of scientific equipment and drugs to cancer institutions, military canteen, United Nations agencies in States, and red cross society etc., are exempted from sale tax.

Conclusion

On the whole, it can be said that the present rate structure of sales tax in the States under study has been formulated with the main object of procuring the maximum revenue from this source. In Uttar Pradesh and Rajasthan most of the commodities are taxable at first point while in Haryana and Punjab tax is levied on the last point basis. The number of rates varied within the range of 10 to 15 in Rajasthan, Haryana and Uttar Pradesh. Luxuries are taxable at higher rates in all the States. Petroleum products are taxed at higher rates in Rajasthan than in Haryana, Punjab and Uttar Pradesh. Exemptions are provided to a limited number of commodities and economic institutions. Agricultural implements are exempted in all the States under study but agricultural machinery is not exempted in Haryana, Punjab and Uttar Pradesh while in Rajasthan water monoblock pumping sets are exempted from levy of tax. Certain exemptions are conditional and others are unconditional. Rate differentiation amongst neighbouring States should be minimised and uniform rates of tax should be applied. Such uniformity would not only facilitate collection of sales tax but also prove more economical and administratively sound.

4

ORGANISATION OF SALES TAX

Introduction

Administration is the keystone of effective taxation system. If the administration fails, the tax must fail.[1] Adequate tax administration is a necessary prerequisite for the maintenance of optimum revenue productivity, equity and taxpayer's morale. In Indian union, States are of federal nature, and have to depend largely on their own sources of revenue. Larger yields from sales taxes can be brought into the treasuries of the States by attempting improvements in fiscal administration. In the absence of proper administrative organisation the object of levying a tax cannot be achieved and, the very purpose of such taxation in particular as well as the fiscal policy of the State in general is defeated. The canon of equity is also threatened because full payment of tax is made by the honest only. Unscrupulous taxpayers are always in search of loopholes to take advantage of administrative weakness and limitations and avoid or evade payment of taxes. In such conditions, the morale of the honest taxpayers is shaken and broken and they too try to take advantage of administrative weakness in tax laws.

The Taxation and Enquiry Commission, 1953-54 amplifies the need for good administration and administrative feasibility for the regulation and enforcement of sale tax laws in these words: "It is true that all taxes are unwelcome and that no tax can be rendered popular by good administration but few taxes can be rendered so unpopular by bad administration as the sales tax."[2]

1. Willan J. Shultz and Lowell Hariss—*American Public Finance*, VI Edition, 1957, p. 296.
2. Government of India, *Report, Taxation and Enquiry Commission*, 1953-54, Vol. III, p. 67.

The sales tax, being a broad based tax, can be collected from relatively few taxpayers since the vendors or retailers serve as the collecting agent for Government, there exist chances of leakage or non-payment of tax. If the administration is not tight enough to check such leakages or evasion of tax, the sales tax structure will collapse. To ensure efficient tax administration having potentiality to produce more and more revenue, it is essential to have a sound organisation system keeping in view the administrative requirements.

In the Indian union, all the State sales tax laws provide administrative machinery to regulate the law within the State. In some of the States, sales tax is administered by State department established solely or principally for that purpose, but in some other States it is also entrusted with the collection of taxes like State excise duty, motor vehicle tax, electricity duty, passengers and goods tax and entertainment tax, etc. Thus, it is essential to have an effective administrative organisation to deal with administration of sales tax laws.

The administration of sales tax departments differs from State to State. Generally speaking the administration of the department is under the charge of a Commissioner. He is invariably assisted by one or more Additional/Joint Commissioners, who subject to general control, exercise all limited powers of the Commissioner. The States are divided in several Zones/Divisions, each under the charge of a Deputy or Assistant Commissioner. The actual assessment work is done by Sales Tax Officers/Commercial Taxes Officers/Excise and Taxation Officers and Assistant Sales Tax Officers/Assistant Commercial Taxes Officers/Assistant Excise and Taxation Officers or any person authorised by the Commissioner as per provision of local sales tax law within a zone, districts and in some cases even part of a district, depending upon the volume of work. A circle is in the charge of a Sales/Commercial/Excise Taxation Officers.[3] Assistant Sales Tax Officers are allotted work on the basis of territorial and pecuniary jurisdiction which vary from State to State. Sales Tax Officers and Assistant Sales Tax

3. Each Officer having same meaning in sales tax point of view, in further Sales Tax and Assistant Sales Tax Officer word has been used as a common authorities.

Officers are assessing authorities in respect of a dealer who carries on business within the limits of their territorial jurisdiction according to pecuniary jurisdiction.

In Rajasthan, a separate department known as Excise and Taxation Department was set up under the charge of Commissioner in 1955.[4] But due to administrative problems it was not possible to run it in effective manner. So, it was bifurcated in two departments in 1964, one known as Excise Department and the other as Commercial Taxes Department. At that time it was assigned administration of the four important taxes, *viz.*, sales tax, taxes on passengers and goods, entertainment tax and electricity duties. The administration of passengers and goods tax was further bifurcated and assigned to the Department of Transport from 1st April, 1974. Therefore, now the administration of Commercial Taxes Department includes administration of sales tax, entertainment tax and electricity duties.

In Uttar Pradesh, there is a separate department for sales tax. Other taxes like passengers and goods tax, electricity duties are not under the jurisdiction of Sales Tax Department.

In Punjab and Haryana, there is single Excise and Taxation Department, which looks after the administration of State excise, sales tax, passengers and goods tax, entertainment tax and show tax, etc. Primarily, Haryana was part of Punjab and Punjab Sales Tax Act, 1948 was applicable there. The Haryana General Sales Tax Act came into force in 1973.[5] Both in Haryana and Punjab, the administration of sales tax is in the hands of Excise and Taxation Department.

It may be concluded that in Uttar Pradesh, a separate department exists for sales tax while in Rajasthan it is combined with entertainment tax and electricity duties. In Haryana and Punjab, it is combined with state excise, passengers and goods tax, entertainment tax, etc. It is, therefore, suggested that where there is a single department to deal with all these taxes (state excise, sales tax, entertainment tax, electricity duties) it should be bifurcated from State excise. Other taxes are not in a position

4. Came into force with effect from 1st April, 1955 *vide* notification No. 13(3) SR/54, dated 2-3-1955, *Rajasthan Gazatte*, Part I-B.
5. *Annual Administration Report*, Excise and Taxation Department, Haryana, 1979-80, p. 11.

to maintain administrative cost separately and also they do not put excessive burden on Sales Tax Department. Separation is suggested because these taxes command great importance from revenue point of view, and every administrative lacuna is dangerous for the State revenue. Although separate department will increase administrative cost yet it may be compensated through sound administration, which will yield more revenue and also check evasion. It is necessary that there should be a proper and efficient administration through separate department.

This Chapter deals with the administrative organisation of sales tax in the States under study. For the study of sales tax administration it is necessary to study the Commercial Taxes Department in Rajasthan, Excise and Taxation Department in Punjab and Haryana and Sales Tax Department in Uttar Pradesh.

Organisation Structure of Sales Tax

The complete organisational set up in regard to sales tax in the States under study is given in Charts 4.1, 4.2, 4.3 and 4.4.

Charts 4.1, 4.2, 4.3 and 4.4 of organisational set up of Sales Tax Departments reveal that in the States under study there is a three tier system of administration, *i.e.*, at State Level, Division/Zone level and District/Circle level. Haryana is the only state where division level organisation does not exist. The enforcement of Sales Tax Act is regulated and controlled by the Commissioner as head of the Department. At the middle level there are Deputy Commissioners, Joint Excise and Taxation Commissioners, Assistant Commissioners of administration, inspection, appeal, legal, revision and anti-evasion, and at the bottom there are Sales Tax Officers who are subordinated by Assistant Sales Tax Officers. The lowest administrative post in the department is Sales Tax Inspectors who assist the assessing authority in recovery, survey and investigations. The administrative units are almost the same in the northern States but in Punjab and Uttar Pradesh the posts of Assistant Excise and Taxation officers as also of Assistant Sales Tax officers have been abolished.

The appointment of the Commissioner and Additional Commissioner is made by the State Government. Commissioner belongs to super time scale of Indian Administrative Services cadre. The Additional Commissioner is also from I.A.S. cadre. In Rajasthan a new post of Additional Commissioner (Anti-evasion) has been created to supervise the anti-evasion activities in the state and the appointment on this post can also be made from Rajasthan Commercial Taxes Service, though it is not a cadre post. At present I.A.S. officers are holding both the posts of Additional Commissioners.

The Commissioner is the highest authority of the department who makes rules of procedure and conducts the administration for the guidance of all persons under him. He also issues notifications as necessitated from time to time under various sections of the Act and Rules made thereunder. He has power to transfer the cases from one assessing authority to another, to determine the jurisdiction (pecuniary as well as territorial) and allow any taxpayer to pay the demand in instalments. He has also the power to allow the stay orders against the demands pending during the period of appeals. He can revise and raise the penalties and interest levied by the assessing authorities. In Rajasthan and Uttar Pradesh, the Commissioner cannot hear any appeal, while in Punjab and Haryana the Commissioner is also the appellate authority.

The Additional Commissioner and Joint Commissioners assist the Commissioner for the supervision and control of work related to various measures and in the matter relating to general day-to-day work of administration and anti-evasion work. Legally, the word 'Commissioner' includes Additional Commissioner. Hence, the Commissioner can delegate the powers of inspection, stay, instalment, but revisional powers of the Commissioner under Sales Tax Act are not delegated by him to his subordinate authorities to the person below the rank of Deputy/Assistant Commissioner.

Deputy Commissioners are appointed from P.C.S. cadre. Deputy Commissioners are assigned various types of work. Deputy Commissioners (Administration) posted as head of the zone, are responsible for the administration of sales tax in their respective zones in Rajasthan, Uttar Pradesh and Punjab, while in case of Haryana there are no zonal headquarters. The Deputy Commissioner is posted as head at District level. The Deputy Commissioner provides link between the Commissioner and assessing authorities.

Deputy Commissioner (Inspection)[6] checks the files assessed by the assessing authorities, investigates the matters reported by the superior authorities or of his own accord. He acts on the general policy laid down by the Commissioner. In Haryana, the check posts are also supervised and controlled by the Deputy Commissioner (Inspection).

Deputy Commissioner (Appeals) is an appellate authority. If any assessee appeals against the order of assessment, refund, penalty, reassessment, etc., Deputy Commissioner (Appeals) decides it. He exclusively does the judicial and appellate work under the taxation measures in each division. The appellate authority gives reasonable opportunity of being heard to the aggrieved dealer and after that he has power to confirm, reduce, enhance or set aside the assessment order and he can remand the case for fresh assessment after making necessary enquiries.

Assessing authority—"Any person authorised by State Government to make any assessment under the Act and to perform other duties as may be required under the Act."[7] In Uttar Pradesh, Haryana and Punjab the Assistant Commissioner is also an assessing authority. Normally assessment work is done by Sales Tax Officers and Assistant Sales Tax Officers. In Punjab the post of the Assistant Excise and Taxation Officer was redesignated as Excise and Taxation Officer.[8] In Rajasthan the assessing authority is Commercial Taxes Officers and Assistant Commercial Taxes Officers. The distinguishing feature in case of Rajasthan is that assessing authority cannot be an officer below the rank of Commercial Taxes Officers and Assistant Commercial Taxes Officers while in case of Punjab, Haryana and Uttar Pradesh, any person authorised by the Commissioner can act as an assessing authority. In every State the minimum turnover limits have been fixed for assessing authorities, as soon as the turnover crosses the particular prescribed limit the file of the dealer is transferred to the senior officer. Assistant Commissioners and

6. In case of Punjab, it is Joint Excise and Taxation Commissioner.
7. Haryana General Sales Tax Act, 1973 under Section 2(9) and Uttar Pradesh and Punjab General Sales Tax Act, under section 2(1).
8. The posts of Assistant Excise and Taxation Officer were redesignated in 1977. *Achievements of Punjab Excise and Taxation Department at a Glance*, 1983-84, p. 11.

Deputy Commissioners are also assessing authorities in certain cases. In case of Uttar Pradesh, Assistant Commissioner assesses those cases only which are related to big companies, firms, industries whose turnover crosses a certain specified limit. The meaning of Sales Tax Officers, Commercial Taxes Officers and Excise and Taxation Officers is the same from sales tax point of view as they perform the same functions of assessment, survey and recovery, etc.

The Sales Tax Officers and Assistant Sales Tax Officers work under the supervision of the Deputy Commissioner (Administration). The jurisdiction of such officers is a circle which is notified by the Commissioner. In Rajasthan special circles have been created to keep watch on revenue collection from important tax payers.[9] It is headed by Commercial Taxes Officers also work as the assessing authority for special circle. In Uttar Pradesh,[10] to investigate the working of circles and check posts and flying squads and to centralise big assessees under one roof, one special investigation cell has been created and accordingly the whole Uttar Pradesh has been divided in three regions. In Haryana and Punjab there is a separate cell to do such work known as flying squad and enforcement wing but in Rajasthan it is anti-evasion wing.

The circles or districts are divided into wards with pecuniary jurisdiction. The jurisdiction of a Sales Tax Officer or an Assistant Sales Tax Officer is confined to his ward. The Sales Tax Officer is responsible for efficient working of the whole circle/ward under him. The powers of assessing authority are as under :—

(*i*) to issue new registration certificate to the dealer who has started business in the territorial jurisdiction of an assessing authority;

(*ii*) to cancel registration certificate if the dealer has got it by fraud or the dealer has closed his business;

(*iii*) to make yearly final assessment or provisional assessment if the dealer has not filed quarterly returns or has not paid monthly returns;

9. *Statistical Abstracts*, Commercial Taxes Department, Rajasthan, 1982-83, p. 11.

10. *Annual Report of Sales Taxes Department*, Lucknow, Uttar Pradesh, 1982-83, p. 53.

(*iv*) to require any dealer to produce before him any books, documents or accounts relating to his business and may inspect, examine and copy the same and make such enquiries from the dealer relating his business as may be necessary;[11]

(*v*) to take steps for recovery of tax by attachment of movable and immovable properties;

(*vi*) to make necessary enquiries regarding any dealer if he is trying to evade liability of tax or other dues under the Sales Tax Act and if anything necessary for the purpose of an investigation into his liability is found in any books, accounts and registers, he may also seize such books and documents and seal the office or godown. He is further empowered to break open office, shop, almirah and take help from the police;[12]

(*vii*) to impose penalties on the dealer in case he contravenes any of the provisions of the Act;

(*viii*) to rectify any mistake apparent on the face of record including legal mistakes and may reopen assessment cases if escapement is there;

(*ix*) to allow refund of any amount deposited in excess and to give effects to the orders of appellate authorities; and

(*x*) to intercept and search any vehicle carrying goods and may seize the vehicle if it is necessary.

The assessing authorities, for the purpose of Sales Tax Act, have the same powers as are vested in a court when trying a suit, in respect of the following matters :

(*a*) enforcing the attendance of any person and examining him on oath or otherwise,

(*b*) compelling the production of documents and impounding or detaining them,

(*c*) issuing commissions for the examination of witnesses,

11. D. Kumar: *Search and Seizure*, Jaipur Printers, Jaipur, 1971, pp. 86-116.
12. Under section 14(3-4) of the Punjab Sales Tax Act, T.R. Tikka—*A Study of Punjab General Sales Tax Act and Central Sales Tax Act*, Pradeep Publications, Jalandhar, 1985, pp. 18-19.
Similar provisions are also given in Uttar Pradesh Sales Tax Act, under section 13, Haryana Sales Tax Act, under section 14 and Rajasthan Sales Tax Act under section 22.

(*d*) requiring or accepting proof of facts by affidavits.

Under the Sales Tax Act, no suit, prosecution or legal proceedings shall lie against any officer or servant of the State Government for anything which is done or intended to be done in good faith.

The above powers of assessing authorities reveal that the implementation of sales tax statute depends upon the efficient assessing authorities. Rai has emphasised that "The linch pin in the sales tax organisation is the Sales Tax Officer, he is the person who initiates all proceedings under the Act".[13] But the question is whether Sales Tax Officers or Assistant Sales Tax Officers are judicial officers. It is clear from the power of assessing authorities that their working is not purely judicial. It is quasi-judicial in nature and the principles of natural justice and judicial procedures too are equally applicable.

Sales Tax Inspectors form the lowest rank in the ladder of the administration set up of the department. Inspectors are not assessing authorities.[14] They mainly give assistance to the assessing authorities in conducting enquiries, anti-evasion surveys and collecting all other relevant information. In fact, they play a key role in contacting the dealer and in executing grass-root level work. The work, they are entrusted with is of great importance. They are "ears and eyes" of the department. But it is a general complaint that most of the Inspectors do not discharge their duties effectively, with the result that the state Government suffers a great loss of revenue. To have better control over the working of inspectors, the incharge of circle and ward should exercise better and effective supervision over the work of Inspectors. They should see that the survey work which is considerably neglected by the Inspectors is properly conducted. The following are the Important duties of inspectors :—

(*i*) to detect new dealers, who though liable to be registered may be carrying on business without obtaining registration certificate;

13. Champat Rai—*Law and Practice of Sales Tax in India*, K. Rai and Company, I Edition, Delhi 1953, p. 15.

14. In case of Punjab, certain inspectors were given powers of assessing authorities *vide* Punjab Government Notification No. S.O. 3/P.A. 46/485-3/80, dated 5th January, 1980.

(*ii*) to collect information as to the extent and scope of business of a dealer;

(*iii*) to enquire about the immovable and movable properties of the dealer for recovery of demand;

(*iv*) to verify challans, *bilties*, declaration forms and sales tax paid vouchers;

(*v*) to investigate the offences made under the Sales Tax Act;

(*vi*) to check the movement of goods; and

(*vii*) to collect taxes and recover arrears of demand.

It is clear from the above analysis that the Sales Tax Inspectors play a key role in contacting the dealer; his work has indeed a great importance in efficient administration.

The organisation structure of Sales Tax Department/Commercial Taxes/Excise and Taxation Department[15] can be studied under following broad heads :—

(*i*) Organisation structure of Head Office;

(*ii*) Organisation structure of Zonal Offices;

(*iii*) Organisation structure of Circle Offices;

(*iv*) Organisation structure of Check Posts;

(*v*) Anti-evasion organisation;

(*vi*) Appellate organisation; and

(*vii*) Revision Organisation.

Organisation Structure of Head Office

The Headquarters of Sales Tax Department is located at Jaipur in Rajasthan, Lucknow in Uttar Pradesh, Chandigarh in Haryana and Patiala in Punjab. The department is headed by a Commissioner who is the overall incharge of the sales tax function in the State. The first tier of administration is almost similar in the northern states. The Commissioner has divided the Headquarters administration in different sections, a brief description of which now follows :

Establishment Section. It deals with establishment functions. In Rajasthan, the incharge of establishment work is Deputy Commissioner (Headquarters) assisted by Commercial Taxes Officer and Assistant Commercial Taxes Officer while in Uttar Pradesh it is done by Assistant Commissioner (Establishment).

15. Hereafter "Sales Tax Department" refer to the Excise and Taxation Department and Commercial Taxes Department.

A joint Excise and Taxation Commissioner (Administration) is assisted by Office Superintendent and Assistant Office Superintendent to look after the establishment part of the administration of the department in Punjab. In Haryana, it is done by Deputy Excise and Taxation Commissioner (Administration). The placement, promotion and other establishment work of the staff is done by these authorities.

Tax Section. The incharge of this section is Deputy Commissioner (Tax) assisted by Sales Tax Officers and Assistant Sales Tax Officers in Rajasthan and Uttar Pradesh. In Punjab it is headed by Assistant Commissioner (Administration) who looks after the work of tax section. The important work of tax section is to see the implementation of tax statutes and to watch the revenue collection from commodities. The tax section plays very important role in deciding the rates in respect of different types of commodities, exemption granted, etc. It also gives new blood to the tax statutes.

Legal Section. This section is headed by Deputy Commissioner (Legal). The Sales Tax Officers, Assistant Sales Tax Officers and Legal Assistants are supporting staff in Rajasthan. In Uttar Pradesh, the Assistant Commissioner is the head of this section and he is supported by Sales Tax Officer (Legal) and researcher. In Punjab, there is a District Attorney and Assistant District Attorney taken on deputation from the state law department, and in Haryana it is only the Deputy District Attorney who supervises the work of legal section. Besides giving legal advice in all taxation matters, supervises the preparation of statements in civil suits/writs filed against the department in the Supreme Court and High Court and other subordinate courts. Deputy District Attorney alone is not in a position to deal all these matters. Therefore, the Haryana sales tax administration needs improvement in its legal section.

Accounts Section. Accounts section is headed by Chief Account Officer in Rajasthan, Haryana and Punjab, while in Uttar Pradesh it is headed by Deputy Commissioner (Accounts) and supported by Accounts Officers, Assistant Accounts Officers and Accountants. Accounts officer is a gazetted rank officer and is solely responsible to the Commissioner for the proper maintenance of departmental accounts at headquarters and divisional headquarters. He is required to consolidate the accounts for each financial year. The important work done is budgeting of expenses for the department, to see the recovery of arrears and to audit the departmental accounts. The accounts wing has a statutory responsibility to submit audit reports to the State Legislature. The scope of internal audit is limited and is done with a view to ensuring that adequate regulations and procedures as framed by the department and to satisfy himself whether such regulations and procedures are adhered to. Internal audit is done with a view to helping the department to keep a check on its own performance. At present, in all the States under study audit work is also done, but there is no separate section for this work. Therefore, it is suggested that the department should establish a separate cell for internal audit work. Moreover, the follow-up of the internal audit is rather poor in all the States which is an alarming situation. It needs more attention of the Government.

Statistical Section. Deputy Director (Statistics)[16] is the head of this section in Rajasthan. He is appointed on deputation from statistical services. In Uttar Pradesh, he works under the supervision of Deputy Commissioner (Headquarters). In Rajasthan, he is supported by Assistant Director and Statistical Officer, and in Uttar Pradesh he is supported by two Statistical officers. The important work of this section is to collect statistical data from circle offices and to publish in the departmental annual report. But in Punjab and Haryana, the reports are not published in a systematic manner due to lack of staff. Therefore, it is suggested that it should follow the working of Rajasthan and Uttar Pradesh in this respect. The work of statistical section is also very important as the tax planning of the whole State depends upon the statistics available. If the statistical section is weak then head of the department will not be able to feed correct position to the Government. During the study it was revealed that no State is in a position to maintain commodity-wise revenue receipts in all cases. In Rajasthan, Haryana and Uttar Pradesh few exercises regarding commodity-wise collections are made. Therefore, it is suggested that all the States should make efforts to collect commodity-wise collections.

Collection Cell/Recovery Cell. At present there is no separate

16. Now the post has been up-graded and it is headed by Joint Director.

collection cell in most of the northern States. The collection of demand work is done by Sales Tax Officers and Assistant Sales Tax Officers who have multifarious duties like assessment, inspection, registration, enquiries and routine office work and hence may not find time to attend hard recovery cases. The result is that the arrears of sales tax revenue are increasing continuously It requires a prompt and effective action against the defaulters to save loss of revenue to the state exchequer otherwise the structure of collection of tax would collapse. In such a situation, creation of a collection cell at the circle level with tax recovery officer[17] is suggested with necessary staff exclusively for the collection so that arrears may be reduced. In Uttar Pradesh, a separate collection cell is also working, which is headed by Deputy Commissioner (Collection) at headquarters but the arrears are still continuously mounting. No efforts have been made to recover from the hard cases. It is suggested that the Government should appoint a Tax Recovery Officer at circle level in each State for speedy realisation of both the old arrears and current demands pending.

Conclusively, the Headquarters administration is almost the same in the states under study but administrative set up of Uttar Pradesh and Rajasthan is more effective in comparison to those of Punjab and Haryana.

Zonal Administration

The whole of Rajasthan is divided into six zones and each zone is headed by Deputy Commissioner (Administration) who is assisted by Commercial Taxes Officers, Assistant Commercial Taxes Officers, Inspectors and Legal Assistants. Uttar Pradesh is divided into twelve zones[18] and each is headed by Deputy Commissioner (Administration). Each zone is further divided into two parts except Meerut and Ghaziabad and each is headed by Assistant Commissioner (Administration) who is assisted by Deputy Collector (Collection) and Sales Tax Officers. In Haryana, Zonal system of administration is not practised. In place of zonal administration there is a district administration, and

17. In some States like Maharashtra, Tamil Nadu and Uttar Pradesh, this has already been done. It was also suggested by *Uttar Pradesh Taxation Enquiry Committee Report*, 1974, p. 221.
18. Uttar Pradesh Sales Tax Department *Report*, 1983-14, p. 1.

each district is headed by Deputy Excise and Taxation Commissioner, who is assisted by Excise and Taxation officers, Assistant Excise and Taxation Officers and Inspectors. Punjab is divided in three divisions[19] and each division is headed by Deputy Excise and Taxation Commissioner (Administration). The supporting staff comprise Assistant Excise and Taxation Commissioner, Excise and Taxation Officers and Inspectors. As regards statuory functions all the above authorities are the same. Deputy Commissioner is empowered and charged with the administration of various taxation measures in his division/zone. He acts as a co-ordinating and supervising officer for the districts in the division and is ultimately responsible to the Commissioner. Deputy Commissioner is the authority who actually sees the proper implementations of the tax laws under his jurisdiction and reports to the Commissioner.

Organisation Structure of Circle Offices

Circle is the level which forms the administrative edifice. If the administrative machinery fails to work efficiently at circle level, the whole system of administrative structure would collapse. Each circle is divided into wards which are headed by Sales Tax Officers and Assistant Sales Tax Officers. Circles and wards work under the supervision of Zonal/Districts administration. In Rajasthan, circles are headed by Commercial Taxes Officers and wards are headed by Assistant Commercial Taxes Officers. Under the supervision of Deputy Commissioner (Administration) presently, 49 circles[20] are working in Rajasthan. Circle authorities are responsible for assessments, collection of demands, etc. In Uttar Pradesh each circle is headed by Sales Tax Officer, grade I and grade II, under the supervision of Assistant Commissioner (Administration) Sub-Division. At the sub-divisional level, Assistant Commissioner (Assessment) is also an assessing authority who assesses big firms and companies. Presently in Uttar Pradesh 99 circles and 8 sub-circles are working and 44 circles are divided into 176 wards.[21] There is also a separate collection cell which is headed by Deputy

19. Punjab Sales Tax Department, *Report*, 1983-84, p. 3.
20. *Statistical Abstract*, Government of Rajasthan, Jaipur 1984-85. p. 1.
21. Annual Report of Sales Tax Department, Uttar Pradesh, *op. cit.*, p. 1.

Collector (Collection) under the supervision of Assistant Commissioner (Administration). In Haryana, 14 districts are operating under the supervision of Deputy Excise and Taxation Commissioners. These districts are also divided in sub-offices. Eight sub-districts are headed by Excise and Taxation Officers and seven are headed by assistant Excise and Taxation Officers.[22] Punjab is divided into 16 districts from sales tax administration point of view. Each district is under the charge of Assistant Excise and Taxation Commissioner. Normally each Assistant Commissioner supervises 7 to 8 wards. At present there are 120 wards. Wards are headed by Excise and Taxation Officers. The Excise and Taxation Officers decide the assessment cases and also work for recovery of demands. The Assistant Commissioners have the responsibility of administering all the taxation measures in the districts.

Organisation Structure of Check Posts

Tax evasion is a common feature in any tax system. It is considered to be a social evil. It is very difficult to quantify the actual evasion of sales tax. The tax dodgers or unscrupulous dealers adopt various methods of avoiding payment of tax. Suppression of purchases and subsequent sales, inflation of stock and non-issuance of cash memos or sale bills are some of the methods which are commonly used by traders. Stringent and effective provisions are, therefore, needed in taxation statutes for curbing such evils. However, efforts have been made to eliminate evasion as far as possible. And for checking evasion of tax, Sales Tax Laws of Rajasthan, Uttar Pradesh, Haryana and Punjab have made special provisions for establishment of check posts.

Section 28 of the Uttar Pradesh Sales Tax Act, 1973 provides that "the State Government, if it is of opinion that it is necessary so to do with a view to preventing evasion of tax or other dues payable under this Act in respect of the sale of goods within the State after their import into the State, may by notification in the Gazette, direct the establishment of check posts or barriers at such places within the State as may be

22. *Annual Report of Haryana Excise and Taxation Department*, 1983-84, p. 1.

specified in the notification."[23] Generally two types of check posts have been set up in the States *viz.*, internal check posts and border check posts. Internal check posts are set up for collection of purchase tax while border check posts or barriers are set up to check the inter-State movement of goods. Sales tax check posts and barriers have been set up at all significant points of contact with territories of other states where information is obtained from the drivers/owners/incharge of goods carrying vehicle, or the goods being imported into the State or being exported out of it. The objective is to transmit the information so gathered to the respective assessing authorities in the State to be used for verification at the time of assessment of the dealer concerned. It is essential that the drivers of the vehicles passing through a check post be required to submit a copy of documents with regard to goods. In suspicious cases the officers of the check posts are empowered to seize the consignment after reasons to be recorded in writing and giving a receipt of the same. The officers may collect the tax and impose the penalties at check posts as per provisions of law of the State. Chart 4.5 gives the organisational set up of check posts during 1983-84, in the States under study.

The check posts class *A* are headed by Sales Tax Officers in each State while in Punjab these are headed by Assistant Excise and Taxation Commissioner. Class *B* check posts are headed by Assistant Sales Tax Officers in Rajasthan, Sales Tax Officers grade II in Uttar Pradesh, Excise and Taxation Officers grade II in Punjab and Assistant Excise and Taxation Officers in Haryana. A few check posts are headed by inspectors also. In Rajasthan, lower division clerks and junior accountants also control check posts. The categorisation of class is done on the basis of revenue collection. At present, there are 87 check posts in Rajasthan, 42 in Uttar Pradesh, 18 in Punjab and 62 in Haryana. Check posts play a vital role in preventing new area of evasion.

23. P.L. Malik—*Uttar Pradesh Sales Tax Act*, 1948, Eastern Book Company, Lucknow, 1982, p. 55.
Similar definitions are given under section 22A of Rajasthan Sales Tax Act, under section 37 of Haryana Sales Tax Act and under section 14B of Punjab Sales Tax Act.

CHART 4.5

Organisation Structure of Check Post during 1983-84

	Rajasthan	*Uttar Pradesh*	*Haryana*	*Punjab*
	C.T.O/ A.C.T.O	S.T.O./ S.T.O.II	A.E.T.C.	
	C.T.I	Inspectors	A.E.T.O.	E.T.O./ E.T.O.II
	Junior Accountants	Police Officers	Inspectors	Inspectors
	L.D.C.		Police guards	Police guards
	Guards			
No. of Check Posts	87	42	62	18

Note: A.E.T.C Stands for: Assistant Excise and Taxation Commissioner.
C.T.O stands for: Commercial Taxes Officer.
A.C.T.O. stands for: Assistant Commercial Taxes Officer.
C.T.I. stands for: Commercial Taxes Inspector.
L.D.C. stands for: Lower Division Clerks.
S.T.O. stands for: Sales Tax Officer.
E.T.O. stands for: Excise and Taxation Officer.
A.E.T.O. stands for: Assistant Excise and Taxation Officer

Abolition of Check Posts

Traders quite often complain that they are harassed by the officers at the check posts in spite of their having proper documents. These complaints should be investigated when such type of complaints are filed to higher authorities. The existence or abolition of check posts depends upon the fact whether they perform any useful function in the context of bringing all inter-State sales within the purview of sales tax or not. This in turn depends on the extent to which information is obtained at check posts and passed on to the assessing authorities who use it effectively for assessment purposes.

Before May, 1977 in Punjab, 34 check posts and barriers were working but all the check posts and barriers were abolished[24] and a new cell Mobile Squad came into existence instead of them. However, administratively it was not possible to

24. Published in *Punjab Gazette*, extraordinary part III, dated 9th May, 1977, pp. 259-60.

prevent evasion without check posts and barriers, so check posts and barriers were established again in Punjab. In this context, it may be observed that the existence of check posts is a must they should not be abolished but it is desirable that they should be manned properly and at the inter-State points strengthened with armed personnel. The superior authorities should occasionally cross-check the vehicles carrying goods other than those specified in the way bill and it should be cross-verified with the dealers accounts so that the dealers dare not skip-off the transactions of the goods dealt by them without incorporating them in the regular books of account. The information collected at the check posts should not be for the sake of collection only but should also be utilised by the assessing authorities. This step, therefore, will not allow the dealers to suppress their turnover and in turn increase the revenue of the State exchequer considerably.

In Rajasthan the administration of check posts is far from being satisfactory. A number of check posts are administered by lower division clerks with one or two guards making it a 'heaven' for the tax evaders. It is a pity on the part of the State Government to expect curbing of evasion from these lower division clerks, who do not even understand the basic tenets of sales tax law. Moreover, there is no armed police guard in Rajasthan at the check posts while in Haryana, Punjab and Uttar Pradesh armed guards have been posted at the important check posts. Therefore, it is suggested that the check posts should be headed by Assistant Commercial Taxes Officer with armed guard and more basic facilities should be provided by the Government. Secondly, weighing machines should be provided at the check post so that chances of evasion may be minimised and system of regular cross verification of the documents must be evolved so that the revenue receipts of the State may not be put to loss.

Anti-Evasion Organisation

Evasion of sales tax is a general problem and to combat with the evasion of sales tax, a separate wing known as Anti-Evasion Wing has been set up in Rajasthan while in Haryana, Punjab and Uttar Pradesh it is known as Enforcement and Flying Squad.

Chart 4.6 shows that in Rajasthan, it is headed by Additional Commissioner (Anti-evasion) who is assisted by a Deputy Commissioner. The subordinate authorities comprise Commercial Taxes Officers, Assistant Commercial Taxes Officers and Inspectors. At present, in Rajasthan 7 flying squads are operating in the area of their specified jurisdiction. There is also a central flying squad at the Headquarters level having jurisdiction over the whole State.

In Uttar Pradesh, flying squad is headed by Deputy Commissioner and at sub-zonal level there is an Assistant Commissioner who is assisted by Sales Tax Officers. There is also a separate wing known as Special Investigation Branch. Presently, 31 flying squads and 19 special investigation branches are working. The special investigation branch is under the charge of Deputy Commissioner who is assisted by Deputy Superintendent of Police and Sales Tax Officers.

In Haryana flying squads are headed by an officer equal to the rank of Deputy Excise and Taxation Commissioner and at district level there is an Excise and Taxation Officer who is assisted by Assistant Excise and Taxation Officers. In Punjab, it is headed by the Chief Enforcement Officer. There is a central wing which checks the anti-evasion activities in the whole State. There are three divisions which are headed by Excise and Taxation Officer (Enforcement).

The overall administrative set up of anti-evasion wing shows some differences. In Punjab and Rajasthan there is a central wing whereas there is no such wing in Haryana. In Uttar Pradesh there is a separate investigation cell. Officers of these wings make surprise raids on the business premises of the suspected dealers to seize unaccounted goods or books of account of such dealers where evasion of tax is suspected. They can also check the road-side vehicles, and if found doubtful, they can seize vehicles with goods and also impose penalties on them. The enforcement organisation is fairly effective in curbing evasion of tax and dishonest practices of traders. Besides this, the enforcement or anti-evasion organisation keeps the normal staff alert and improves their functioning and helps in increasing the revenue of the State. The ultimate objective of anti-evasion wing in all the States under study is to check evasion of sales tax. Nomenclature of tax officers may be different but all of them are alike dedicated to the same goal.

Appellate Organisation

The necessity of appeal arises because of the abuse of discretionary powers of the assessing authorities. To impart justice to the dealers and to check the discretionary powers of assessing authorities, there is a provision of appeal under Sales Tax Laws. Assessment of tax, penalty, interest, cancellation of registration, etc., are subject to appeal. The appellate authority has power to ask the dealer to produce books of account and other relevant documents before him at the time of hearing of appeal and if the appellant does not produce them, the authority can proceed to make *ex parte* orders. The appellate authority shall send a copy of the memorandum of appeal to the concerned assessing authority asking him to send the record of the order appealed against together with his comments, if any.[25] The appellate authority has power to maintain the assessment order passed by the assessing authority and can restore the order. Alternatively the appellate authority can also remand the assessment for fresh orders. Appellate authorities in the States under study are given in Chart 4.7.

In Rajasthan, an aggrieved person or party may appeal first to the Deputy Commissioner (Appeals). However, any order passed by the Commissioner is appealable at the tribunal. Any order passed by the appealate authority is also appealable as second appeal in the tribunal. Previously, there was a Board of Revenue for revision cases.

In Uttar Pradesh, the assessing authority is also Assistant Commissioner, and any order passed by him is appealable to Deputy Commissioner (Appeals). If remaining assessing authorities (Sales Tax Officer, grades I and II) pass any order, that would be appealable to the Assistant Commissioner (Judicial). Any order passed by Commissioner and appellate authorities, is appealable as second appeal to the tribunal.

In Haryana and Punjab almost similar procedure is in practice. But there is a major difference that the Commissioner of the department also has the power to hear appeal, if any

25. Jai Kumar Jain—*Law of Sale and Purchase Tax in Rajasthan*, Anand Prakashan, Jaipur, 1980, p. 372.

CHART 4.7

Appellate Authorities in Rajasthan, Uttar Pradesh, Haryana and Punjab during 1983-84

RAJASTHAN		*UTTAR PRADESH*		*HARYANA*		*PUNJAB*	
Authority Passing Original Order	*Appellate Authority*	*Authority Passing Original Order*	*Appellate Authority*	*Authority Passing Original Order*	*Appellate Authority*	*Authority Passing Original Order*	*Appellate Authority*
	First Appeal		**First Appeal**		**First Appeal**		**First Appeal**
1. The assessing authorities passing any order	Deputy Commissioner (Appeal)	1. The assessing authority Assistant Commissioner passed any order	Deputy Commissioner (Appeal)	1. The assessing authority passing any order	The Deputy Excise and Taxation Commissioner (Appeal)	1. The assessing authority passing any order	The Deputy Excise and Taxation Commissioner (Appeal)
2. Any order passing by Commissioner	The Tribunal	2. The assessing authority Sales Tax Officer passed any order	Assistant Commissioner (Judicial)	2. Deputy Excise and Taxation Commissioner	The Commissioner	2. Deputy Commissioner (Excise & Taxation)	The Commissioner
		3. The Commissioner	The Tribunal	3. The Commissioner	The Tribunal	3. The Commissioner	The Tribunal

	Second Appeal		**Second Appeal**		**Second Appeal**		**Second Appeal**
3. Any order passed by Deputy Commissi-oner (Appeal)	The Tribunal	4. Any order passed by appellate authority	The Tribunal	4. Any order passed by Deputy Commissioner on an appeal	The Tribunal	4. Any order passed by Deputy Commissioner on an appeal	The Tribunal

order is passed by the Deputy Excise and Taxation Officers. The second appeal provision is uniform in all the States under study.

Table 4.1 gives the number of appellate offices in Rajasthan, Uttar Pradesh, Haryana and Punjab.

TABLE 4.1

Number of Appellate Offices as on 31st March, 1983

States	*Number of Appellate Offices*	*Name of Division*
RAJASTHAN	6	Jaipur, Jodhpur, Alwar, Ajmer, Bikaner, and Udaipur division.
UTTAR PRADESH	24	Agra, Aligarh, Allahabad, Bareilly Bulandshahr, Bijnor, Faizabad, Gorakhpur, Kanpur, Lucknow, Meerut, Moradabad, Muzaffar-nagar, Saharanpur, Varanasi, Jhansi, Nainital, Dehradun, Ghaziabad, Mainpuri, Etawah, Hathras, Sitapur and Fatehgarh sub-division.
HARYANA	3	Rohtak, Ambala and Faridabad division.
PUNJAB	3	Jullundur, Patiala and Ferozepur division.

Table 4.1 reveals that in Rajasthan, Haryana and Punjab, appellate offices are located at divisional level and in Uttar Pradesh they are located at sub-divisional levels.

Revision Organisation

Section 40 of the Haryana Sales Tax Act—1974 provides that "Commissioner may at his own motion call for the record of any case pending before, or disposed of by, any assessing authority or appellate authority other than the tribunal, for the purposes of satisfying himself as to the legality or propriety of any proceeding or of any order made therein and may pass such order in relation thereto as he may think fit."[26] The Commissioner may delegate his power to Deputy Commissioner or

26. M.L. Pullani—*Haryana General Sales Tax Act with Rules*, Legal Book House, Chandigarh, 1984, pp. 35-36.

such officer not below the rank of Deputy Commissioner or Assistant Commissioner. In Rajasthan, the revision authority is Deputy Commissioner (Headquarter) and also the Deputy Commissioner (Revision) at Ajmer who is assisted by Commercial Taxes Officer, Assistant Commercial Taxes Officers and Legal Assistant. Revisional authority can reassess the turnover and pass orders for levying tax on escaped turnover. In Uttar Pradesh the revision authority is Assistant Commissioner while in Punjab and Haryana the Commissioner has powers to revise cases which are generally delegated to Joint Excise and Taxation Commissioner. In Rajasthan, Haryana, Punjab and Uttar Pradesh *suo-moto* revision can also be filed by the Commissioner.

The tribunal is an appellate body both in respect of the facts and the laws. Appeal to the tribunal may be made be any dealer objecting to an order passed or proceedings recorded by the appellate authority or Deputy Commissioner's authority or Deputy Commissioner *suo-moto* or any order passed by the Commissioner. Among other things the tribunal has power to confirm, reduce, enhance the annual assessment or the penalty amount. The tribunal has also power to award costs and the amount of such costs shall be recoverable from the person as land revenue. Ordinarily, the tribunal is the final authority in determintng the question of fact, which cannot be agitated in a reference to the High Court.

Tribunal is working in all the States under study. It is a separate body to decide cases. In Uttar Pradesh, 14 tribunal benches were working during 1982-83 and the Chairman of the tribunal is working at Lucknow. Punjab and Haryana also have a tribunal. In Rajasthan tribunal has been established in 1985, having headquarters at Ajmer and its bench at Jaipur.

Training Programme

The handling the tax work is a very technical task. Training is essential to develop individual efficiency of persons who deal with tax as statutes. An effective recruitment may supply intelligent persons with high mental aptitude, but to utilise their efficiency effectively it is essential to organise training programmes by the Department, particularly, in sales tax where every leakage of tax is dangerous to the State exchequer. It is necessary that officers should be provided with an opportunity to exchange information constantly regarding difficult points about the administration of sales tax. In this context a training school was started in the Punjab Excise and Taxation Department on 15th May, 1968.[27] Every year this school familiarises the departmental officers and field staff with up-to-date knowledge of the Act and Rules. The Head of the school is an officer of the rank of Deputy Commissioner assisted by Assistant Commissioner and Excise and Taxation Officers. Haryana has also provided a training school under the charge of Joint Excise and Taxation Commissioner. In Rajasthan, previously there was a commercial taxes training school. However, now the training is imparted by the Harish Chandra Mathur State Institute of Public Administration. It is suggested that the other States should also follow this programme. The main object of the training school is to familiarise the officers with the latest judicial decisions. In this context the present training programme should be streamlined to arrange tax administration seminars, workshops, group discussions, lectures by seniors/retired officers, eminent lawyers and professional auditors. Such training programmes are essential in the wake of the fact that the officers of the Sales Tax Department are not well acquainted with the latest judicial pronouncements.

Sales Tax Advisory Committee

Public relations is the most neglected part of the organisation structure. As suggested by the Taxation Enquiry Committee, it would help remove the lacuna in the structure of tax and difficulties of the traders resulting from operating of tax.[28] If the traders face any problem regarding the operation of sales tax, they can bring it to the notice of the advisory committee. In this regard, the Bhoothalingam Committee suggested that the sales tax advisory committee should consist of members of State Legislature, retired sales tax officers and trade representative and should meet at least once in an year at the headquarters to hear the particular problems in the different regions.

27. Administrative Report, Excise and Taxation Department, Punjab, *op., cit.*, 23.
28. Taxation and Enquiry Committee, *Report, op. cit.*, p. 75.

Purohit (1975)[29] has found the role of the public relations as that of an extra-player in the game. He cited the role of these committees in the State of Rajasthan (1958), Delhi and Haryana. According to him, the reason for their being inactive is the attitude of the Government in accepting their recommendations because of the apprehension of losing revenue. Recently in Rajasthan, the Commissioner has again made a good beginning by forming vigilance committees at zonal and district headquarters. These committees meet monthly to solve the problems of dealers.

Conclusively, advisory committee plays a very important role in the operation of sales tax. It is recommended that, to eliminate the gap between administrative authorities and traders, all States should organise a separate sales tax advisory committee which may include members of the trade organisations, advocate and retired seniors of the department and vigilance committees may be formed on the pattern of Rajasthan.

Conclusion

Although the administrative machinery of Sales Tax Department in the States under study is quite satisfactory, it is essentially felt that there should be a separate intelligence section in the office of the Commissioner to review continuously the organisation and method of working of the department. The audit programme should be made more extensive and separate audit wing at Zonal/District levels should be established. At present, the departments are in a very poor position to collect and summarise data. It may be suggested particularly in case of Punjab that the statistical base research agency should be established. The collection of demand, correlated with assessing authority should be bifurcated and should follow the pattern of Uttar Pradesh by creating recovery circles.

Appellate organisation is a part of general organisation. Administrative officers are working under the direct control of the Commissioner. This procedure is objectionable because there are chances of biased and prejudiced judgments. In this connection, the view of the Law Commission of India regarding

29. M.C. Purohit—*Sales Taxation in India*, Sultan Chand and Sons, New Delhi, 1975, p. 184.

income-tax are illuminating. It says on principle, it may appear objectionable that an agency which is under the direct control of the Central Board of Revenue should be vested with jurisdiction to hear appeals from the orders of the Income-tax Officers. Justice should not only be done, but should appear to be done and inspire confidence in the person concerned. It is an elementary principle of law that a person should not be judged in his own case.[30] It is, therefore, suggested that the appellate organisation must be separated from the general organisation. Appellate authorities are not given any training in judicial work which they are required to perform. Therefore, they should be duly trained by judiciary before their placement on job. In Rajasthan the appellate authorities are appointed from State Civil Service, which is highly undesirable because officers without any background of sales tax work can do justice neither to the dealers and nor to the State. Therefore, it should be appointed from State Taxation Service. Last but not the least, the effectiveness of the organisation structure, can be judged by frequent reviewing of its operation.

30. Government of India—Twelfth Report, Law Commission of India, Ministry of Law, 1968, para 89, p. 43.

5

OPERATIONAL ANALYSIS OF SALES TAX

Introduction

Tax administration is the key to the effective policy which is universally acclaimed, but virtually ignored in practice in operation of sales tax. Sigbren Cnossen has observed that, "there is a widespread preoccupation with what should be done rather than with how to do it"[1] Sales tax is no exception to this rule. So the operation of sales tax like that of administrative organisation demands special attention because the operation of sales taxation is directly linked with higher tax yield. In the words of Dr. G.K. Srivastava, "The productivity of any tax is correlated with the principles and procedures for the registration of dealers, assessment, collection of tax, appeals, revisions and references and offences and penalties."[2] A larger proportion of the criticism of sales tax seems to arise because of the operations of the sales tax and not because of its structure. It is, therefore, essential that operation of sales tax must be looked into carefully.

Administrative machinery in general, has to face many problems in order to provide an efficient fiscal administration of the sales tax. Structural difficulties, under-assessment, evasion, delinquency and lack of sufficient statistical information are some of the basic problems of the Sales Tax Department in the States. If a tax policy is to be carried out perfectly, a feasible solution to these difficulties of administration and the problems of the taxing process should be found. In fact, larger yields can be affected in the States by attempting to improve

1. Sigbren Cnossen: *Excise System. A Global Study of the Selective Taxation of Goods and Service*, The John Hopkins University Press, Baltimore and London, 1977, p, 99.
2. Dr. G.K. Srivastava—*Commercial Taxes in India*, Pitaliya Publications Jaipur, 1975, p. 160.

fiscal administration, To quote Prof. Gopal,[3] the efficiency of the tax administration and the successful functioning of a tax system must satisfy a few criteria. Firstly, the arrears of tax should be as small as possible. Next, evasion should be promptly dealt with, so as to discourage attempts of evasion and make the evader himself feel guilty. Thirdly, it must engender in the taxpayer a degree of trust in the administration's efficiency, impartiality and sense of fairness. It must so administer the taxes that the feeling of harassment in the procedure is minimised. These virtues in any administration are ideal and efforts should be made to acquire them. It is further suggested that tax dodgers must be dealt with deterrent actions and honest tax payers encouraged in order to get the tax evaders from the economy out. Full taxpayers may also be motivated through pecuniary benefits.

Registration of Dealers

Sales tax is payable by dealers under every local Sales Tax Act. The dealers who are liable to pay tax are required to get themselves registered. Every Sales Tax Act makes a provision for the registration of dealers which is necessary for the establishment of suitable operating procedures for the handling of tax returns, money received and for the ascertainment of delinquent firms not filing and paying on time.[4] Registration is one of the corner-stones of the sales tax structure. The efficiency of this aspect of administration directly influences the amount of revenue receipts and is useful in the preparation of statistical data and the enforcement programmes. Further Moak and Cowan have emphasised that, "Registration can be viewed as the 'alpha' and 'omega' of sales tax administration."[5] In all the States, there is a provision for statutory compulsory registration of dealers under certain prescribed conditions. The dealers have also been given an option of voluntary registration even if prescribed conditions do not exist. In voluntary regis-

3. M.H. Gopal: "Tax Administration as a Factor in Economic Growth in India", *Southern Economic Review*, Vol. 1, April, 1972, p. 198.
4. John F. Due: *State Sales Tax Administration*, Public Administration Service, Illinois, 1963, p. 48.
5. Moak and Cowan: *Administration of Local Sales and Use Taxes*, Municipal Finance Association of U.S. and Canada, Illinois, 1961, p. 89.

tration, a dealer who is not liable to pay tax can get himself registered voluntarily. If the dealer gets himself registered, he gets some benefits in the operation of his business. Registration enables a dealer to charge sales tax from customers which is an offence and punishable in the absence of registration. S.D. Singh has emphasised that the registration means putting the dealers on the list of assessees and it confers certain privileges on them to which they would otherwise not he entitled.[6] Registration enables a registered dealer to purchase goods on declaration forms without paying any tax. It further enables manufacturers to purchase raw materials as tax free or at concessional rate. In case of inter-State dealings, a registered dealer under the Central Sales Tax Act is entitled to obtain goods from outside the State at the concessional rate. A registered dealer is invariably required to display his registration number prominently in his shop and is further required to mention the same on his printed cash or credit memos, failing which he is punishable under the sales tax statute.

Application for Registration

Every dealer who is liable to pay sales tax makes an application in the prescribed form and manner to the assessing authority in whose circle/ward the business firm is situated, accompanying a treasury receipt of the specified fee for registration. The registration fee varies from State to State. It is ten rupees in Rajasthan, five rupees in Haryana and Punjab while in Uttar Pradesh, the fee payable by the dealer for registration is seventy-five rupees for the first assessment year and fifty rupees for each subsequent year.[7] If a dealer has branches or places of business at several places within the State he will have to move the application at his principal place of business and state the name of branches in application form. If the branches of the dealer are spread over in two or more States, he will have to secure registration in each such State not only for the registration under the State law but also under Central Sales Tax Act. In case of loss of registration certificate,

6. S.D. Singh: *The Principles and Law of Sales Tax*, Eastern Book Company, Lucknow, 1973, p. 436.
7. Substituted by Uttar Pradesh Sales Tax Act 12 of 1979 with effect from 1st April, 1978.

a duplicate copy can be obtained from the assessing authority concerned by submitting an application accompanied by treasury receipt. According to John F. Due there are two schools of thought on the question of fee. One believes that business firms should pay an amount sufficient to cover the costs of handling the registration, the other believes that registration is of primary importance to the State and the vendor should not be charged on this account.[8] In this context it may be pertinent to note the views of the Lokanathan and Bhoothalingam Committees regarding registration fee. The Lokanathan Committee (1963)[9] has suggested a compulsory registration of dealers irrespective of their turnover and further stated that the registration fee should be in two slabs, *i.e.*, Rs. 5 for petty dealers and Rs. 10 for other dealers. The Bhoothalingam Committee[10] has recommended an increase in the registration fee from Rs. 6 to Rs. 20 or Rs. 25 per annum. In Rajasthan, Haryana and Punjab the present registration charges have been in vogue for a long time and do not reflect the change in the price level or in the cost of administration. The State Governments should, therefore, consider the revision of registration charges by fixing it at Rs. 50 to cover registration costs.

The application for registration must he filed within 30 days from the date on which the dealer becomes liable to pay tax. The application is put before the Sales Tax Officer or Assistant Sales Tax Officer. Sales Tax Inspector investigates the genuineness of the case and reports to the issuing authority. The concerned authority examines it, and if found in order he issues a registration certificate within a period of 60 days from the date of receipt of application. Generally, the whole process takes a long time due to inefficiency of inspectors and excess burden on assessing authorities, The period of 60 days is very long. It is desirable to prescribe a period of 30 days as a limit within which the registration certificate must be issued. It is essential that the work of inspectors should be checked by senior authorities. Recently Commissioner, Commercial Taxes,

8. John F. Due: *op. cit.*, p. 49.
9. P.S. Lokanathan—*Sales Tax System in Andhra Pradesh: A Review*, National Council of Education and Research, New Dehli, 1963, p. 32.
10. S. Bhoothalingam—*Review of Sales Tax in Andhra Pradesh*, NCEAR, New Delhi, p. 58.

Rajasthan has issued a circular to all the assessing authorities to issue registration certificate within 30 days from the date of receipt of application for registration. Any delay in issuing such certificate has been viewed seriously in the meetings of vigilance committee held from time to time.

Provisions Relating to Security

There are provisions in the Sales Tax Act of different States for a demand of a reasonable security for the proper payment of tax from a dealer applying for the registration. Security may be demanded at the time of registration or after the registration is granted. But this power may be exercised only if the sales tax authorities consider it necessary for the security of the revenue of the State. If the dealer does not deposit the required security then the authority may refuse to grant the registration certificate unless the required security is furnished.[11] The amount of security should depend on the nature of business, its turnover and the amount of tax payable thereon. If unreasonable amount of security is demanded by the assessing authority, the order may be referred to the appellate authority. No dealer should be required to furnish any security under Sales Tax Act unless he has been given an opportunity of being heard. Security may bé deposited as cash, bonds or in the form of bank guarantee.

In Rajasthan, the amount of security has been fixed in the statute which cannot exceed Rs. 5,000.[12] Additional security may also be demanded from defaulting dealers. In Uttar Pradesh the security amount cannot exceed the tax payable as assessed by authorities on the turnover of the dealer for the assessment year,[13] while in Punjab, the maximum limit of security which can be demanded by the assessing authority is Rs. 50,000.[14] If once security has been demanded and after

11. *Report of the Committee For Drafting the Rajasthan Sales Tax Bill*, Government of Rajasthan, 1973, p. 96.
12. Rajasthan Sales Tax Act 1954, Section 6(7).
13. Uttar Pradesh Sales Tax Act, 1948, Rules 8 (1) (2). Almost the same provision is given in Haryana Sales Tax Act, section 23(1).
14. Substituted by Punjab Sales Sax Act No. 9 of 1974 section (3) as published in *Punjab Gazette*, Extraordinary Part I, dated 30th April, 1974, p. 33.

that assessing authority thinks that the security furnished is inadequate, additional security can also be demanded.

Amendment or Cancellation of the Registration Certificates

The assessing authority may amend or cancel any certificate of registration after giving a reasonable opportunity of being heard to the holder of registration certificate. The registration certificate is cancelled if any dealer changes the name or place or nature of business or class of goods and does not inform about it to the assessing authority. It may also be cancelled if it has been obtained by fraud or misrepresentation. Similarly, the amendment in registration certificate can also be made after making necessary inquiries if the dealer applies for the same.

Registration Under Central Sales Tax Act

Sub section (1) and (2) of section 7 of the Central Sales Tax Act, 1956 contain the provisions for the registration of dealers under Central Sales Tax Act. Every dealer who sells goods in inter-State trade or commerce is liable to pay tax under this Act, and therefore, he must apply for registration under sub-section (1) not later than 30 days from the date on which he becomes liable to pay the tax.[15] Registration under sub-section (2) is, however, voluntary. A dealer who is liable to pay tax under State Sales Tax Act, may apply for the registration even under the Central Sales Tax Act, though he is not liable to pay tax thereunder. The application for registration must be sent alongwith a court fee in stamps worth Rs. 5.[16] After receiving the application, the prescribed authority examines it, and if it is found satisfactory and in conformity with the provisions of the Act, he shall register the application and issue a certificate of registration. If the dealer has misplaced his certificate, the authority will grant a fresh duplicate copy of the certificate on payment of a fee of Rs. 2 for[17] each such copy.

Trend in Sales Tax Registration

After a brief description of the existing registration proce-

15. K.R. Chaturvedi: *Central Sales Tax Law*, Eastern Law House (P) Ltd., Calcutta, 1965, p. 122.
16. *Ibid.*
17. *Ibid.*

dure in the States, it would be pertinent to analyse the trend in sales tax registration under State Sales Tax and Central Sales Tax Acts. Table 5.1 gives the trend in Sales Tax registration in the States under study for the period from 1974-75 to 1983-84.

It can be seen from Table 5.1, that the number of registrations under the Rajasthan Sales Tax and Central Sales Tax Act is continuously increasing. Under Rajasthan Sales Tax Act, it was 1,02,790 in 1974-75 which increased to 1,48,087 in 1983-84, the increase being of 44 per cent. Under Central Sales Tax Act, from 60,175 in 1974-75, it increased to 1,08,066 in 1983-84, marking an increase of 80 per cent. Further, during this period the registrations under the Rajasthan Sales Tax Act as percentage to total registrations showed a declining trend. It was 63.07 per cent in 1974-75 which dropped down to 57.81 per cent in 1983-84. Under the Central Sales Tax Act it showed an increasing trend and rose from 36.93 per cent in 1974-75 to 42.19 per cent in 1983-84. It may be considered as a reflection of the growing importance of inter-State trade or commerce of the State.

In Uttar Pradesh the registration numbers showed a trend different from that of Rajasthan, Haryana and Punjab. The number of firms registered under Uttar Pradesh Sales Tax Act was 1,53,000 in 1974-75 which increased to 2,24,000 in 1977-78. After that it dropped down to 2,08,000 in 1978-79 due to cancellation of a large number af registrations. Further, in the two succeeding years it increased but soon declined to 2,18,000 in 1981-82. Finally, it again increased to 2,37,000 in 1983-84. Similar trend was also seen under the Central Sales Tax Act. Under Uttar Pradesh Sales Tax and the Central Sales Tax Act, the percentage of registered dealers to total number of registered dealers showed fluctuating trend during the study period. Under the Uttar Pradesh Sales Tax Act it was 66.23 in 1975-76 which marginally declined to 65.18 in 1976-77. After that it registered a steady growth and reached 72.47 in 1978-79, but again declined and came down to 71.82 in 1979-80 and further to 71.28 in 1980-81, but it again increased to 80.15 in 1981-82. However, again dropped down to 78.41 in 1982-83. Finally, it declined to 76.95 in 1983-84. Under the Central Sales Tax Act, the percentage of registered dealers to total number of registered dealers was 33.77 in 1974-75 which increased to 34.82 in

TAELE 5.1

Trend in Sales Tax Registrntion in Selected States Under Study 1974-75 to 1983-84

Year	RAJASTHAN			UTTAR PRADESH			HARYANA			PUNJAB		
	RST ACT	*CST ACT*	*TOTAL*	*UPST ACT*	*CST ACT*	*TOTAL*	*HGST ACT*	*CST ACT*	*TOTAL*	*PGST ACT*	*CST ACT*	*TOTAL*
1974-75	102790	60175	162965	153000	78000	231000	34556	29558	64114	65703	52285	117988
	(63.07)	(36.93)		(66.23)	(33.77)		(53.90)	(46.10)		(55.69)	(44.31)	
1975-76	111156	65757	176913	161000	86000	247000	36284	31918	68202	70643	63255	133898
	(62.83)	(37.17)		(65.18)	(34.82)		(53.20)	(46.80)		(52.76)	(47.24)	
1976-77	121396	72458	193854	181000	87000	278000	40768	36345	77113	73316	66996	140312
	(62.62)	(37.38)		(67.54)	(32.46)		(52.87)	(47.13)		(52.25)	(47.75)	
1977-78	123487	74305	197792	224000	87000	311000	44532	40142	84674	78740	72640	151380
	(62.43)	(37.57)		(72.03)	(27.97)		(52.59)	(47.41)		(52.01)	(47.99)	
1978-79	130462	80688	211150	208000	79000	287000	48211	43666	91877	83868	70861	154729
	(61.79)	(38.21)		(72.47)	(27.53)		(52.47)	(47.53)		(54.20)	(45.80)	
1979-80	138323	86958	225281	237000	93000	330000	50740	46627	97367	88628	75083	163711
	(61.40)	(38.60)		(71.82)	(28.18)		(52.11)	(47.89)		(54.14)	(45.86)	
1980-81	144185	92950	237135	268000	108000	376000	54546	49779	104325	94592	81493	176085
	(60.80)	(39.20)		(71.28)	(28.72)		(52.28)	(47.72)		(53.72)	(46.28)	
1981-82	148315	97645	245960	218000	54000	272000	57981	53545	111526	100486	87235	187721
	(60.30)	(39.70)		(80.15)	(19.85)		(51.99)	(48.01)		(53.33)	(46.47)	

1982-83	144233	101464	245697	236000	65000	301000	60438	55769	116207	105603	90534	196137
	(58.70)	(41.30)		(78.41)	(21.59)		(52.01)	(47.99)		(53.84)	(46.16)	
1983-84	148087	108066	256153	237000	71000	308000	64430	59581	124011	106609	92462	199071
	(57.81)	(42.19)		(76.95)	(23.05)		(51.96)	(48.04)		(53.55)	(46.45)	

Source: Admtnistrative Reports of Rajasthan Commercial Taxes Department, Haryana Excise and Taxation Department, Punjab Excise and Taxation Department and Uttar Pradesh Sales Tax Department.

1975-76. It showed a decreasing trend from 1976-77 to 1978-79. But in the next two years it showed an increasing trend. It again dropped to 19.85 in 1981-82 but increased to 21.59 in 1982-83 and finally reached 23.05 in 1983-84. The registration under the Uttar Pradesh Sales Tax Act showed an increase of 54.90 per cent whereas under the Central Sales Tax it declined by 8.97 per cent during the period of study.

Under the Haryana Sales Tax Act the percentage of registered dealers to total registered dealers showed a declining trend. It was 53.90 in 1975-76. After that, it registered a steady fall in the succeeding five years and reached 52.11 in 1979-80. It marginally increased to 52.28 in 1980-81 and finally, dropped down to 51.96 in 1983-84. Under the Central Sales Tax Act, the percentage of registered dealers to total number of registered dealers showed an increasing trend upto 1979-80 but it slightly declined to 47.72 in 1980-81 from 47.89 in 1978-79. It again increased to 48.01 in 1981-82 but marginally dropped down to 47.99 in 1982-83. Finally, it reached 48.04 in 1983-84. In absolute terms, the number of registered dealers under the Haryana Sales Tax Act and the Central Sales Tax Act has shown an increase throughout the period of study. The number of registrations under the Haryana General Sales Tax Act showed an increase of 86 per cent whereas under Central Sales Tax Act, of 102 per cent during the study period.

In Punjab, the number of registered dealers under Punjab General Sales Tax Act was 65,703 in 1974-75. After making a steady growth throughout the study period it reached 1,06.609 in 1983-84 and under the Central Sales Tax Act it was 52,285 in 1975-76 which increased to 92,462 in 1983-84. The number of registered dealers under Punjab General Sales Tax Act showed an increase of 62 per cent and under Central Sales Tax Act of 77 per cent during the study period. The number of registered dealers as a percentage to total registered dealers showed a declining trend upto 1977-78 but it increased to 54.20 per cent in 1978-79 from 52.01 per cent in 1977-78. After that it showed a decreasing trend in the succeeding four years and finally reached 53.55 per cent in 1983-84. Under the Central Sales Tax Act, the number of registered dealers was 44.31 per cent of the total number of dealers in 1975-76 which showed an increasing trend and reached 47.99 per cent in 1977-78. It slipped to 45.80 per cent in 1978-79, but after showing marginal increase it reached 46.45 per cent in 1983-84.

As a whole the registration number under Sales Tax Act increased by 44 per cent in Rajasthan, 55 per cent in Uttar Pradesh, 86 per cent in Haryana and 62 per cent in Punjab. It shows that trade and commerce activities has increased more in Haryana followed by Punjab, Uttar Pradesh and Rajasthan. The trend of registrations under the Central Sales Tax Act also signifies the importance of inter-State trade and commerce activities in the States. Registrations under the Central Sales Tax Act shows an increase of 80 per cent in Rajasthan, 102 per cent in Haryana and 77 per cent in Punjab whereas it declined by 8.97 per cent in Uttar Pradesh during the period from 1974-75 to 1983-84. It reveals that in Haryana and Punjab inter-State trade activities increased much faster in comparison to those in Rajasthan. On the basis of declining trend of registration in Uttar Pradesh, as a result of cancellation of forged registrations it may be suggested that the other States should also take necessary steps like Uttar Pradesh.

Submission of Returns and Payment of Tax

A return is a prescribed form in which dealers prepare a statement of their sales and purchases for a particular period and submit it to the assessing authority.[18] Every dealer who is liable to pay tax and gets himself registered with the department is required to submit the returns within 30 days in prescribed form and manner alongwith treasury challans. Unregistered dealers may also be required to furnish a return or returns, if prescribed authority issues a notice to file return. Returns may be presented personally or may be sent by post. All the registered dealers are required to submit their returns on 'Quarterly basis'.[19] In case of Punjab and Haryana there is a provision for submission of monthly returns in case of doubtful dealers. And in Rajasthan, there is provision of monthly returns in case of newly established business during the first 12 months from the date of issue of the certificate of registration. Revised returns

18. M.L. Jain: *Rajasthan Sales Tax Act, 1954*, P.K. Prakashan, Jaipur, 1982, p. 171.
19. Quarter will be calculated on the basis of an accounting year of the dealer.

can be submitted in case of wrong submission of the information in the return. It should be submitted before the submission of next return. In the words of S.K. Agarwala, "If a dealer discovers some omission or other error in the return filed, he may file a revised return at any time before the time prescribed for furnishing the next return."[20]

Rule 25 (3) of Rajasthan Sales Tax Act provides for some exception to the periods and time allowed for filing the returns. Firstly, a dealer whose taxable turnover does not exceed one-tenth of his gross turnover in the previous year, can apply within 3 months of the commencement of the year of his accounts and assessing authority can allow him to submit his returns annually. Secondly, a dealer who has no taxable turnover in any year of accounts, may submit an annual return in form S.T. 21 not later than 60 days after the end of such accounting year. Thirdly, a dealer whose gross turnover in the previous year does not exceed Rs. 50,000, may submit his return annually in form S.T. 5 not later than 60 days after the end of the year. The Punjab Sales Tax Act provides that the dealer dealing exclusively in goods liable to tax at first stage of sale and who has paid tax on purchase of such goods within the States has been allowed to file returns annually within 30 days from the expiry of his accounting year. Conclusively it may be observed that provisions of quarterly returns are useful in the interest of the regular flow or revenue to the Government.

The amount of tax is paid by the dealers at the time of the submission of returns. Every return of turnover should be accompanied by a receipt showing the deposit of the full amount of tax due on the basis of return within thirty days of the close of the quarter. The state government may permit a class of dealers to compound for the tax by paying a lump-sum amount in lieu of tax. If the return is not accompanied by a receipt for the deposit of tax, the assessing authority shall not be bound to take any cognisance of the returns and assessing authority may issue a show-cause notice to the dealer. Non-filing of returns and non-payment of tax is punishable under the provisions of law.

20. S.K. Agarwala: *All India Sales Tax Manual*, Central Law Agency, Allahabad, 1952, p. 50.

Assessment Proceedings

The word 'assessment' is used in different connotations depending upon its context. Sometimes it may refer to computation of turnover, sometimes the amount of tax payable and sometimes to the whole procedure laid down in the Act for imposition of tax. In a broader sense it includes quantification of tax, penalty, interest and fees. B.P. Khaitan has observed that ascertainment or quantification of liability is generally known as assessment though sometimes the expression assessment not merely means the determination of the amount of tax payable but also includes the computation of turnover and even the whole procedure laid down in the Act for imposing liability of tax.[21]

Assessment proceedings is a necessary consequence of the imposition of tax. The assessment provisions are the cornerstones of any taxing statute which makes the charging section effective for all practical purposes. "If machinery of the Act to quantify the liability is defective or incompetent or invalid the charging section will almost remain paralysed with no capacity to move its limbs in spite of all its willingness."[22] The assessing authorities have power to make provisional and best judgement assessment in case of non-filing of returns by the dealer and also in case of evasion of tax.

Provisional Assessment on Failure to Submit Returns

If a dealer fails to submit a return for a particular period within prescribed time, the assessing authority after making enquiry as it deems fit and after giving the dealer a reasonable opportunity of being heard may assess the tax provisionally for that period to the best of his judgement. Best judgement assessment can be made against a dealer who is a defaulter in supplying informations. The authority must not act dishonestly, or vindictively, or capriciously because he must exercise best judgement in the matter. To decide cases, he must be able to take into consideration local knowledge and repute in regard to the assessee's circumstances, and his own knowledge of previous returns and the assessments of the assessee, and all

21, B.P. Khaitan: *Evolution of Sales Tax in India*, National Law Publication, Indore, 1963, p. 210,

22. *Ibid.*, p. 202.

other matters which he thinks, will assist him in arriving at a fair and proper estimate.[23] The main purpose of provisional assessment is to deprive a dealer of taking undue advantage of not depositing the tax in time. The demand created under this section is required to be paid within a reasonable time, otherwise, it is recoverable as an arrear of land revenue.

Provisional Assessment in Case of Evasion

Section 10 of the Rajasthan Sales Tax Act provides that "If an assessing authority has reason to believe that a dealer has evaded or avoided tax, he may after giving the reasonable opportunity of being heard, determine at any time and for any period the taxable turnover of such dealer and assess the tax to the best of his judgement."[24] Irregular payment of tax is not evasion of tax. Assessment under this section is also provisional and can be made for any period but if final assessment becomes due no provisional assessment is justified as per latest judgement of the High Courts.

Circumstances for Best Judgement Assessment

The power to make assessment to the best of his judgement is conferred upon the assessing authority by sales tax laws of all the States. Following are the circumstances under which the assessing authority can make best judgement assessment:

(*i*) Where the dealer has not filed the return within prescribed time.

(*ii*) Where the dealer does not comply with the notice calling upon him to produce accounts, documents and such other evidence: as he may be required in support of a return.

(*iii*) Where the assessing authority is not satisfied with the correctness or completeness of the returns.

(*iv*) Where the dealer liable to pay tax, fails to get himself registered under appropriate law of the State.

Normally, the dealers are not satisfied with the best judgement assessment because they feel that the machinery has not

23. K.R. Chaturvedi: *The Principles of Sales Tax Laws*, Eastern Law House (P) Ltd., Calcutta, 1967, pp, 428-29.

24. Similar provision has been made under Uttar Pradesh, Haryana and Punjab Sales Tax Acts.

worked honestly. It was observed in the case of B.N. Banerjee and others *Vs.* Commercial Taxes Commissioner and others that "An assessee may be bad enough but there is no reason why the assessing authorities must be worse and must not conform to the requirements of law in making a best judgement assessment."[25] Therefore, it may be said that while making best judgement assessment, the assessing authority must be guided by judicial considerations and by rules of justice, equity and conscience. The final assessment can be made on the basis of returns, on the basis of evidence adduced and on the basis of best judgement of the assessing authorities.

Assessment of Small Dealers Under Self Assessment Scheme

In all the States under study, sales tax laws provide for assessment on the basis of returns. This is called as self assessment without calling the dealers in the sales tax offices. Small dealers whose gross turnover does not exceed Rs. 3 lacs in Rajasthan, and Rs. 2 lacs in Punjab and Uttar Pradesh are required to submit their returns in prescribed form and in order to ensure that the claims of deductions, refund, reductions are genuine and correct, these dealers are required to enclose a list of accounts books maintained, Trading account, Profit and Loss account, evidence regarding deposit of tax during the year, declaration forms etc. alongwith the last return. These dealers are required to calculate tax themselves, and if the assessing authority finds any mistake in calculations, he will correct it and make additional demand of tax from the dealer. If the dealer is importer or manufacturer and the assessment is the first and last then he will not be assessed under self-assessment scheme. In Punjab, 15,000 small dealers were assessed under this scheme in 1979-80. In Rajasthan 14,417 and in Uttar Pradesh 13,018 cases were assessed in 1983-84. The benefit of self assessment has been provided on the pattern of income-tax laws.

During the course of present study it was revealed that in practice almost all dealers are called in the office of assessing authority with their accounts etc. which is a clear cut violation

25. B.N. Banerjee, Jhagru Shah and others *vs.* Commissioner of Commercial Taxes and others, 17, *S.I.C.* 130, Calcutta.

of the policy of the Department. Hence, it is suggested that inspecting authorities should regularly watch the performance of the self assessment scheme so that the real benefits of the policy can reach the small traders. In case where returns have been filed *suo-moto*, assessment should be done by the assessing authorities. The Commissioner should prescribe certain specific forms for informations to be submitted by the dealer at the time of assessment. After finalisation of assessment on order to check lapses 10 to 20 per cent cases should be scrutinised by the investigating officers in detail. It is suggested that all the States should follow the self-assessment scheme with changes as suggested above.

Pending Assessment Cases

The number of pending assessment cases are increasing in each State. Delay in assessment is a common complaint.[26] It is caused due to either incomplete and defective returns submitted or adjournment in the course of assessment sought by dealers. These incomplete and defective returns cause much inconvenience to the assessing authorities. Therefore, in order to avoid delay in the assessment of sales tax the dealer should be exhorted to file returns with greater care. On the part of administration delay is due to the lack of staff, result is that the officers have excess burden of work. An assessing authority has multifarious duties such as assessment, recovery, survey, investigation of offences and day-to-day work.

Trend of assessment and pending cases

The number of assessments and pending cases are given in Table 5.2.

26. Almost all Sales Tax Simplification Committee Reports have insinuated this fact, for example:
 —*Report of Taxation Enquiry Committee*, Govt. of India, 1953-54, p. 70.
 —P.S. Lokanathan: *Report on Simplification and Improvement of Sales Tax System in Madras*, Government Press, Madras, 1957, p. 27.
 —P.S. Lokanathan. *Sales Tax in Andhra Pradesh, op. cit.*, p. 31.
 —Federation of Indian Chamber of Commerce and Industry, *Sales Tax: A Plea for Simplification*, New Delhi, 1969, p. 18.

TABLE 5.2

Trend of Assessment Cases and Pendency in States Under Study

States	*Upto 1976-77*	*1977-78*	*1978-79*	*1979-80*	*1980-81*	*1981-82*	*1982-83*	*1983-84*
Rajasthan								
Cases	84,163	87,642	96,767	1,26,203	1,29,687	1,30,438	1,41,256	1,32,638
Assessed		(+4.13)	(+9.73)	(+30.42)	(+2.76)	(+.58)	(+8.29)	(– 6.10)
Cases	1,37,665	1,55,484	1,79,276	1,73,130	1,71,245	1,73,024	1,70,382	1,61,824
Pending		(+12.94)	(+15.30)	(—3.43)	(–1.09)	(+1.11)	(—1.53)	(—5.02)
Uttar Pradesh								
Cases	2,81,099	3,12,044	3,67,929	3,66,505	3,16,605	2,89,807	3,02,558	2,55,736
Assessed		(+11.01)	(+17.91)	(—3.87)	(—13.64)	(—8.46)	(+4.40)	(—15.48)
Cases	4,24,586	4,57,847	4,37,819	3,65,852	3,56,320	3,71,790	3,75,647	4,16,743
Pending		(+7.83)	(—4,37)	(—16.44)	(—2.61)	(+4.34)	(+1.04)	(+10.94)
Haryana								
Cases	63,038	80,163	81,156	81,936	97,799	97,553	99,074	1,05,865
Assessed		(+27.17)	(+1.24)	(+.96)	(+19.36)	(—.25)	(+1.56)	(+6.85)
Cases	44.940	38,784	32,575	36,471	31,970	35,244	39,377	40,310
Pending		(—13.69)	(—16.01)	(+11.96)	(—12.34)	(+10.24)	(+11.73)	(+2.37)
Punjab								
Cases	67,499	1,14,258	1,09,009	1,10,412	1,19,622	1,68,686	1,33,483	1,81,113
Assessed		(+69.27)	(—4.59)	(+1.29)	(+8.34)	(+41.02)	(—20.87)	(+35.86)
Cases	83,577	98,205	1,37,935	1,79,624	2,26,629	2,11,669	2,39,447	2,54,223
Pending		(+17.50)	(+40.46)	(+30.22)	(+26.17)	(—6.60)	(+13.12)	(+6.17)

—Figures in brackets shows percentage increased or decreased over previous year.

—Assessment cases and pending cases include Sales Tax cases and Central Sales Tax cases.

Source: *Administrative Reports* of Rajasthan, Uttar Pradesh, Punjab and Haryana Sales Tax Departments.

It is clear from Table 5.2, that in Rajasthan the number of cases assessed increased continuously. The cases assessed were 84,163 upto 1976-77 which increased by 4.13 per cent in 1977-78, 9.73 per cent in 1978-79 and spurted by 30.42 per cent in 1979-80. After that, it made minor growth upto 1982-83, but finally it dropped by 6.10 per cent in 1983-84 over the previous year. The cases pending for assessment were 1,37,665 upto 1976-77 which increased by 12.94 per cent in 1977-78 and by 15.30 per cent in 1978-79. However, in the succeeding two years the pending assessment cases decreased but again marginally increased by 1.11 per cent in 1981-82. The number of cases pending for assessment again decresed by 1.53 per cent in 1982-83 and finaliy, it plummeted by 5.02 per cent in 1983-84.

In Uttar Pradesh, the assessment work done by the assessing authorities was 2,81,099 cases upto 1976-77 which increased by 11.01 per cent in 1977-78 and by 17.91 per cent in 1978-79. Further during the three succeeding years, it showed a declining trend. It fell by 3.87 per cent in 1979-80, 13.64 per cent in 1980-81 and 8.46 per cent in 1981-82. However, it again increased by 4.40 per cent in 1982-83. The pending cases were 4,24,586 in 1976-77 which increased by 7.83 per cent in 1977-78 In the successive three years, the pending cases decreased but after that they increased continuously and recorded a phenomenal increase of 10.94 per cent in 1983-84. The problem of pending assessment cases is a great challenge for the state.

In case of Haryana, the number of cases assessed was 63,038 upto 1976-77. The assessed cases showed increasing trend upto 1980-81 but marginally declined by .25 per cent in 1981-82. After that they increased by 1.56 per cent in 1982-83 and further by 6.85 per cent in 1983-84. The pending cases were 44,940 upto 1976-77 which declined by 13.69 per cent in 1977-78 and further by 16.01 per cent in 1978-79. However, it increased by 11.96 per cent in 1979-80 but again declined by 12.34 per cent in 1980-81. After that, in the three succeeding years it marked a rising trend and increased by 10.24 per cent in 1981-82, 11.73 per cent in 1982-83 and finally by 2.37 per cent in 1983-84.

In Punjab, the number of cases assessed was 67,499 upto 1976-77 which hiked to 1,14,258 in 1977-78. It dropped by

4.59 per cent in 1978-79 but marginally increased by 1.29 per cent in 1979-80 and further by 8.34 per cent in 1980-81. It marked a tremendous growth of 41.05 per cent in 1981-82, but again dropped by 20.87 per cent in 1982-83. Finally, in 1983-84 it increased by 35.86 per cent over the previous year. The pending assessment cases were 83,577 upto 1976-77 which increased by 17.50 per cent in 1977-78, 40.46 per cent in 1978-79, 30.22 per cent in 1979-80, and by 26.17 per cent in 1980-81. It dropped by 6.60 per cent in 1981-82 but again increased by 13.12 per cent in 1982-83 and finally by 6.17 per cent in 1983-84.

Thus, it may be concluded that the number of pending cases is a great problem of sales tax department in all the States under study. In Rajasthan, it showed an increase upto the year 1981-82. Thereafter, it showed a declining trend. In Uttar Pradesh, the number of pending cases declined in 1978-79, 1979-80 and 1980-81, but then showed an increasing trend in the last three years of study. In Haryana, it showed some fluctuations upto 1980-81 but during the last three years it increased with greater speed. The number of cases pending in Punjab showed continuous increase except in 1981-82. The growth rate of pending cases is more in Punjab followed by Haryana, Uttar Pradesh and Rajasthan. Rajasthan is little better than other States. It has been observed that because of the increase in the number of assessing authorities, the rate of assessed cases has been increasing and the rate of pending cases declining. The delay in assessment, therefore, seems more to be a function of the assessing authorities. In case of Punjab, it is recommended that the number of assessing authorities should be increased so that the pending cases could be settled.

Normally, old cases for assessment remain unassessed for a long time. It has been observed that the assessing authorities are tempted to tackle new cases in order to show larger number of cases assessed. Therefore, incentives for the disposal of complicated cases should also be given. Timely disposal of the assessment cases is must for the sales tax administration because it yields more revenue to the department and lessens the work of the assessing authorities.

Arrears of Sales Tax Revenue

Collection of tax and recovery of demand are two aspects of taxation. Collection of tax means payment of advance tax by the dealer subject to adjustment at the time of final assessment and recovery of demand means a demand for which demand notice has been issued. If a dealer has not paid demand in compliance with the notice of demand within specified time, the recovery of demand can be made through attachment of movable and immovable properties. Such demand is recoverable as an arrear of land revenue. The arrears of sales tax pose a menacing problem and destroy most of the productivity of revenue to the State exchequer. They increase unnecessary workload, are a burden to the administrative machinery, and also increase the compliance cost of the department. Mounting arrears can defeat the very purpose of taxation. The main reason of increase in arrears is the increasing number of appeals and delay in their disposal. In certain cases the dealers close their business and start another business under different name. As a consequence, the amount cannot be collected in time and the unrealised amount of tax becomes an arrear.

Problems of Delinquency

The problems of delinquency refer to the increasing arrears of the tax.[27] The term implies that the dealer has either failed to file returns and pay tax or has filed returns but failed to pay tax. In fact, it increases arrears and adds to the problems of the administration. So the list of tax payers must be so maintained that tax payer's non-payment may immediately be detected and after the due date, a notice for demand should be made at the earliest. Prompt action will help in minimising delinquency. If the necessary step is not taken in time then demand would gradually become ineffective. Generally, dealers attitude to hold money and invest it in their business increases the arrears. According to Due the greatest weakness in handling delinquents is the failure to analyse delinquency scientfically.[28] A survey undertaken by the Economic and Statistical

27. John F. Due—*op. cit.*, p. 88.
28. *Ibid.*

Adviser to the Government of Punjab, in Patiala District shows that in 1960-61, out of 573 dealers 100 did not file returns. Thus, there were 17.4 per cent delinquents. The survey reports that "They were dealing in commodities which subject to General Sales Tax in the beginning but were declared tax free at a later date or they had closed down their business."[29] Purohit observes the delinquency was greatest among hardware dealers, manihari dealers and dealers in gems and precious stones in Rajasthan.[30] Therefore, the problem of delinquency needs very prompt and strict handling. It is essential that the authority should watch the tax payers from time-to-time and delay should be dealt with deterrent actions, so that the regular flow of tax may be maintained. Extension of time may be given on justifiable grounds. The old arrears should be cleared through attachment or any other procedure. Special campaign must be started to clear the arrears. During campaign routine work should be stopped.

Trend of arrears of Sales Tax

The arrears of sales tax in Rajasthan, Uttar Pradesh, Haryana and Punjab are presented in Table 5.3.

Arrears of sales tax in absolute terms in all the States unders tudy have been increasing as shown in Table 5.3. In Rajasthan, it was 627.99 lakhs in 1976-77 which increased by 15.79 per cent in 1977-78. In the next two years, arrears dropped by 24.51 per cent and 2.40 per cent respectively. They rose by 86.38 per cent in 1980-81 and further hiked by 229.99 per cent in 1981-82. After rising by 15.74 in 1982-83, they finally increased by 19.73 per cent in 1983-84 over the previous year. In terms of its relation with sales tax yield, the arrears amounted to 7.45 per cent in 1976-77 but fell to 7.25 per cent in 1977-78, to 4.82 per cent in 1978-79 and further to 3.95 per cent in 1979-80. They again increased to 6.88 per cent in 1980-81.

29. Economic and Statistical Advisei to Government, Punjab, *Survey and Analysis of General Sales Tax in Patiala District for 1960-61*, Economic and Statistical Organisation Publication No. 37, Chandigarh, 1963, p. 5.
30. M.C. Purohit—*Sales Taxation in India*, Sultan Chand and Sons (Pvt.) Ltd., New Delhi, 1975, p. 178.

TABLE 5.3
Trend in Sales Tax Arrears

States	1976-77 Rs.	Increase or decrease over previous year	1977-78 Rs.	Increase or decrease over previous year	1978-79 Rs.	Increase or decrease over previous year	1979-80 Rs.	Increase or decrease over previous year	1980-81 Rs.	Increase or decrease over previous year	1981-82 Rs.	Increase or decrease over previous year	1982-83 Rs.	Increase or decrease over previous year	1983-84 Rs.	Increase or decrease over previous year
Rajasthan	627.99 (7.45)	+13.77	727.15 (7.25)	+15.79	548.93 (4.82)	−24.51	535.73 (3.95)	−2.40	998.49 (6.88)	+86.38	3294.92 (17.70)	+229.99	3813.65 (17.19)	+15.74	4566.36 (18.27)	+19:73
Uttar Pradesh	7316.00 (30.09)	—	9126.00 (37.09)	+24.74	10442.00 (38.35)	+14.92	13433.00 (43.97)	+28.64	19407.00 (61.81)	+44.47	21698.00 (47.86)	+11.81	24060.00 (49.41)	+10.89	29056.00 (54.78)	+20.76
Haryana	298.61 (4.67)	—	514.29 (7.39)	+72.23	643.36 (8.07)	+25.10	1011.29 (11.23)	+57.19	1004.93 (9.30)	−.63	1489.08 (10.76)	+48.18	1919.48 (11.96)	+28.90	2174.29 (11.46)	+13.27
Punjab	877.31 (9.13)	+271.63	629.41 (5.85)	−28.26	682.72 (5.72)	+8.47	1210.50 (9.33)	+77.31	633.27 (3.96)	−47.69	957.05 (4.99)	+51.13	1823.83 (8.29)	+90.57	4642.15 (18.57)	+154.28

Note: Figures in brackets show per cent of Sales Tax arrears to sales tax revenue.
Arrears include Sales Tax arrears and Central Sales Tax arrears.

Sources: *Administrative Reports* from Sales Tax Departments.

After that the arrears as percentage to sales tax revenue hiked to 17.70 per cent in 1981-82, to 17.19 per cent in 1982-83 and finally reached 18.27 per cent in 1983-84.

In Uttar Pradesh the arrears of sales tax have been increasing continuously and have spurted from Rs. 7,136 lakhs in 1976-77 to Rs. 29,056 lakhs in 1983-84 an increase of 297 per cent. The percentage increase over the previous year has been fluctuating. It increased by 24.74 per cent in 1977-78, by 14.42 per cent in 1978-79 and further by 28.64 per cent in 1979-80. It hiked by 44.47 per cent in 1980-81, by 11.81 per cent in 1981-82, by 10.89 per cent in 1982-83 and finally increased by 20.76 per cent in 1983-84. The arrears as a percentage to sales tax revenue showed an alarming trend. It was 30.09 per cent in 1976-77, after a steady growth it reached 61.81 per cent in 1980-81, further it dropped to 47.86 per cent in 1981-82. It again increased to 49.41 per cent in 1982-83 and finally rose to 54.78 per cent in 1983-84. Uttar Pradesh is facing a great problem regarding arrears. It affects cumulatively and defeats the very purpose of sales taxation.

The amount of arrears was Rs. 298.61 lakhs in Haryana in 1976-77. It increased in the three succeeding years but marginally slipped by Rs. 6.36 lakhs in 1980-81. After that, it increased continuously throughout the period and finally reached Rs. 2174.29 lakhs in 1983-84, an increase of 628 per cent over 1976-77. The percentage of arrears growth over preceding year was 72.23 in 1977-78, 25.10 in 1978-79 and 57.19 in 1979-80. It slightly declined by .63 in 1980-81. After that, it showed an increasing trend *i.e.* 48.18 per cent in 1981-82, 28.90 per cent in 1982-83 and finally 13.27 per cent in 1983-84. Arrears as a percentage to sales tax revenue has been making a steady growth throughout the period. It varies between 4.67 to 11.96 per cent during 1976-77 to 1983-84.

In Punjab, the arrears of sales tax were Rs. 877.31 lakhs in 1976-77 which declined to Rs. 629.41 lakhs in 1977-78 but increased to Rs. 682.72 lakhs in 1978-79 and further to Rs. 1210.50 lakhs in 1979-80. They dropped to Rs. 633.27 lakhs in 1980-81 and after making a continuous increase in the three succeeding years they finally reached Rs. 4642.15 lakhs in 1983-84, there being an increase of 429 per cent over 1976-77.

The percentage change over the previous year has been showing wide fluctuations. It increased by 271.63 per cent in 1976-77 while it declined by 28.26 per cent in 1977-78. It again increased by 8.47 per cent in 1978-79 and further by 77.31 per cent in 1979-80. However, it dropped by 47.69 per cent in 1980-81 but again increased in the succeeding period *i.e.* by 51.13 per cent in 1981-82, by 90.57 per cent in 1982-83, and finally hiked by 154.28 per cent in 1983-84. The arrears as a percentage of sales tax revenue has been varying in the range of 3.96 to 9.33 per cent during 1976-77 to 1982-83, but in 1983-84 it increased to the alarming size of 18.57 per cent.

The problem of arrears is common to all the States. In Rajasthan, arrears had fallen in 1978-79 and 1979-80. In Haryana, they marginally fell in 1980-81 and in Punjab, they fell in 1977-78 and 1980-81 but again registered a rise in other years. The arrears increased to 7.27 times in Rajasthan, 3.97 times in Uttar Pradesh, 7.28 times in Haryana and 5.29 times in Punjab during 1976-77 to 1983-84. In fact, the growth of arrears is low in Uttar Pradesh but Uttar Pradesh is the only State where arrears highly affect the revenue and administration of sales tax. The major cause is that the old arrears generate further new arrears. In Uttar Pradesh the arrears to the sales tax revenue were in the range of 30.09 to 61.81 per cent during the period of study which is an alarming situation. In Rajasthan they were in the range of 3.95 to 18.27 per cent, in Haryana 4.67 to 11.96 per cent and in Punjab 3.96 to 18.57 per cent throughout the period under study. The continuous increase in sales tax arrears is an unhealthy feature, it causes extra burden on the consumers through more and more taxes. States should concentrate more on recovery proceedings by introduction of special recovery campaigns twice in a year.

Problem of Evasion

No tax can be successful in attaining the desired objectives unless it is collected with reasonable effectiveness. Evasion or avoidance results not only in loss of revenue and inequity but also creates serious competitive disturbance in economy. It is generally believed that there is a considerable amount of tax evasion but it is difficult to estimate the exact amount of sales tax evasion. Lokanathan Committee (1963)[31] estimated avoidance and evasion of sales tax for the ten agricultural commodities produced in Andhra Pradesh in 1959-60. The yield of the sales tax of these commodities was Rs. 230 lakhs in 1959-60 (or 32 per cent of the optimum y eld) whereas the optimum yield should have been Rs. 711 lakhs. The Committee estimated the turnover escaping tax in those goods and others around 40 per cent. The evasion of taxes causes inflationary pressure on economy. Basu emphasised that "The main ill effect of widespread tax evasion is that it fosters a sense of injustice in society."[32] In case of the study in 'rice' in Andhra Pradesh Dr. A. Venkata Rayudu observed that the sales tax evasion was as high as 57 per cent on an average during the five years period ending 1978-79.[33] No studies have been made so far in case of Rajasthan, Punjab, Haryana and Uttar Pradesh regarding the quantum of evasion of sales tax. Sita Ram Kesari, General Secretary of All India Congress Committee once said that Rs. 1500 crores are being earned by sales tax inspectors through mal-prac tices during the year 1982-83. Sri Bhikku Ram Jain, also demanded to abolish "Inspector Raj" from sales tax department. It shows that there is a big evasion by the dealers with the connivance of the departmental officers.

Generally, dealers employ following methods to evade tax (*i*) misreporting or under-reporting of purchases and sales by maintaining secret books of accounts, (*ii*) under billing and showing under weight, (*iii*) misuse of '*C*' forms in connection with inter-state sales and goods transfer to depot in any other State, (*iv*) misuse of delivery notes, (*v*) maintenance of duplicate bills, cash memos, (*vi*) carrying business without registration certificate, (*vii*) splitting of business etc.

Measures to Check Evasion

Adoption of the following measures would be helpful in controlling evasion of sales tax in the States:

31. P.S. Lokanathan—*op. cit.*, p. 43.
32. Basu Kaushik—"Inflation and Evasion", *Economic and Political Weekly*, March 4, 1984, p. 506.
33. Dr. A Venkata Rayudu: *Taxation and Economic Development in India*, Chugh Publications, Allahabad, 1981, p. 157.

(*i*) Compulsory registration should be enforced for all dealers. This would enable the department to know the turnover of producers and importers of each commodity which would help checking cross entries of other dealers. Besides, this would help the department to get a hold of the business from the very beginning.[34]

(*ii*) Rate differentiation among the States should be avoided. In the words of J.F.J. Toye "the rate differentiation beyond a very simple level quickly destroys the administrative advantages. Then net revenue is eaten away, either through increased evasion or by steeply rising cost of collection."[35]

(*iii*) Proper training and refresher courses to newly recruited authorities and working authorities should enable to plan administrative process to detect evasion and loopholes of tax structure.

(*iv*) In the selection of assessing authorities the law and commerce graduates should be given preference.

(*v*) Some incentives must be given to authorities who detect and decide the evasion cases.

(*vi*) Inter-State co-ordination should be sought in getting the information in regard to '*C*' forms so that misuse may be checked. Moreover, the co-operation of neighbouring States will help to check cross entries and checking of under estimation of imported goods.

(*vii*) Regular system of cross verification of the *bilties*, challans, sales tax forms and other documents should be developed in the circle offices.

(*viii*) Surprise raids must be organised on specific complaints.

(*ix*) State Governments should appoint a committee to look into the problems of sales tax evasion and suggest various ways and means to minimise the problem of evasion.

(*x*) A permanent sales tax settlement commission should also be established to settle the seizure cases.

34. Similar suggestion was made by M.C. Purohit, *op. cit.*, p. 181.
35. J.F.J. Toye: "How Progressive are Indian Consumption Taxes", *Economic and Political Weekly*, March 20, 1976, p. 469.

Appeals, Revisions and References Under Sales Tax Laws

'Appeal' means to "take a question to a higher court for rehearing and a new decision."[36] According to J.H. Burton "An appeal is, in principle an action by a disgruntled tax payer or rather person or body on whom an assessment to tax has been made."[37] Under sales tax laws of all the States, it is provided that an appeal can be made against any assessment, reassessment, refund, penalty order or rejection of application for registration certificate. Appeal can be filed against all the orders under the sales tax laws. The appeal should be filed in prescribed manner within prescribed time. In Rajasthan, Haryana and Punjab the time limit is 60 days from the day when notice of demand relating to the assessment or penalty order objected to is served or when the copy of refund is served upon the assessee. However, in case of Uttar Pradesh it should be filed within 30 days. After receiving the application, the authority will check that the application has been submitted in the prescribed manner. After giving a reasonable opportunity of hearing, the appellate authority can either confirm or reduce or enhance the assessment order or remand the case to assessing authority for making further enquiries and to pass fresh orders. In the states under study the sales tax law also provides provision of second appeal to Tribunal/Board of Revenue.

The jurisdiction of revision is generally conferred on superior authority to look into the legality or propriety of the orders passed by the subordinate authorities. The revisional authorities are different in different States. It is either the Commissioner, Board of Revenue, Financial Commissioner or Tribunal or any other person appointed by government as revising authority. The powers of revisional authorities are almost the same in the States under study. In Uttar Pradesh a revision would lie for purpose of satisfying the revising authority as to the legality or propriety of any order passed by the assessing or appellate authority. In Rajasthan the Commissioner may revise any order

36. A.S. Hornby, A.P. Cowie, J. Windsor Lewis—*Oxfold Advanced Learner's Dictionary of Current English*, Oxford University Press, London, 1974, p. 36.
37. J.H. Burton—*How to Appeal Against Tax Assessments*, A Jordan Publications, London, 1950, p. 3.

if he considers that it is illegal or improper or erroneous and prejudicial to the interest of revenue. In Punjab and Haryana the revising authority, Commissioner of Excise and Taxation, Financial Commissioner, and Joint Excise and Taxation Commissioner have been given wide powers. They may, upon application or *suo-moto* revise any order passed under sales tax law of the state. The revising authority have been empowered to call necessary records and examine the orders passed by assessing and appellate authority and also having power to issue stay orders against tax and penalty amount. The application for the revision is submitted in prescribed manner and within prescribed time *i.e.* 3 years for the assessing authority and 6 months for the dealer in Rajasthan, from the service of the order.[38] It is 180 days in Punjab and and one year in Uttar Pradesh. The Commissioner can revise all the cases but cannot revise the tribunal cases.

The references are made to High Court when any question of law arises in any case. Reference can be made by the dealer or assessing authority within 120 days from the passing of such order in Rajasthan, 90 days in Uttar Pradesh and 60 days in Punjab and Haryana. If it is made by dealer, he has to put up an application accompanied with prescribed fee of Rs. 100 in case of Haryaua, Punjab and Rajasthan and Rs. 200 in case of Uttar Pradesh. If the authority is not satisfied regarding the question of law, it may refuse to make such reference. The dealer may withdraw his application and may appeal to High Court against such refusal. The High Court may demand such cases from the concerning authority. If it thinks that the refusal is justified, it may refer the case back to the revising authority to make such additions or alteration as the High Court directs in the particular cese.

Trends of Institution, Disposal and Balance of Appeals

Table 5.4 gives the trend of institution of appeal cases and disposed cases by the appellate authorities and also gives the number of cases remaining undisposed and the trend of filing

38. Provision has been replaced after establishment of Sales Tax Tribunal. The period limitation for Department is 180 days and for the dealer 90 days.

appeal against the assessment cases in the States under study. The trend in the institution of appeal and percentage change over the previous years would not give an exact position of trend in the institution of appeals unless it relates to the number of cases assessed during the relevant years. This is necessary because the number of appeals instituted depends mainly upon the number of cases assessed.

Table 5.4 reveals that in case of Rajasthan the number of institution of appeals increased from 6,583 in 1977-78 to 8,781 in 1983-84. Although in the years 1977-78, 1978-79, 1982-83 and 1983-84 it registered a fall yet during the years 1979-80, 1980-81 and 1981-82 it registered an increase of 21.19, 45.99 and 7.82 per cent respectively over the respective previous year. The percentage increase over previous years was really alarming in 1979-80 and 1980-81. The percentage of appeals instituted to the number of cases assessed gives a different story. It was 7.82 per cent in 1976-77 which registered a fall to 7.51 per cent in 1977-78, to 5.56 per cent in 1978-79 and further to 5.17 per cent in 1979-80. In the succeeding two years it marked an increase of 7.34 per cent and 7.88 per cent respectively. However, it again declined to 6.60 per cent in 1982-83 and finally reached 6.62 per cent in 1983-84. The trend of disposal and resultant balance shows that 5,801 cases were disposed of in 1976-77 in Rajasthan. The figure decreased to 4,459 in 1977-78. In the succeeding three years, it increased to 5,493 to 6,705 and to 6,854 respectively but dropped to 5,115 in 1981-82. It again hiked to 10,226 in 1982-83 and finally it can be seen at 11,515 in 1983-84. The balance of appeals was 10,115 in 1976-77 which hiked by 21.00 per cent in 1977-78. However, it slightly dropped by .88 per cent in 1978-79 and by 1.48 per cent in 1979-80 but rose by 2.24 per cent in 1980-81 and again shot up by 35.26 per cent in 1981-82. It dropped by 4.6 per cent in 1982-83 and finally plummeted by 12.61 per cent in 1983-84.

In Uttar Pradesh, the number of appeals instituted was 84,429 in 1976-77. It declined by 2.02 per cent in 1977-78, by 13.91 per cent in 1978-79, by 16.95 per cent in 1981-82 and by 9.29 per cent in 1983-84, while it increased by 1.54 per cent in 1979-80, .26 per cent in 1980-81 and .65 per cent in 1982-83. It shows that institution of appeals is not very much preferred

TABLE 5,4

Trend in Institution, Disposal and Balances of Appeals

States	Particulars	1976-77	1977-78	1978-79	1979-80	1980-81	1981-82	1982-83	1983-84
Rajasthan									
	(*a*) Institution	6585	6583	5385	6526	9527	10272	9316	8781
			(—.03)	(—18,20)	(+21.19)	(+45.99)	(+7.82)	(—9.31)	(—5.74)
	(b) Disposal	5801	4459	5493	6705	6854	5115	10226	11515
			(—23.13)	(+23.19)	(+22.06)	(+2.22)	(−25.37)	(+99.92)	(+12.61)
	(c) Balance	10115	12239	12131	11952	14625	19782	18872	16138
			(+21.00)	(—.88)	(—1.48)	(+2.24)	(+35.26)	(−4.6)	(—14.49)
	(d) Percentage of institution of appeal to the number of cases assessed	7.82	7.51	5.56	5.17	7.34	7.88	6.60	6.62
Uttar Pradesh									
	(a) Institution	84429	82725	71220	72316	72504	60213	60607	54979
			(—2.02)	(—13.91)	(+1.54)	(+.26)	(−16.95)	(+.65)	(—9.29)
	(b) Disposal	64095	62807	79574	80256	72182	64626	64193	73781
			(—2.01)	(+26.70)	(+.86)	(—10.06)	(—10.46)	(—.67)	(+14.94)
	(c) Balance	100053	119971	111617	101309	101631	97074	93159	74254
			(+19.90)	(—6.96)	(—9.24)	(+.31)	(—4.54)	(—3.98)	(—20.29)
	(d) Percentage of institution of appeal to the number of cases assessed	30.04	26.51	19.36	19.73	22.90	20.77	20.03	(21.50)
Haryana									
	(a) Institution	—	2953	—	3285	2906	2948	3851	3757
			—			(—11.54)	(+1.44)	(+30.63)	(—2.44)

(b) Disposal	—	1991	—	3277	2160 (—34.09)	2878 (+33.24)	3933 (+36.66)	4020 (+2.21)
(c) Balance	1229	2191 (+78.28)	2758 (+25.88)	2766 (—.29)	3503 (+26.64)	3573 (+2.00)	3491 (–2.29)	3228 (—7.53)
(d) Percentage of institution of appeal to the number of cases assessed	—	3.68	—	4.01	2.97	3.02	3.89	3.55
Punjab								
(a) Institution	—	5680	5278 (—7.1)	4326 (—18.04)	4348 (+.51)	3631 (—16.49)	3255 (—10 36)	3638 (+11.77)
(b) Disposal	—	3567	5134 (+43.9)	5751 (+12.02)	4971 (—13.56)	3085 (—37.94)	3853 (+24.89)	4227 (+9.71)
(c) Balance	2229	4442 (+99.3)	4586 (+3.24)	3161 (—31.07)	2538 (—19.71)	3084 (+21.5)	2486 (—19.4)	1897 (—23.7)
(d) Percentage of institution of appeal to the number of cases assessed	—	4.97	4.84	3.92	3.63	2.15	2.44	2.01

—Figures in brackets show percentage change over previous year.

—Appeals filed before Deputy Commissioner are shown in the table but in case of U.P. it also include the appeal before the Assistant Commissioner (Judicial).

Source: *Administration Reports* from Sales Tax Departments.

in Uttar Pradesh. However, the absolute study of the institution of appeals is not sufficient unless it is compared with the number of cases assessed during the respective year.

The percentage of appeals instituted to the number of cases assessed was 30.04 in 1976-77. It fell to 26.51 in 1977-78 and to 19.36 in 1978-79, but again increased to 19.73 and further to 22.90 in the succeeding two years. This percentage again slightly declined to 20.77 in 1981-82 and further to 20.03 in 1982-83 but finally reached 21.50 in 1983-84. The number of disposed of appeals was 64,095 in 1976-77. It slightly dropped by 2.01 per cent in 1977-78 but increased by 26.70 per cent in 1978-79 and by .86 per cent in 1979-80 and again dropped by 10.06 per cent in 1980-81, by 10.46 per cent in 1981-82 and .67 per cent in 1982-83 but finally increased by 14.94 per cent in 1983-84 over the respective previous year. The number of pending appeals was 1,00,053 in 1975-76. It hiked by 19.90 per cent in 1976-77. In the succeeding two years it fell by 6.96 per cent and by 9.24 per cent respectively but it marginally increased by .31 per cent in 1980-81. After that it showed a declining trend and dropped by 4.54 per cent in 1981-82 by 3.98 per cent in 1982-83 and finally by 20.29 per cent in 1983.84.

In Haryana, the number of institution of appeals was 3,285 in 1979-80. It decreased by 11.54 per cent in 1980-81. Although it registered an increase of 1.44 per cent in 1981-82 and further of 30.63 per cent in 1982-83 yet in 1983-84 it decreased by 2.44 per cent over the respective previous year. The percentage of appeals instituted to the number of cases assessed was 3.68 in 1977-78 which increased to 4.01 in 1979-80. However, it declined to 2.97 per cent in 1980-81 but again rose to 3.02 per cent in 1981-82 and further to 3.89 per cent in 1982-83. Finally, it came down to 3.55 per cent in 1983-84. The number of disposed of appeals was 3,277 in 1979-80. It declined by 34.09 per cent in 1980-81. After that, it spurted by 33.24 per cent in 1981-82, by 36.66 per cent in 1982-83 and finally by 2.21 per cent in 1983-84 over the respective previous year. The number of pending appeals was 1,229 in 1976-77. It increased by 78.28 per cent in 1977-78, by 25.88 per cent in 1978-79, by .29 per cent in 1979-80, by 26.64 per cent in 1980-81 and further by 2 per cent in 1981-82, but it decreased by 2.29 per cent in

1982-83 and finally by 7.53 per cent in 1983-84.

In Punjab, the number of appeals instituted was 5,680 in 1977-78. It decreased by 7.1 per cent in 1978-79 and further by 18.04 per cent in 1979-80. It slightly increased by .51 per cent in 1980-81, but the next two years witnessed a decrease of 16.49 per cent and 10.36 per cent respectively and finally, it rose by 11.77 per cent in 1983-84. The percentage of appeals instituted to the number of cases assessed was 4.97 in 1977-78. In the next four years it registered a fall and reached 4.84, 3.92, 3.63 and 2.15 respectively. However it increased to 2.44 in 1982-83 but finally decreased to 2.01 in 1983-84. The number of disposed of appeals was 3,567 in 1977-78. It increased by 43.90 per cent in 1978-79 and further by 12.02 per cent in 1979-80. In the succeeding four years it fell by 13.56 per cent and 37.94 per cent respectively but it again rose by 24.89 per cent in 1982-83 and by 9.71 per cent in 1983-84 surpassing last year's fall. The number of pending appeals was 2,229 in 1976-77. It shot up by 99.3 per cent in 1977-78 and by 3.24 per cent in 1978-79. It plummeted by 31.07 per cent in 1979-80 and by 19.71 per cent in 1980-81 but increased by 21.5 per cent in 1981-82. It again fell by 19.4 per cent in 1982-83 and finally by 23.7 per cent in 1983-84.

Conclusively it may be observed that in case of Rajasthan, the increase in the institution of appeals was the highest in 1979-80 and 1980-81 *i.e.* by 21.19 per cent and 45.99 per cent respectively. In Uttar Pradesh it shows a downward trend, only the years 1979-80 and 1980-81 showed slightly increasing movement by 1.54 per cent and .26 per cent respectively. In Haryana it made an increase of 1.44 per cent in 1981-82 and 30.63 per cent in 1982-83 and in Punjab of .51 per cent in 1980-81 and of 11.77 per cent in 1983-84. However it declined in the other years of study. It shows that in Uttar Pradesh the position of institution of appeals is much better than those in Rajasthan, Haryana and Punjab.

However, the percentage of appeals instituted to the number of cases assessed shows a different picture. It varies between 5.17 to 7.88 in Rajasthan, 19.36 to 30.04 in Uttar Pradesh, 2.97 to 4.01 in Haryana and 2.01 to 4.97 in Punjab during the period of study. It shows that in Uttar Pradesh the number of appeals was high in the face of assessments made. This is an alarming position. The trend of increasing appeals is mainly due to the following causes: (*i*) the penalties by the assessing authorities in many cases are more than warranted, (*ii*) the best judgement assessment in most cases is not acceptable to the dealers (*iii*) the procedural mistakes are committed by the assessing authorities (*iv*) the fee for appeal is quite meagre.

Therefore, it is suggested that the fee for appeals should be revised. The work of assessing authorities should be evaluated on the basis of their performance keeping in view the demands they create at the time of assessment and which are not maintained by the appellate authorities. The Commissioner must ensure that cases of wilful legal and procedural mistakes by assessing authorities are properly punished. To reduce the number of appeals the idea of "Lok Adalats" may be introduced in the sales tax. Cases of unwarranted and petty penalties may be settled by both the parties without going for further appeals. This will reduce the burden of appellate authorities and state will not be put to loss by making expenditure on appellate work.

The number of disposed appeals has shown a fluctuating trend in the states under study. The balance of appeals increased by 59.5 per cent in Rajasthan, by 16.2 per cent in Haryana while in Uttar Pradesh and Punjab it showed a decrease of 25.8 per cent and 14.9 per cent respectively. Therefore, the administration of Rajasthan and Haryana needs to take necessary steps to increase the disposal of appeals.

Trends of Revision Cases

Table 5.5 gives the comparative analysis of revision cases disposed and pending in Rajasthan, Uttar Pradesh, Haryana and Punjab.

Table 5.5 reveals that in Rajasthan 821 revision cases were disposed of in 1980-81. It decreased by 22.53 per cent in 1981-82 but marginally increased by 1.42 per cent in 1982-83 and finally dropped by 19.53 per cent in 1983-84. The number of pending revision cases before the Board of Revenue was 2,147 in 1980-81. It dropped by 7.08 per cent in 1981-82, but in-

TABLE 5.5

Trend of Revision Cases

	Rajasthan		Uttar Pradesh		Haryana		Punjab	
	Cases disposed	*Cases pending*	*Cases disposed*	*Cases pending*	*Cases disposed*	*Cases pending*	*Cases disposed*	*Cases pending*
1980-81	821	2147	9625**	31518	—	—	385	1101
1981-82	636	1995	16654	34277	—	872	327	1134
	(—22.53)	(—7.08)		(+8.75)			(—15.06)	(+3.00)
1982-83	645	2155	16371	41112	498	900	894	666
	(+1.42)	(+8.02)	(—1.70)	(+19.94)		(+3.21)	(+173.39)	(—41.27)
1983-84	519	2656	15691	45408	455	1179	630	532
	(—19.53)	(+23.25)	(—4.15)	(+10.45)	(—8.63)	(+31.00)	(—29.53)	(20.12)

*In case of Rajasthan it was Board of Revenue for revision purpose. Now Sales Tax Tribunal has been constituted with effect form 1st May, 1985, accordingly pending cases has been transferred to the Tribunal.

**In case of Uttar Pradesh, the Tribunal started work with effect from 3rd October, 1981. Therefore, pending revision cases 28157 has been transferred to Tribunal.

Source: *Administrative Reports* of the Sales Tax Departments.

creased by 8.02 per cent in 1982-83 and finally by 23.25 per cent in 1983-84.

In Uttar Pradesh, the number of cases disposed of by the Tribunal was 9,625 in the last six months of 1980-81 which increased to 16,654 in 1981-82. It dropped by 1.70 per cent in 1982-83 and finally by 4.15 per cent in 1983-84. The pending revision cases have been increasing continuously after the constitution of the tribunal. It was 31,518 in 1980-81. It increased by 8.75 per cent in 1981-82, further by 19.94 per cent in 1982-83 and finally by 10.45 per cent in 1983-84.

In Haryana, the Tribunal disposed of 498 cases in 1982-83. The number dropped by 8.63 per cent in 1983-84. The number of pending cases was 8,72 in 1981-82. It increased by 3.21 per cent in 1982-83 and finally spurted by 31 per cent in 1983-84.

In Punjab, the number of revision cases disposed of was 385 in 1980-81, however, it dropped to 3,27, in 1981-82 but hiked to 8.94 cases in 1982-83 (an increase of 173.39 per cent over 1981-82). Finally, it dropped to 630 cases in 1983-84. The number of pending revision cases was 1101 in 1980-81. It increased by 3 per cent in 1981-82, after that it declined by 41.27 per cent in 1982-83 and finally by 20.12 per cent in 1983-84.

Comparatively, it may be said that, in Rajasthan, the number of revision cases disposed of was declining while the number of pending cases was increasing. The tribunal is the only solution which has been constituted in 1985. In Uttar Pradesh the number of pending revision cases was also increasing. It is suggested that more tribunal benches should be constituted. In Haryana, the number of pending revision cases increased more in 1983-84. Punjab is the state where tribunal was working more efficiently and effectively. It disposed of 173.39 per cent more cases during 1982-83 in comparison to 1981-82. It is felt that in case of Rajasthan and Uttar Pradesh the position of pending revison cases is alarming. It defeats the very purpose of revision because the saying "justice delayed means justice denied" is equally applicable in case of Uttar Pradesh and Rajasthan. To solve the problem it is suggested that additional members should be included in the tribunal to clear the pending work. Secondly, tribunal should make camp-courts at the district headquarters to impart quick justice to the assessees.

Cost of Collection of Sales Tax

The importance of administrative and collection costs has been long recognised in economic and public finance literature, so far as the cost of tax administiation is concerned, it is well recognised that the tax may not be adopted if it is very costly to administer. The importance of least cost of collection has been recognised in Smith's canon that "Every tax ought to so contrived as both to take out and keep out of the pockets of the people as little as possible, over and above what it brings into the public treasury of the state.[39] Mahfooz Ahmed emphasised that the "Different taxes do not have the same cost implications. Minimisation of the cost of tax collection must be an important objective of budgetary policy."[40] Further in the words of M.M. Ansari, "an excessive cost on tax administration in relation to the net yield may result in uneconomical use of tax and persistence of higher costs are not desirable in the interest of a sound fiscal policy."[41] Therefore, only the revenue outlay of tax is not an important factor but the cost of administration and collection is also kept in view, because continuous increase in cost of collection is an indicator of inefficiency in the Department.

Nature of Sales Tax Collection Costs

Two major kinds of costs are incurred in the administration and collection of sales tax. The administrative and collection costs associated with the maintenance expenses for necessary enforcement and collection of tax machinery. Specially, such expenditure would include outlays for salaries of administrative authorities and investigators, office equipment, rent, telephone

39. Adam Smith: *Wealth of Nations*: The Modern Library, Random House, New York, 1937, p. 778.
40. Mahfooz Ahmed: "Cost of Tax Collection in India", *Economic and Political Weekly*, February 17, 1968, p, 339.
41. M.M. Ansari: "Resource Mobilisation and Cost Efficiency of the States' Taxes", *Margin*, Vol. 15, No. 2, January 1983, p. 90.

and travelling expenses etc. In addition to such costs, tax payers have to bear certain costs in complying with tax system. These costs result from (*i*) preparing returns, (*ii*) obtaining judicial or administrative interpretation, (*iii*) adjusting procedures and operations to minimise tax liability.[42] The compliance cost are in the form of both money and non-money. In money cost, tax payers make payments to lawyers and other tax experts as consultation fee, the non-money cost comprises the physical and psychological botherations and the wastage of time in complying with the taxes. It arises mainly due to the complexities in the tax laws and other procedural difficulties. A clear distinction between administrative cost and the compliance costs is that the administrative cost is met from state exchequer while compliance cost burden falls on the tax payers. The higher compliance costs encourage the tax payer to evade or resent imposition of tax. In India, to measure the compliance cost is very difficult due to statistical problem and no attempt has so far been made in this context. The low administrative cost is also not a sure indicator of better performance of the tax administration.

The study of Prof. Due on European countries sales taxation suggests that relatively low sales tax administration cost reflects completely inadequate enforcement programmes and a state of high population density and income, and optimum expenditure for collection of a three per cent tax rate would be 1.7 per cent of revenue.[43]

NIPFP study found that the cost of collection of sales tax in Bihar as percentage of sales tax revenue has declined from 1.5 per cent in 1970-71 to 1.1 per cent in 1977-78 which is considered not very high.[44]

Dr. Venkata Rayudu, in his study found that in Andhra Pradesh the cost of collection was 4.28 per cent in 1960-61

42. Clinton V. Oster and Arthur D. Lynn: "Compliance Costs and the Ohio Axle Mile Tax—A case study"– *National Tax Journal*, June 1955, p. 209. Quoted in Clinton V. Oster—*Sales Retail Sales Taxation*, Bureau of Business Research Publication, Columbus, 1957, pp. 158-59.
43. John F. Due—*op. cit.*. p. 227.
44. National Institute of Public Finance and Policy, *Sales Tax System in Bihar*, Somaiya Publication (Pvt.) Ltd., Bombay, 1981, p. 96.

which declined upto 2.03 per cent in 1980-81, probably due to faster increase in sales tax yields.[45]

Comparative Analysis of Collection cost

It is very difficult to calculate the accurate cost of the administration of sales tax because some costs are always mixed up with other taxes in a department operating more than one taxes. However, since the budget estimates of the state governments provide for the estimates of costs of sales tax under the head of sales tax expenditure, the trend may be studied with the help of such estimates. The table 5.6 gives such estimates of cost of sales tax in Rajasthan, Haryana, Punjab and Uttar Pradesh during 1978-79 to 1983-84.

Table 5.6 reveals that the collection cost was Rs. 2.31 crores for operation of sales tax in Rajasthan in 1978-79. It increased throughout the study period and finally reached Rs. 4.68 crores in 1983-84. The percentage of collection cost to sales tax yield was 2.03 in 1978-79. It dropped to 1.78 in 1979-80 but again increased to 1.96 in 1980-81, and dropped to 1.77 in 1981-82. Further during the two succeeding years it marginally increased to 1.84 and 1.89 respectively.

In Uttar Pradesh, the collection cost increased from Rs. 6.15 crores in 1978-79 to Rs. 12.76 crores in 1983-84 making an increase of 107 per cent. The percentage of collection cost to sales tax revenue was 2.67 in 1978-79 which increased to 2.79 in 1979-80. In the further two succeeding years it declined to 2.76 and 2.57 respectively. The percentage mounted to 3.10 in 1982-83, but finally, it dropped to 2.84 in 1983-84.

In Haryana, the collection cost was Rs. 1.70 crores in 1978-79 which reduced to Rs. 1.65 crores in 1979-80. After that it marked a steady growth in the succeeding three years *i.e.* Rs. 2.16 crores, Rs. 2.69 crores, and Rs. 3.52 crores respectively and finally dropped to Rs. 3.51 crores in 1983-84. The percentage of collection cost to sales tax revenue was 2.26 in 1978-79, it declined to 1.97 in 1979-80 and increased to 2.14 in 1980-81 but again dropped to 2.02 in 1981-82. The percentage again registered an increase and reach 2.30 in 1982-83 and finally dropped to 1.97 in 1983-84.

45. D. Venkata Rayudu—*op. cit.*, p. 166.

TABLE 5.6
Trends of Collection Cost

(*Rs. in crores*)

	Rajasthan		*Uttar Pradesh*		*Haryana*		*Punjab*	
	Collection cost Rs.	*Sales Tax Revenue* Rs.	*Collection cost* Rs.	*Sales Tax Revenue* Rs.	*Collection cost* Rs.	*Sales Tax Revenue* Rs.	*Collection cost* Rs.	*Sales Tax Revenue* Rs.
1978-79	2.31 (2.03)	113.68	6.15 (2.67)	230.08	1.70 (2.26)	75.03	1.59 (1.43)	110.88
1979-80	2.42 (1.78)	135.86	7.16 (2.79)	256.92	1.65 (1.97)	83.79	1.83 (1.50)	122.14
1980-81	2.84 (1.96)	145.00	8.33 (2.76)	301.56	2.16 (2.14)	101.07	2.32 (1.51)	153.23
1981-82	3.30 (1.77)	186.21	9.75 (2.57)	379.42	2.69 (2.02)	132.76	2.57 (1.40)	183.28
1982-83	4.09 (1.84)	222.23	12.73 (3.10)	410.74	3.52 (Revised Estimates) (2.30)	152.65	2.93 (Revised Estimates) (1.33)	219.33
1983-84	4.68 (1.89)	248.00	12.76 (2.84)	449-47	3.51 (1.97)	177.99	—	—

— Figures in brackets show the percentage of collection cost to sales tax yields.
—Sales tax revenue includes—General Sales Tax revenue and Central Sales Tax revenue.

Sources: (1) Collection costs have been compiled from *States Budget Study from 1980-81 to 1984-85*. In case of Punjab figures of collection cost after 1980-81 has been compiled from *States' Public Finance*, Government of Punjab, 1982-83, p. 10.
(2) Sales tax revenue figures compiled from *Reserve Bank of India Bulletins*.

In Punjab the collection cost was increasing continuously. It was Rs. 1.59 crores in 1977-78 which increased to Rs. 2.93 crores in 1982-83. The percentage of collection cost to sales tax yield was 1.43 in 1978-79 which increased to 1.50 in 1979-80 and further to 1.51 in 1980-81. After that, it dropped to 1.40 in 1981-82 and further to 1.33 in 1982-83.

Conclusively, the cost of collection in absolute amount has been increasing in the states under study except in case of Haryana, it marginally declined in 1979-80. The collection cost in operating the sales tax in the states under study is not increasing in comparison to increase in sales tax revenue but at present it is decreasing. In Rajasthan the percentage of total collection cost to sales tax revenue varied between 1.77 to 2.03 while in Uttar Pradesh 2.57 to 3.10, in Haryana 1.97 to 2.30 and in Punjab 1.33 to 1.51 during the period of study. It shows that Punjab is the only state where collection cost is very low in comparison to other states. But a low percentage certainly does not always signify the increasing efficiency of tax administration and it might be the result of faster increase in sales tax yields due to increase of business activities. In Uttar Pradesh the percentage of collection cost to sales tax is very high, being 3.10 per cent in 1982-83 which however, declined to 2.84 per cent in 1983-84. The change in percentage of total cost is because of the streamlining of the anti-evasion organisation. However, 2.84 per cent is not an unreasonable figure and it is hoped that strengthening of the enforcement wing may bring more revenue.

In the collection cost, there is no provision of depreciation on building, furniture, vehicle and other fixed assets. So the collection cost figures do not show actual position. It is recommended that all the states should make a provision for depreciation on departmental assets.

Cost Elasticity of Sales Tax Revenue in States Under Study

The cost elasticity of sales tax revenue in Rajasthan, Haryana, Uttar Pradesh and Punjab has been estimated for the period 1978-79 to 1983-84 according to the following formula:[46]

46. Shyam Nath: "Level Growth and Composition of the Tax System in Rajasthan", *Rajasthan Economic Journal*, Vol. I, Jan., 1977, p. 12.

$$E=\frac{\dfrac{T_1-T_0}{Y_1-Y_0}}{\dfrac{T_1+T_0}{Y_1+Y_0}}=\frac{\Delta T}{\Delta Y}\times\frac{Y_1+Y_0}{T_1+T_0}$$

E=Stands for elasticity of the collection cost with respect to sales tax revenue.

T=Stands for collection cost

Y=Stands for sales tax revenue

T_1, T_0, Y_1, Y_0=Postcripts 0 and 1 represent the base year (1978-79) and current year (1983-84) respectively.

The results are as under:

E=In Rajasthan=.91, in Uttar Pradesh=1.08, in Haryana =.85 and in Punjab=.90

The cost elasticity of sales tax revenue indicates that one per cent increase in sales tax revenue leads to .91 per cent, (Rajasthan), 1.08 per cent (Uttar Pradesh), .85 per cent (Haryana) and .90 per cent (Punjab) increase in the cost of collection. It is less than one in case of Haryana, Punjab and Rajasthan which is a welcome indication from the viewpoint of improving its administration. In case of Uttar Pradesh it is higher than one which is not a good position and efforts are needed to effect a cut in collection cost for the part of the Department.

Conclusion

It is evident from the foregoing analysis that the operation of sales tax requires improvement. In this connection we would like to give the following few suggestions to obtain the desired results. Registration must be made compulsory for all the dealers irrespective of their turnover and fee levied should be atleast Rs. 50. The problems of assessment and arrears should be tackled more promptly and carefully. The position of Uttar Pradesh in regard to arrears which are increasing continuously is far from being satisfactory. The state should take necessary steps to finalise old arrears and assessment as early as possible. Besides this, the appellate structure should be bifurcated from the sales tax department and only such officers who have administrative and legal background must be appointed on the post of Deputy Commissioner (Appeals). Assessing and appellate authorities must be imparted training from time to time so that they may acquire necessary legal knowledge. Evasion of taxes should be minimised by placing honest and efficient officers in the wing doing the evasion work. Conclusively machinery in the sales tax departments should be revamped and there should be a co-ordination cell at all offices of Commissioners so that ultimate objective of high tax collection may be achieved by all the states alike. We believe that sincere implementation of the above suggestions would go a long way towards insuring smooth and efficient functioning of the sales departments of the states under study.

6

INCIDENCE OF SALES TAX

Introduction

In formulation and analysis of any tax policy, it is essential to consider the incidence aspect of taxation. It provides a clear view of the distribution of the burden of taxation. The incidence of taxation also helps in determining as to on whom the direct money burden of tax falls. According to De Viti, De Marco, "It is of great economic and social interest to consider as to how this burden is distributed among citizens with different income levels."[1] If the tax incidence does not correctly identify equity canon then any tax programme is bound to create and foster lopsidedness in the tax system to the disadvantage of economy as a whole. If the burden of taxes is heavy, people try to evade tax. The incidence concept is also useful in preparation of budgets. Therefore, incidence of taxation has a paramount importance in our economy.

Concept of Incidence

The concept of incidence in tax theory has always been elusive. The question 'who pays the tax' and 'who bears the burden of tax are different concepts of taxation.[2] In determination of who pays the tax is a simple matter of tax liability as defined by the statutes. Tax incidence theory is concerned with

1. The phenomenon occurs when the tax which law imposes on a tax payer, who is called the tax payer 'de jure', is unloaded by the latter, in whole or in part, upon other citizens, who are called the tax payers 'de facto'. Marco De, De Viti Antonio: *First Principles of Public Finance*, Jonathan Cape, London, 1950, p. 141.
2. Edger K. Browning and Jacquenleme M. Browning: *Public Finance and Price System*, Macmillan Publishing Company, New York, 1979, p. 273.

determining who bears the real burden of taxation. Hugh Dalton states that the problem of incidence is just the problem of finding on whom the direct money burden and real burden of a tax. Real burden of a tax is associated with loss of economic welfare in terms of sacrifice undergone by the tax payers.[3] Pechman and Okner emphasised that burden of tax and incidence of tax are the same and could be used synonymously.[4] Seligman, on the other hand, draws a distinction between "impact" and 'incidence'. The impact of tax is said to be on those persons on whom it is at first (legally) imposed. Shifting is the process by which a tax payer transfers his money burden (or payment of tax) to others in the course of his normal economic transactions with them. Incidence is stated to be on those persons from whom further shifting of tax could not take place.[5] According to Due, by incidence is meant the pattern of the final distribution of the burden resulting from the tax, after all readjustments are complete.[6]

Musgrave has also suggested two terms, *viz*., 'effective incidence' and 'impact incidence'. The term effective incidence is used to denote the actual change in distribution that results as a given tax is imposed or tax substitution is made. The term impact incidence is used to refer to the change that would result if the income position of new tax payers were reduced by the amount of tax addition or the income position of a former tax payer were improved by the amount of tax remission while the position of all others remains unchanged.[7]

On the track of Musgrave, Ursula K. Hicks also emphasied two types of incidence *i.e.* 'formal incidence' and 'effective incidence'. Formal incidence deals with the money burden of taxes

3. Hugh Dalton: *Principles of Public Financc*—Allied Publishers Private Limited, New Delhi, 1978, p. 36.
4. Pechman A. Joseph, and Okner A. Benjamin: *Who Bears the Tax Burden?* Studies in Government Finance, The Brooking Institution, Washington, 1976, p. 3.
5. E.R.A. Seligman: *The Shifting and Incidcnce of Taxation*, Columbia University Press, New York, 1932, p. 1.
6. John F. Due: "The Incidence of General Sales Tax", *Public Finance*, Vol. 5, 1950, pp. 222-39.
7. R.A. Musgrave: *The Theory of Public Finance*, Mcgraw Hill, New York, 1959, p. 217.

and on the other hand effective incidence deals with the tax payer's reaction to a change of tax and its consequences.[8]

The Taxation Enquiry Commission defined 'incidence' as the money burden as intended by the taxing authority to fall, the amount paid in tax is thus measured as per cent of income of different income groups.[9]

Lennox, Moak and Frank Cowan, state that the tax incidence is usually the final resting place of the burden of the tax.[10] Kenyon E. Poole observes that "Formidable difficulties may face the attempt to determine who bears the burden of a tax. The person who initially pays the tax incurs its impact and the burden or incidence of the tax is said to be on the one on whom it rests after further shifting becomes impossible."[11] In this way the theory of tax incidence has become increasingly complicated over the years and it is difficult to present a simple statement of the analysis in its various ramifications. In this chapter concept of the burden of tax and incidence of tax has been used synonymously.

Direct and Indirect Tax Incidence

In direct taxes, it can be easily determined that who bears the burden of tax. For example, in case of Income-tax, the incidence clearly falls on the person earning the income. But in case of indirect taxes, different types of buyers and sellers are in the economy, burden of sales tax may be on the buyer or the seller or it may be divided in any proportion between them, depending upon the elasticity of demand for a particular commodity on which tax has been imposed. If the demand for a particular commodity is perfectly inelastic the price will rise by full amount of tax and incidence will fall completely on the

8. Ursula K. Hicks: *Public Finance*, Cambridge University Press, Cambridge, 1971, Chapter IX, pp. 130-140.
9. Government of India: *Report of the Taxation Enquiry Commission*, 1953-54, Vol. I, p. 45.
10. Lennox, Moak and F. Cown: *Administration of Local and Uses Taxes*, Municipal Finance Officers Association of the United States and Canada, Illinois, 1961, p. 16.
11. Kenyon E. Poole: *Public Finance and Economic Welfare*, Rinehart and Company, New York, 3rd edition, p. 117.

buyer, on the other hand, if demand is perfectly elastic, the seller reduces selling price by reducing his profit margin by the full amount of tax and incidence will be entirely on the seller.

Theory of Sales Tax Incidence

The application of incidence theory to the taxation on sales has been complicated by a wide variety of institutional circumstances surrounding this kind of tax. The taxation of sales may take place at the retail, wholesale or manufacturing stages. The tax may be general sales tax or it may be applicable only to the selected commodities. Under sales tax it may be that virtually nothing is exempted or alternatively necessaries of life such as housing, food, and clothing may be removed from the tax base. Some commodities are taxed at higher rates and some at lower rates and rate differentiation in the states also prevails.

Generally, sales tax is shifted to the buyer but the extent to which this shift takes place cannot be quantified. The impact of sales tax is on the seller as he pays it in the first instance. It is thus but natural to resist and try to avoid the taxing over of its burden. He tries to shift it by raising the prices of the taxed commodity. Besides this, it is a tax on the sales. It is payable even when there is no profit. It is, therefore, an addition to the cost of the dealer and enters into price.[12] The shifting of sales tax may depend on a number of factors, *viz.*, the elasticity of supply and demand of the taxed commodity and nature of competitive conditions. The greater the elasticity of supply, the more is the likelihood of the tax being shifted to the purchaser and *vice versa.* On the other hand, the greater the elasticity of demand, the more is the chance of tax borne by the producer or the seller. Under the conditions of pure competition, the tax is fully shifted to the buyer in the long run.[13] As for monopoly the analysis becomes difficult as the monopolist will add the

12. B. Das Gupta: *Provincial Taxation Under Autonomy*, Oxford Universito Press, London, 1948, p. 137.
13. See for shifting of Sales Tax under different Competitive conditions—
    (*a*) Elmer D. Fagan: "Shifting of Sales Taxes Under Joint Costs", *Public Finance*, Vol. 8, 1953, pp. 338-554.
    (*b*) A.G. Buehler: *General Sales Taxation—Its History and Development*, Business Course, New York, 1932, p. 179.

tax only if his profits are greater after he adds the tax than if he absorbs it.[14]

The burden of sales tax should not be assessed in isolation. The regressivity of sales tax is lessened if it is considered simultaneously with the benefit accrued from public expenditure. Raja J. Chelliah has observed that taxation is used as a tool for promoting economic development, the incidence of benefits can be expected to be progressive. The incidence of benefits will depend on the pattern of investment. If priority is assigned to increasing the supply of wage-goods, the poorer sections can improve their economic position over time and the volume of employment can expand steadily.[15]

Review of Earlier Studies

The first systematic attempt to measure tax incidence was made by the Taxation Enquiry Commission (1953-54).[16] It measured the tax burden by using the household consumer expenditure data furnished by National Sample Survey in its 4th round. The burden was expressed by certain household expenditure classes. Later, two more attempts were made by the Ministry of Finance[17] to measure the incidence of indirect taxes for 1958-59 and 1963-64 on the basis of same methodology. In this direction National institute of Public Finance and Policy, New Delhi has attempted to estimate the incidence of indirect taxation by National Sample Survey expenditure groups for the year 1973-74.[18] In these studies, revenue collected from the tax on each commodity or base is allocated to various National Sample Survey expenditure groups on the basis of the proportionate consumption or use of that particular commodity or base in each group in rural and urban sectors.

14. *Ibid.*
15. Raja J. Chelliah: *Fiscal Policy in Underdeveloped Countries* (With Special Reference to India), 1960, p. 104.
16. Government of India, 1953-54, Vol. I, *op. cit.*, pp. 45-84.
17. Ministry of Finance: *Incidence of Indirect Taxation 1958-59, and 1963-64*, Government of India, New Delhi, 1961, and 1969.
18. Raja J. Chelliah and R.N. Lal: "Incidence of Indirect Taxation in India 1973-74", published in Government of India, Ministry of Finance, *Report of the Indirect Taxation Enquiry Committee*, part II, January, 1978, pp. 87-116 and 463-516.

National council of Applied Economic Research in its studies of the State of Gujarat (1970)[19] and Mysore (1972)[20], undertook full scale surveys of family budgets, specially designed to serve the objective of estimating the tax incidence on various income groups in both rural and urban areas of Mysore. The Taxation and Enquiry Commission, Uttar Pradesh (1974)[21] attempted to calculate the tax incidence in different income expenditure groups in rural and urban groups. The committee adopted in toto the methodology used by Taxation Enquiry Commission (1953-54) and Tax research unit for the allocation of the state indirect taxes directly on the basis of the tax payment revealed by the survey schedules.

The 1968 study of Chandra Sekhar[22] calculated inter-state disparities in the burden of state taxes as a whole (13 states), and in particular of land revenue and general sales tax (in 1960-61 and 1965-66) and expressed the tax burden in the terms of state incomes. Mr. Goswami[23] also studied 17 states of India for the period of 1962-63 and 1969-70, and analysed the total tax burden and sales tax burden in terms of state income. The Purohit (1971)[24] study presents the estimates of the incidence of sales tax for the capital of Rajasthan by using the usual assumption that the tax is borne by the consumers according to their expenditure on taxed commodities. The study suggests that there is regressivity upto the income group of Rs. 301-500, but progressivity is also witnessed in the income group higher than that.

Dr. Srivastava has studied incidence of commercial taxes of five states (Rajasthan, Uttar Pradesh, Madhya Pradesh, Punjab and Bihar) from the period 1961-72. He calculated per capita incidence in terms of population and states income and found

19. NCAER: *Incidence of Taxation in Gujarat*, New Delhi, 1970.
20. NCAER: *Incidence of Taxatin in Mysore State*, New Delhi, 1972.
21. Government of Uttar Pradesh: *Uttar Pradesh Taxation Enquiry Committee Report*, 1974, pp. 83-100.
22. S. Chandra Sekhar: "Inter-State Disparities of Tax Incidence in India", *Economic and Political Weekly*, June, 1968, pp. 845-849.
23. Bhawar Pury Goswami: "Expanding Scope of General Sales Taxes", *Southern Economist*, January 26, 1972, pp 37-9.
24. M.C. Purohit: "Incidence of Sales Tax: An Empirical Analysis" *Indian Journal of Economics*, Vol. No. 205 Oct. 1971, pp. 158-70.

that in Punjab, the per capita incidence is the highest in comparison to other states.[25]

Shyam Nath[26] (1980) study reveals that at all levels of expenditure, the urban households have borne higher tax incidence than the rural households.

Finally, to measure tax incidence is a very complicated process and inadequate availability of data in this regard is a great problem. No state is in a position to make a complete commodity-wise collection and to determine expenditure according to different income groups and it is not possible to ascertain actual household expenditure. In this study an attempt has been made to calculate per capita incidence in terms of population and state income.

Inter-State Comparisons of per Capita Sales Tax Incidence

Various methods may be used to find out tax incidence, but the most simple method of measuring it is to divide the tax revenue in a particular year by the estimated population of that year. This, however, gives only a partial picture of tax incidence of the states, because it does not relate to the per capita income or expenditure. Even if the rates of the tax and level of administrative efficiency are the same in the different states, the per capita sales tax would differ, if income levels or tax base and size of the population vary. In this method population cannot be divided in various income groups on the basis of their income slabs and the tax incidence thereon cannot be calculated. The only possible method to estimate tax incidence is to divide the tax revenue by population. If the per capita incidence is increased in spite of increase in population, it denotes an increase in the consumption of such goods and services which are subject to sales tax. Therefore, per capita sales tax incidence would serve only as a broad indicator of the levels of sales tax incidence.

25. Dr. Girish K. Srivastava—"Incidence of Commercial Taxes in Rajasthan", *Eastern Economist*, June 7, 1974, p. 1116.
26. Shyam Nath—"Incidence of Indirect Taxation in Rajasthan", *Margin*, Vol. 12, No. 3, April, 1980, pp. 60-73.

Methodology

The present study aims at computing money burden of sales tax. To arrive at the per capita tax incidence the following formula can be used :—

$I=\frac{T}{P}$ in which I Stands for tax incidence

T Stands for particular tax revenue in particular year

P Stands for population in particular year.

The population figure of different states has been estimated by using different decennial compound growth rates pertaining to the census of 1971 and 1981 were applied. The growth rate per year has been calculated on the basis of interpolation extrapolation formula.

$r=n\sqrt{\frac{pn}{po}}-1$ in which

r Stands for rate of growth

n for number of years intervening

Pn for year at the end

Po for year of start

Population after the year 1981 has been calculated on the basis of extrapolation formula.

Inter-state comparison of per capita sales tax incidence is presented in Table 6.1 (given on page 170 & 171).

Table 6.1 reveals that in Rajasthan the per capita incidence of sales tax has shown a rising trend throughout the period of study. It went up from Rs. 22.70 in 1975-76 to Rs. 67.80 in 1983-84 *i.e.* an increase of 198.7 per cent. Index number of per capita sales tax incidence also showed an increasing trend. It increased by 21.23 per cent in 1976-77 over the year 1975-76. After that it registered a rise in the succeeding four years *i.e.* by 15.56 per cent, by 10.22 per cent, by 16.55 per cent and by 3.47 per cent over the respective previous year. It increased very sharply by 25.89 per cent in 1981-82, by 16.72 per cent in 1982-83 and finally by 9.16 per cent in 1983-84.

In Uttar Pradesh, the per capita incidence of sales tax amounted to Rs. 21.05 in 1975-76 which increased to Rs. 24.03 in 1976-77 but slightly declined to Rs. 23.75 in 1977-78. After that it marked a steady growth and increased to Rs. 25.70 in

TABLE 6.1
Inter State Comparisons of Per Capita Sales Tax Incidence

Year	*RAJASTHAN*				*UTTAR PRADESH*				*HARYANA*				*PUNJAB*			
	Sales Tax Revenue (Rs. in crores)	*Population (in crores)*	*Per capita incidence (in Rs.)*	*Index number of per capita incidence (Base 1975-76)*	*Sales Tax Revenue (Rs in crores)*	*Population (in crores)*	*Per capita (incidence (in Rs.)*	*Index number of per capita incidence (Base 1975-76)*	*Sales Tax Revenue (Rs. in crores)*	*Population (in crores)*	*Per capita incidence (in Rs.)*	*Index number of per capita incidence (Base 1975-76)*	*Sales Tax Revenue (Rs. in crores)*	*Population (in crores)*	*Per capita incidence (in Rs.)*	*Index number of per capita incidence (Base 1975-76)*
1975-76	67.60	2.978	22.70	100.00	208.26	9.893	21.05	100.00	49.50	1.137	43.54	100.00	73.16	1.509	48.48	100.00
1976-77	84.29	3.063	27.52	121.23 (21.23)	243.17	10.121	24.03	114.16 (+14.16)	63.95	1.167	54.80	125.86 (+25.86)	96.12	1.541	62.38	128.67 (+28.67)
1977-78	100.25	3.152	31.80	140.09 (15.56)	246.03	10.359	23.75	112.83 (—1.17)	69.62	1.197	58.16	133.58 (+6.13)	107.51	1.574	68.30	140.88 (+9.49)
1978-79	113.68	3.243	35.05	154.41 (10.22)	272.25	10.592	25.70	122-09 (+8.21)	79.68	1.228	64.89	149.04 (+11.57)	119.31	1.607	74.24	153.14 (+8.70)
1979-80	135.86	3.337	40.85	179.96 (16.55)	302.52	10.836	27.91	132.59 (+8.60)	90.05	1.260	71.47	164.15 (+10.14)	129.79	1.641	79.09	163.14 (+6.53)
1980-81	145.00	3.430	42.27	186.21 (3.47)	313.97	11.090	28.31	134.49 (+1.43)	108.00	1.290	83.27	191.25 (+16.51)	160.00	1.680	95.23	196.43 (+20.41)
1981-82	186.21	3.502	53.17	234.42 (25.89)	453.35	11.316	40.06	190.31 (+41.50)	138.37	1.319	104.90	240.92 (+25·97)	191.82	1.712	112.04	231.11 (+17.66)
1982-83	222.23	3.578	62.11	273.61 (16.72)	486.98	11.542	42.19	200.42 (+5.31)	160.48	1.348	119.05	273.43 (+13.49)	219.93	1.744	126.11	260.13 (+12.56)

1983.84 R.E.)	248.00	3.658	67.80	298.68 (9.16)	530.38	11.768	45.06	214.06 (+6.81)	189.70	1.377	137.76	316.40 (+15.72)	249.95	1.776	140.74	290.31 (+11.60)

†Sales tax revenue includes state sales tax, central sales tax, motor spirit tax and purchase tax on sugarcane.

††Population has been calculated on the basis of interpolation extrapolation formula.

Figures in brackets shows percentage change over previous year.

Source: (*i*) Revenue figures has been comprised by *Reserve Bank of India Bulletins*.

(*ii*) Population figures of 1980-81 has been compiled from *Statistical Abstract*, Directorate of Economics and Statistics, Rajasthan and other year's population has been calculated on the basis of interpolation extrapolation formula.

1978-79, to Rs. 27.91 in 1979-80, to Rs. 28.31 in 1980-81 and reached a phenomenal height of Rs. 40.06 in 1981-82, Rs. 42.19 in 1982-83 and finally Rs. 45.06 in 1983-84. This high growth reflects that during the last three years of the study the sales tax revenue has increased considerably. The per capita incidence increased by 114.06 per cent in 1983-84 over 1975-76. The index number of per capita sales tax incidence increased by 14.16 per cent in 1976-77 but declined by 1.17 per cent in 1977-78. Further it has shown an increasing trend throughout the period of study but the year 1981-82 witnessed a sharp rise *i.e.* 41.50 per cent over the previous year.

In Haryana the per capita sales tax incidence increased from Rs. 43.54 in 1975-76 to Rs. 137.76 in 1983-84 marking an increase of 216.40 per cent. The index number of per capita sales tax incidence increased by 25.86 per cent in 1976-77, by 6.13 per cent in 1977-78, by 11.57 per cent in 1978-79, by 10.14 per cent in 1979-80, by 16.51 per cent in 1980-81 and further sharply by 25.97 per cent in 1981-82, by 13.49 per cent in 1982-83 and finally by 15.72 per cent in 1983-84 over the respective previous year. The higher incidence indicates that in Haryana, sales are mobilised properly in view of sales tax and trade activities which increased much faster than in Rajasthan and Uttar Pradesh.

In Punjab, the per capita incidence of sales tax increased from Rs. 48.48 in 1975-76 to Rs. 140.74 in 1983-84 marking an increase of 190.3 per cent. The per capita incidence of index number showed a steady growth throughout the period of study. It increased by 28.67 per cent in 1976-77, by 9.49 per cent in 1977-78, by 8.70 per cent in 1978-79, by 6.53 per cent in 1979-80 and spurted by 20.41 per cent in 1980-81, by 17.66 per cent in 1981-82, by 12.56 per cent in 1982-83 and finally by 11.60 per cent in 1983-84 over the respective previous year.

As a whole, the states where population is not increasing faster, the per capita incidence of sales tax is higher. In this regard in Punjab and Haryana which are less populous states and where the industrial and agricultural advancement is very fast, the per capita sales tax incidence was found being Rs. 140.74 and Rs. 137.76 respectively while in Uttar Pradesh and Rajasthan it was only Rs. 45.06 and 67.80 in 1983-84. In Uttar Pradesh the per capita sales tax incidence is very low in comparison to Haryana, Punjab and Rajasthan. The per capita incidence of sales tax in 1983-84 increased by 2.98 times in Rajasthan, by 2.14 times in Uttar Pradesh, by 3.16 times in Haryana and by 2.90 times in Punjab over 1975-76. Uttar Pradesh is in a poor position so far as per capita incidence of sales tax is concerned.

Comparison of per Capita Sales Tax to per Capita Total Tax

Table 6.2 (p. 174) gives per capita sales tax and per capita total tax burden.

Table 6.2 reveals that in Rajasthan, the per capita total tax incidence increased from Rs. 68.94 in 1975-76 to Rs. 183.72 in 1983-84, while the per capita incidence of sales taxes increased from Rs. 22.70 in 1975-76 to Rs. 67.80 in 1983-84. The percentage of per capita incidence of sales tax to per capita total tax was 32.93 in 1975-76 which registered a steady growth in the successive four years and reached 42.85 in 1979-80 *i.e.* the highest percentage throughout the period of study. Further, it dropped to 36.96 in 1980-81 to 36.63 per cent in 1981-82 and finally, reached 36.90 per cent in 1983-84.

In Uttar Pradesh, the per capita incidence of total tax amounted to Rs. 65.72 in 1975-76 which increased to Rs. 158.02 in 1983-84. The incidence of sales tax was only Rs. 21.05 in 1975-76 which mounted to Rs. 45.06 in 1983-84. The percentage of sales tax incidence to total tax incidence was 32.03 in 1975-76 and 33.40 in 1976-77 which dropped to 32.43 in 1977-78. However, it marginally increased to 32.97 in 1978-79 but fell to 26.73 in 1979-80 and 26.31 in 1980-81. It again increased to 29.54 in 1981-82 but decreased to 28.57 in 1982-83 and finally to 28.51 in 1983-84.

In Haryana, the per capita incidence of total taxes increased from Rs. 126.73 in 1975-76 to Rs. 352.34 in 1983-84. The per capita sales tax incidence was Rs. 43.54 in 1975-76 which increased to Rs. 137.76 in 1983-84. The percentage of per capita sales tax incidence to total tax incidence showed variations. It was 34.36 in 1975-76 which increased to a phenomenal height of 40.57 in 1976-77. After that it remained fluctuating continuously and finally reached 39.10 in 1983-84.

In Punjab, the per capita total tax and sales tax incidence is

TABLE 6.2

Comparison of Per Capita Sales Tax Incidence and Total Tax Incidence

Year	RAJASTHAN			UTTAR PRADESH			HARYANA			PUNJAB		
	Per Capita total tax revenue (Rs.)	Per Capita sales tax revenue (Rs.)	Percentage of per capita sales tax to per capita total tax	Per Capita total tax revenue (Rs.)	Per Capita sales tax revenue (Rs.)	Percentage of per capita sales tax to per capita total tax	Per Capita total tax revenue (Rs.)	Per Capita sales tax revenue (Rs.)	Percentage of per capita sales tax to per capita total tax	Per Capita total tax revenue (Rs.)	Per Capita salas tax revenue (Rs.)	Percentage of per capita sales tax to per capita total tax
1975-76	68.94	22.70	32.93	65.72	21.05	32.03	126.73	43.54	34.38	139.81	48.48	34.68
1976-77	75.32	27.52	36.54	71.94	24.03	33.40	135.09	54.80	40.57	156.76	62.38	39.79
1977-78	81.44	31.80	39.05	73.23	23.75	32.43	154.77	58.16	37.58	176.19	68.80	38.76
1978-79	89.19	35.05	39.30	77.96	25.70	32.97	165.82	64.89	39.13	194.62	74.24	38,15
1979-80	95.00	40.71	42.85	104.41	27.91	26.73	199.49	71.47	35.83	233.03	79.09	33.94
1980-81	114.36	42.47	36.96	107.60	28.31	26.31	229.00	83.27	36.36	253.64	95.24	37.55
1981-82	145.16	53.17	36.63	135.62	40.06	29.54	271.91	104.90	38.58	306.32	112.04	36.58
1982-83	168.55	62.11	36.85	147.69	42.19	28.57	303.63	119.05	39.21	338.14	126.11	37.30
1983-84	183.72	67.80	36.90	158.02	45.06	28.51	352.34	137.76	39.10	368.68	140.74	38.17

Note : Total taxes revenue includes the states own direct and indirect taxes and share in central taxes.
Per capita tax revenue has been calculated by using the same formula as used in Table 6.1

too high in comparison to Rajasthan and Uttar Pradesh. The per capita total tax incidence increased from Rs. 139.81 in 1975-76 to Rs. 368.68 in 1983-84 while the per capita sales tax incidence increased from Rs. 48.48 in 1975-76 to Rs. 140.74 in 1983-84. The sales tax as a percentage to total tax incidence varied between 33.94 to 39.79 during period of study.

The per capita burden of sales tax and total tax of states under study reveals that the burden is the highest in Punjab followed by Haryana, Rajasthan and Uttar Pradesh. The percentage of sales tax burden to total tax burden varies between 32.93 to 42.85 in Rajasthan, 28.51 to 33.40 in Uttar Pradesh, 34.36 to 40.57 in Haryana and 33.94 to 39.79 in Punjab. Uttar Pradesh is the only state where sales tax has contributed small share in total tax revenue while in Punjab, Rajasthan and Haryana it is too high.

Burden of Sales Tax—Income Analysis

The method of calculating per capita incidence of sales tax on the basis of population ignores the level of income prevailing in the different states in different years which effects the actual burden of sales tax. The effects of tax burden depends upon the marginal utility of money. If the level of income increases, the marginal utility of money goes down and a person has to sacrifice more.

Professor Vito Tanzi in his article "International Tax Burden"[27] has defined the tax burden as the ratio of tax revenue to the part of national income which is above the subsistence level so it is:

$$E = \frac{T}{Y-S}$$

where

E = burden,

T = tax revenue,

Y = national income, and

S = that part of national income required to provide a defined subsistence standard of living to the population.

27. Tazi Vito, Milnes and R. Myddetron: *Taxation—A Radical Approach*, The Institute of Economic Affairs, London, 1970, p. 9.

But for the purpose of this formula, it is not possible to collect the data regarding income at the subsistence level in the states.

Mr. V.P. Gandhi (1966)[28] attempted to study the incidence of direct and indirect taxes in agriculture on the basis of the net or fiscal tax burden *i.e.* the burden taking into consideration the benefits of the public expenditure. He also suggested the following formula to measure tax incidence.

$$B_2 = \frac{t}{f\,(Y-S,\ W,\ w,\ i)e}$$

Where B_2=tax incidence, t=per capita tax paid, Y=per capita income, S=per capita subsistence requirement, W=per capita wealth, w=wealth inequality measure, i=income inequality measure, e=a constant denoting the desired degree of progressivity, and f=function.

Gandhi's estimates, however, do not appear to have made much headway on account of the great dearth of statistical data relating to such variables as per capita subsistence requireiments, per capita wealth, wealth and income inequality, included in his measure of incidence. The absence of reliable data has forced him to make some assumptions, such as e=1.5, about the number of variables.

In our study it is asssumed that the entire sales tax burden is passed forward to the consumers and in calculating the sales tax incidence, it is assumed that expenditure is approximately equal to income. To measure liability of sales tax per rupee the following formula has been used and then by taking the average liability of sales tax per rupee for the study period (ET/EY) as the standard (index=100), the index numbers for different years have been found out:

$$R = \frac{T}{Y}$$

Where R denotes per rupee sales tax liability;
T denotes the total revenue from sales tax; and
Y denotes net state domestic products as state income.

Table 6.3 (p. 178) gives the comprehensive results of per capita

28. V.P. Gandhi: *Tax Burden in Indian Agriculture*, The Law School of Harvard University, Cambridge, 1965, p. 31.

burden of sales tax in a rupee. It reveals that the per rupee tax rate of sales tax in Rajasthan was 2.697 paisa in 1975-76. It reflects a steady growth in the succeeding two years increasing to 2.958 paisa and 3.152 paisa respectively but it dropped to 3.129 paisa in 1978-79. It again reached a phenomenal height of 4.018 paisa in 1979-80 but decreased to 3.468 paisa in 1980-81 and further to 3.372 paisa in 1981-82. It again rose to 3.833 paisa in 1982-83 and finally dropped to 3.533 paisa in 1983-84. The index number of sales tax incidence was 77.72 in 1975-76. After registering a growth in the successive two years it reached 85.24 in 1976-77 and 90.83 in 1977-78, while it slipped to 90.17 in 1978-79. After that, it increased very sharply similar to per rupee tax rate and reached 115.79 in 1979-80 which was the highest throughout the period of study. It again fluctuated in the succeeding period and finally reached 101.82 in 1983-84 marking an increase of 31 per cent over 1975-76.

In Uttar Pradesh, the per rupee sales tax rate was 2.973 paisa in 1975-76, It increased to 2.989 paisa in 1976-77 but dropped to 2.599 paisa in 1977-78. It again increased to 2.791 paisa in 1978-79 and further to 2.931 paisa in 1979-80. However, it marginally slipped to 2.236 paisa in 1980-81 but again increased to 3.073 paisa in 1981-82. It again dropped to 2.918 paisa in 1982-83 and finally to 2.847 paisa in 1983-84. The index number of sales tax incidence was 105.80 in 1975-76. It increased to 106.37 in 1976-77. In the succeeding years it fluctuated continuously and finally reached 101.32 in 1983-84, registering decrease of 4.24 per cent over 1975-76.

In Haryana, the burden of sales tax was 3.062 paisa in a rupee in 1975-76 which increased to 3.362 paisa in 1976-77 but marginally dropped to 3.323 paisa in 1977-78. Although, it registered a growth in the succeeding two years reaching 3.463 and 3.717 paisa respectively yet it dropped to 3.640 paisa in 1980-81. After that it increased continuously and finally reached the phenomenal height of 4.391 paisa in a rupee in 1983-84. The index number of sales tax incidence was 80.09 in 1975-76 which showed fluctuations in the study period but in the last three years of the period of study it rose sharply and reached 114.86 in 1983-84 an increase of 43.4 per cent over 1975-76.

TABLE 6.3

Burden of Sales Tax—Taking Net Domestic Products in the States

(Rs. in crores)

Year	RAJASTHAN				UTTAR PRADESH				HARYANA				PUNJAB			
	Sales Tax Revenue (Rs.)	State Income (Rs.)	Per Rupees Tax Rate (in Paisa)	Index of Tax incidence	Sales Tax Revenue (Rs.)	State Income (Rs.)	Per Rupees Tax Rate (in Paisa)	Index of Tax incidence	Sales Tax Revenue (Rs.)	State Income (Rs.)	Per Rupees Tax Rate (in Paisa)	Index of Tax incidence	Sales Tax Revenue (Rs.)	State Income (Rs.)	Per Rupees Tax Rate (in Paisa)	Index of Tax incidence
	T	Y	T/Y	ET/EY =100	T	Y	T/Y	ET/EY =100	T	Y	T/Y	ET/EY =100	T	Y	T/Y	ET/EY =100
1975-76	67.60	2506.00	2.697	77.72	208.26	7005.00	2.973	105.80	49,50	1616.40	3.062	80.90	73.16	2598.90	2.815	83.14
1976-77	84.29	2849.90	2.958	85.24	243.17	8135.00	2.989	106.37	63.95	1902.2	3.362	87.94	96.12	3061.8	3.139	92.71
1977-78	100 25	3179.8	3.152	90.83	246.03	9464.0	2.599	92.49	69.62	2095.2	3.323	86.92	107.51	3454.7	3.112	91.91
1978-79	113.68	3632.9	3.129	90.17	272.25	9756.0	2.791	99.32	79.68	2300.6	3.463	90.58	119.31	3718.8	3.208	94.74
1979-80	135.86	3381.5	4.018	115.79	302.52	10320.0	2.931	104.31	90.05	2422.7	3.717	97.23	129.79	4219.6	3.076	90.84
1980-81	145.00	4180.3	3.468	99.94	313.97	14041.0	2.236	79.57	108.00	2967.0	3.640	95.21	160. 0	4577.1	3.495	103.22
1981-82	186.21	5006.5	3.372	97.18	453.35	14755.0	3.073	109.36	138.37	3373.1	4.102	107.30	191.82	5339.1	3.593	106.11
1982-83	222.23	5797.6	3.833	110.46	486.98	16687.43	2.918	103.84	160.48	3834.37	4.185	109.47	219.93	6081.77	3.616	106.79
1983-84 (R.E.)	248.00	7019.44	3.533	101.82	530.38	18632.52	2.847	101.32	189.70	4319.73	4.391	114.86	249.95	6743.71	3.706	109.45

Source : (1) Net States Domestic Products upto 1981-82 has compiled from *Central Statistical Organisation Department of Statistics*, Ministry of Planning, Government of India, New Delhi, 1984, figures after 1981-82 are Provisional estimation which has been supplied by Directorate of Economic and Statistics Department, Rajasthan.

(2) Sales Tax Revenue has been compiled from *Reserve Bank of India Bulletins*.

Per rupee tax rate of sales tax in Punjab was 2.815 paisa in 1975-76 which increased to 3.139 paisa in 1976-77. It marginally dropped to 3.112 paisa in 1977-78 but again increased to 3.208 paisa in 1978-79. However, it again dropped to 3.076 paisa in 1979-80 but registered a speedy growth in the remaining period of study and reached 3.706 paisa in 1983-84. The index number was 83.14 in 1975-76. It also showed a trend similar to rupee tax rate of sales tax. It finally reached 109.45 in 1983-84 marking an increase of 31.65 per cent over 1975-76.

The comparative study showed that the per rupee tax rate of sales tax was the highest (4.395 paisa) in Haryana followed by Punjab (3.706 paisa), Rajasthan (3.533 paisa) and Uttar Pradesh (2.847 paisa) in 1983-84. The percentage of sales tax increased by 31 in Rajasthan, by 43.3 in Haryana, by 31.65 in Punjab while in Uttar Pradesh it declined by 4.24 over 1975-76. The per rupee tax rate shows that the state has been collecting very negligible part of sate income. Punjab and Haryana are advanced states in regard to agriculture and industry where state income is too high but sales tax occupies only 2.815 to 3.706 paisa and 3.062 to 4.391 paisa in rupee respectively. In Rajasthan sales tax occupies 2.697 to 4.018 paisa while in Uttar Pradesh 2.236 to 3.073 paisa in a rupee during the period of study. It is, therefore, necessary to improve the administration and check the evasion of sales tax. To check the evasion, it should be made necessary that the goods consigned to a businessman in any part of the state should be delivered after the necessary documents are submitted to the concerning sales tax officer, besides this, frequent surprise checking of the stock registers of the dealers should also be done to minimise the evasion of tax.

Commodity-Wise Importance

A state-wise analysis of the sales tax revenues in terms of their commodity-wise importance could throw useful light on aspects such as the strains and weakness of their tax measures, revenue concentration etc. D.T. Lakdawala and K.V. Nambiar have observed that the per capita revenue is much higher for food items in Kerala, Tamil Nadu and Gujarat.[29] Lack of data

29. D.T. Lakdawala and K.V. Nambiar: *Commodity Taxation in India*, Sardar Patel Institute of Economic and Social Research, Ahmedabad, 1972, p. 75.

TABLE 6.4

Commodity-Wise Incidence of Sales Tax in 1983-84

Commodity-wise group	*RAJASTHAN*		*UTTAR PRADESH*		*HARYANA*	
	Revenue each Commodity-wise (Rs. in lakhs)	*Per Capita Incidence (Rs.)*	*Revenue each Commodity-wise (Rs. in lakhs)*	*Per Capita Incidence (Rs.)*	*Revenue each Commodity-wise (Rs. in lakhs)*	*Per Capita Incidence (Rs.)*
1. Food items	4467,97 (18.02)	12.21	8540.24 (19.00)	7.26	3276.39 (18.40)	23.79
2. All kinds of Cotton, Yarn, Silk woollen etc.	666.26 (2.69)	1.82	883.79 (1.97)	.75	631.34 (3.54)	4.58
3. Timber, woods their products	89.04 (.36)	.24	563.52 (1. 06)	.48	382.87 (2.15)	2.78
4. Building Materials	2217.49 (8.94)	6.06	2541.81 (5.66)	2.16	1044.61 (5.87)	7.59
5. Medicine and Drugs	415.32 (1.67)	1.14	1311.91 (2.92)	1.11	282.84 (1.59)	2.05
6. Motor and Motor Parts	1761.37 (7.10)	4.82	3019.02 (6.72)	2.57	1978.62 (11.12)	14.37
7. Scientific Equipments and Machinery	825.67 (3.33)	2.26	1575.8 (3.51)	1.34	73.49 (.41)	.53
8. Electrical goods	399.5 (1.61)	1.09	1760.5 (3.92)	1.49	246.39 (1.38)	1.79

9. Photographic goods	19.41 (.08)	.05	9.83 (.02)	.01	8.25 (.05)	.06
10. Iron and Steel and their products	556.69 (2.24)	1.52	1630.02 (3.63)	1.39	856.03 (4.81)	6.21
11. Bullion and Jewellery items	11.19 (.05)	.03	152.46 (.34)	.13	10.02 (.06)	.07
12. Fuel items and their products	3939.41 (15.88)	10.77	2502.35 (5.57)	2.13	795.82 (4.47)	5.78
13. Crokery, cutlery and cosmetics, items	91.65 (.37)	.25	321.19 (.71)	.27	236.21 (1.33)	1.72

Figure in brackets shows the percentage to sales tax revenue (Sales tax revenue + central sales tax revenue). In calculation of per capita incidence, each commodity revenue has been divided by projected population in 1983-84.

Sources : Commodity-wise groups are given in *Appendix IV*.

is a problem in this regard. However, attempts have been made to collect data by Rajasthan, Haryana and Uttar Pradesh. These data are partial and some of these are of overlapping nature also but still they give us some idea of the commodity group concentrations as may be seen from Table 6.4 (given on p. Nos. 180 & 181).

The table reveals that revenue from food items accounted for a significant portion of sales tax in the state of Rajasthan, Uttar Pradesh and Haryana, but the tax components were different. In Rajasthan the revenue was mainly derived from foodgrains, oils and oilseeds, in other states foodgrains were also an important source but in Uttar Pradesh and Haryana the gur shaker, kirana, and vanaspati ghee contributed more revenue to sales tax. The percentage of revenue from food items to sales tax revenue was 18.02 in Rajasthan, 19.00 in Uttar Pradesh, and 18.40 in Haryana in 1983-84 while other items did not contribute such high percentage. The per capita incidence of food items was Rs. 12.21 in Rajasthan, Rs. 7.26 in Uttar Pradesh while in Haryana such a high (Rs. 23.79) per capita incidence was due to agricultural and industrial development

The percentage of revenue from cotton, woollen and their products to sales tax revenue was also highest in Haryana followed by Rajasthan and Uttar Pradesh. It was 2.69 in Rajasthan, 1.97 in Uttar Pradesh and 3.54 in Haryana. The per capita incidence in Uttar Pradesh was very low (Rs. 0.75) while in Haryana it was Rs. 4.58 in comparison to Rs. 1.82 in Rajasthan.

The contribution of timber and their products, medicine and drugs, photographic goods, crockery and cutlery, bullion and jewellery, scientific goods and electrical goods was very meagre in sales tax revenue in each state. The per capita incidence on these items was also below Rs. 2 in Rajasthan, Uttar Pradesh and Haryana (except medicines and drugs and timbers).

The percentage of revenue from building materials to sales tax revenue was 8.94 in Rajasthan, 5.66 in Uttar Pradesh and 5.87 in Haryana. It shows that in Rajasthan the building materials (bricks, cement) produce and give more tax revenue in inter-state transactions. The per capita incidence was highest in Haryana (Rs. 7.59) while it was lowest in Uttar Pradesh (Rs. 2.16) and Rajasthan (Rs. 6.06) in 1983-84.

Sales tax on transport vehicles constitutes a high percentrge of revenue in case of Haryana, Rajasthan and Uttar Pradesh with more or less uniform tax rates in these states. The variations in sales tax collections may be due to the number of motor vehicles and their parts sold in each state. It contributes 7.10 per cent in Rajasthan, 6.72 per cent in Uttar Pradesh and 11.12 per cent in Haryana to total sales tax revenue. In Haryana motor vehicles industry is more developed than other states. The per capita incidence in 1983-84 was Rs. 14.37 in Haryana, Rs. 4.82 in Rajasthan and in Uttar Pradesh it was the lowest *i.e.* Rs. 2.57.

Iron and steel are important components in steel tube industry which is also more developed in Haryana contributing 4.81 per cent to sales tax revenue. In Uttar Pradesh the percentage of its revenue to sales tax in 1983-84 was 3.63 and in Rajasthan only 2.24. The per capita incidence in 1983-84 was Rs. 6.21 in Haryana followed by Rajasthan (Rs. 1.52) and Uttar Pradesh (Rs. 1.38).

Fuel and other products generate high percentage of sales tax revenue in Rajasthan because petrol is also taxable under Sales Tax Act while in Haryana and Uttar Pradesh it is separately taxed under Motor Spirit Act. The per capita incidence was Rs. 10.77 in Rajasthan, Rs. 5.78 in Haryana and Rs. 2.13 in Uttar Pradesh in 1983-84.

Conclusively, the five items, *viz.*, food, building materials, motor vehicles and their parts, scientific equipments and fuel, contribute more than half of the sales tax revenue in Rajasthan while in Uttar Pradesh and Haryana these items contribute more than 40 per cent. The per capita incidence of all items except that scientific goods, bullion and jewellery and fuel items is highest in Haryana.

Conclusion

The per capita incidence of sales tax is higher in Haryana and Punjab which are developed states regarding industry and agriculture while in Rajasthan and Uttar Pradesh which are industrially backward states, the per capita incidence of sales tax is lower. The share, of sales tax in state income is negligible in each state. Punjab and Haryana are in a better position than Rajasthan and Uttar Pradesh. The burden of sales tax on food items was heavy in each state. Uttar Pradesh shows a poor position in comparison to other states.

7

SUMMARY OF FINDINGS AND SUGGESTIONS

Introduction

Generally speaking, Sales Tax is a tax on the sale of commodities at the retailing, wholeselling or manufacturing stages and it is a wide connotation which includes purchase tax too. Sales tax is a levy on the sales or elements incidental to sales. The modern form of sales taxation is of very recent origin in India but in the world history it came into existence during the depression period after the second world war. The earliest traces of sales tax can be found in Greece. Next to it one finds references of such a levy in old Indian scriptures. Manu Samriti and Kautilya Arthasastra mention such a levy like sales tax in olden times. In ancient Rome, it was also imposed in the 6 A D. and in France it existed in 1292, in Italy it was prevalent in the fifteenth century. Spain introduced "Alcabala" as a national tax in 1342. Adam Smith had condemned it as a major factor in the decay of Spain. In India, the sales tax existed during Mauryan, Rajput and Cholan periods. It also existed during Hindu period and during the time of Shershah and Akbar. However, Firuz Shah and Jehangir attempted to abolish such taxes but abolition was done only on papers and it was duly collected in spite of abolition orders not only during their periods but its existence also continued upto the Aurangzeb period and further during the East India Company rule. During the 18th and the 19th centuries, except for India and England, sales tax did not find favour with other countries due to development of democratic government.

Originally, sales tax was justified as temporary source of revenue during the period of crisis only, but after the first world war, sales tax as an important fiscal measure attracted many nations to cope with the financial stringencies created by the world war I. Germany and France were the major countries who first adopted this tax after the war. After the second world war, it became a permanent source of revenue of the nations.

However, sales taxes have acquired particular importance in India in the present century only. The Government of India Act, 1935 envisaged federal character with a provision of provincial autonomy. Naturally provinces required adequate financial resources to carry on the function allotted to them. The Bombay province was the pioneer to levy tax on tobacco in limited areas in 1938. Second in line was Central Provinces (Madhya Pradesh) which levied a retail sales tax on motor spirit and lubricants in January, 1939. The general sales tax for the first time was imposed in 1939 by Madras. Following Madras, many provinces resorted to sales tax during and after the second world war and presently all states levy this tax. In Punjab it was introduced in 1941 as East Punjab General Sales Tax Act. The present Sales Tax Act was made applicable with effect from May 9, 1949. The Uttar Pradesh Sales Tax Act, 1948 came into operation with effect from April, 1948, while Rajasthan Sales Tax Act, 1954 came into existence with effect from April 1, 1955 and in Haryana it was introduced with effect from 5th May, 1973, previously Haryana was the part of Punjab.

The prevalent forms of sales taxes can be classified in general, according to scope, *i.e.* general and selective and according to the legal basis of imposition, *i.e.* on buyers or on sellers. General sales taxes may be further classified according to the point of levy into (*i*) single point and (*ii*) multiple point tax. Some of more important forms of sales tax family are the Canadian Manufacturer's Sales Tax, the Turnover Tax of Germany, and the Value Added Tax of France. At present in Uttar Pradesh and Rajasthan, most of the commodities are taxable at first point while in Haryana and Punjab the last point of taxation is in vogue.

Financial Dependence of States on Sales Tax

India is a federal country where the Central Government is

more powerful having more elastic source of revenue. States are dependent on centre to some extent but they have some independent sources also, particularly, the sales tax which is the most elastic source of revenue of the states. It is based on expenditure which is regarded superior to income basis taxation due to its incentive effects on savings, economic growth and wide coverage. The role of sales tax in state's finances has now become very important. Its yield has increased by leaps and bounds. Its share in states own tax revenue was only 28.91 per cent in 1955-56. It increased to 58.94 per cent in 1983-84. The position of sales tax in individual states undoubtedly indicates that it has become "KAMDHENU" for them. Its share in states indirect taxes varies from 61.9 to 71.66 per cent in Rajasthan, 61.61 to 67.33 per cent in Uttar Pradesh, 49.7 to 53.06 per cent in Haryana and 46.99 to 52.70 per cent in Punjab during the period of study (1975-76 to 1983-84). It also contributes major share in states own taxes revenue which varies in the range of 51.68 to 64.74 per cent in Rajasthan, 52.40 to 55.10 per cent in Uttar Pradesh, 42.34 to 47.67 per cent in Haryana and in Punjab 42.00 to 47.59 per cent during 1975-76 to 1983-84. The percentage of sales tax in state's total revenue (Tax+Non-Tax revenue) shows that every fourth and fifth paisa in a rupee springs from the sales tax. The importance of sales tax has grown enormously since its imposition and it has grown comparatively much more than any other tax. Sales tax revenue has increased 3.67 times in Rajasthan, 3.83 times in Haryana, 3.42 times in Punjab and 2.55 times in Uttar Pradesh during the period of study. It indicates that sales tax as a source of revenue is increasing faster in Haryana followed by Rajasthan, Punjab and Uttar Pradesh. The growth of sales tax is also much higher than the total tax growth and other states taxes growth, which shows a significance of the role of sales tax in state exchequer. Uttar Pradesh is the only state, where revenue has not kept pace with the total taxes revenue and states taxes revenue. The state should made efforts to improve this situation.

It being a major source of revenue, the state governments are not ready to abolish sales tax. Abolition of sales tax cannot be considered a wise step because it will make the states more dependent on the centre and the centre-state financial conflicts which are already so acute would become all the more complicated. The alternative proposals for replacement of sales taxation are (*i*) the replacement of sales tax by additional excise duties or (*ii*) introduction of value added tax in place of sales tax. Regarding the first proposal, the complete shifting of sales tax by additional excise duties could not be possible due to states financial autonomy and coverage of additional excise duties. However, the central government may extend the additional excise duties and distribute the revenue on a rational, fair and equitable basis among the states. The commodities which may be extended to additional excise duties may comprise cement, paper products, petrol and petroleum products, hydrogenated oils and medicines which are recommended by Tripathi Committee. Other commodities which may come in this ambit are iron and steel and coal.

As regard the second proposal, in view of the constitutional and administrative problem, it is felt that the introduction of VAT is neither feasible nor desirable at this juncture in India. Therefore, the need of the hour is to simplify the sales tax laws and to minimise the complexities in their operation.

Rate Structure of Sales Tax

With the increasing importance of the sales tax its structure has also undergone changes. It has been revised, its base has been expanded and exemptions have been added or subtracted but no common rate structure has emerged so far and different commodities are taxed at different rates.

Any dealer whose turnover does not exceed the prescribed limit is not liable to pay tax. If the minimum turnover limit is low, sales tax administration faces many problems such as that of coverage and the problem of coping up with the increased work load etc. In case of importer, the minimum turnover limit is Rs. 10,000 in Rajasthan while in Haryana, Punjab and Uttar Pradesh there is no limit. In case of manufacturers, in Rajasthan and Haryana the limit of sale proceeds is Rs. 25000 as a minimum turnover limit while in Uttar Pradesh and Punjab it is Rs. 50,000 and Rs. 40,000 respectively. In case of other dealers there is uniformity in Haryana, Punjab and Uttar

Pradesh where the limit is Rs. 1,00,000. In Rajasthan the dealers who are dealing in tax paid goods are not liable to pay tax and to registration irrespective of any quantum of turnover. For liability to pay sales tax in Rajasthan both the conditions of gross turnover of Rs. 75,000 and taxable turnover of Rs. 5,000 in previous accounting year must be fulfilled simultaneously. This provision provides a heaven for tax evaders by issuing forged tax paid vouchers.

Regarding points of taxation, single point levies may be confined to items which are produced or imported in large scale and also where the trade is well organised. Where production and trade are such that they cannot be adequately taxed at one stage in the process of production or distribution they could be brought under multiple point levy. But in practice the goods having multiple point of taxation are vouched arbitrarily at low prices, causing a big loss to the revenue. So a combined system of single point (first-last) levy according to the suitability of the item would, in a large measure, minimise the shortcomings of either systems adopted exclusively. In Rajasthan and Uttar Pradesh most of the commodities are taxable at first point while in Haryana and Punjab most of the commodities are leviable at the last point In the states under study Rajasthan is the only state where multiple point of taxation on gems, stones and pearls is adopted.

The general rate of sales tax shows some sort of uniformity. It is 8 per cent in Rajasthan, Uttar Pradesh and Haryana while it is slightly lower in case of Punjab (7 per cent). Rate on selective commodities shows wide rate disparity. It is the most distinguishing characteristic of the sales tax. Wide varieties of rate differentiation gives incentives to diversion of sales from one state to another. Rate differentiation also prevail within the state. Different type of commodities are taxed at different rates. Luxurious goods are taxable at 10 to 12 per cent in Rajasthan, 12 per cent in Haryana and Uttar Pradesh while in Punjab such items are taxable at the rate of 10 per cent. Rates of these items have reached its peak point and any further increase in one state would not produce additional revenue and administratively it will create difficulties by providing greater incentive to evade taxes. Mineral oils are taxable at higher rates in Rajasthan resulting in smuggling of these goods in Rajasthan from other states.

Foodgrains and other essential commodities are taxable in the range of 1 to 4 per cent in Rajasthan while in Haryana, Punjab, Uttar Pradesh most of these commodities are taxable at the rate of 4 per cent.

Rate of sales tax on hydrogenated oils are 10 per cent in Rajasthan and Uttar Pradesh which is very high as compared to Haryana (7 per cent) and Punjab (8 per cent). The rate of sales tax on deshi ghee is 3 per cent in Rajasthan, 6 per cent in Uttar Pradesh and 4 per cent in Punjab. Hydrogenated oil which is used by lower income groups is taxable at high rates while deshi ghee which is used by higher income groups is taxable at low rates of taxation. These types of anomalies would scrap the idea of welfare state and should be removed.

In each state 10 to 15 types of rates are in vogue which is very difficult for a dealer to maintain separate accounts for different types of sales but it is obligatory under the provisions of the law. Rate differentiation according to commodity prices is even more complex. In hosiery items such type of system prevails in Haryana which gives birth to widespread evasion of tax through under-invoicing. Thus, it is suggested that not more than three or four different rates of sales tax should be determined for different types of commodities. Goods which are declared and are of special importance under Central Sales Tax Act may be subjected to at the rate of 4 per cent, luxuries items may be taxed at higher rate (say 10 per cent); lower rate of tax *i.e.* 2 to 3 per cent may be levied on food and other necessaries and finally narcotic goods may be taxed at even higher rates (say 15 per cent).

Under the existing arrangement of Central Sales Tax Act, the tax is collected by the exporting state while the incidence of tax is borne by consumers of the importing state. However, the residents of the importing state do not get any benefit from the tax revenue derived by the exporting state. It creates inter-state jealousies and a fiscal inequity. States, which are industrially developed derive more share in central sales tax revenue. Therefore, it is suggested that such a provision should be revised and assessment and collection power be given to importing states. This will increase the revenue of relatively financially backward states like Uttar Pradesh, Bihar and Rajasthan. Developed states have surplus commodities but in case of branch transfer/depot sales, the exporting states do not get any revenue and also on inter-state transactions tax is easily evaded. Therefore, special cells at the headquarters of tax administration in the states should be established to cross check such transaction of sales. The 46th amendment to the constitution of India has rightly given the power to levy the consignment tax but no common consensus has been developed among the states regarding levy and rate of such tax so far. The earlier it is done, the better.

Purchase tax is also levied under states sales tax law. Livestock are taxable on per head basis in Haryana. It may be observed that the states have not provided for set off of the excess tax paid on purchases of goods which are used in manufacturing process, which should be done to encourage industrial development.

Exemptions are also provided in the states tax law. The items which come closest to the universalities are salt, vegetables, meat, milk, books and periodicals etc. Some of the commodities are fully exempted and others are conditionally exempted. Food and other essential commodities are not exempted because in India the coverage of direct taxes is extremely limited and a very large section of population can be reached only through indirect taxes. Raw materials and intermediates of producer goods are not exempted. It is recommended that states should adopt a uniform policy within the state on the pattern of central excise duties (Modified value added tax). Exemptions are also provided to promote village and cottage industries, and institutions of non-profitable nature. This is not a suitable method, because given the exemption to any one industry create a political pressure for additional exemption of similar nature. Therefore, exemption from sales tax should not be preferred to granting of subsidies if it is felt desirable to promote such industries. Agriculture implements are exempted in all the states under study but agricultural machinery is not exempted. Rajasthan is the only state where water monoblock pumping sets are exempted.

Rate differentiation prevails in the states which gives widespread evasion of sales tax. To avoid rate differentiation, it is essential to adopt the policy of common rate structure for all the states. If the common consensus is not developed on rate structure then the whole nation may be divided into five zones (North, South, East, West and Central) to develop a common regional structure of sales tax.

Organisation of Sales Tax

In all the states under study the states sales tax law provides administrative machinery to regulate flow of tax. In Rajasthan it is known as Commercial Taxes Department which deals with Sales Tax, Entertainment Tax and Electricity Duties while in Uttar Pradesh, a separate department known as Sales Tax Department deals with Sales Tax only. In Haryana and Punjab, there is a single department known as Excise and Taxation Department which looks after the administration of Sales Tax, State Excise, Passengers and Goods Tax, Entertainment Tax etc. It would be advisable to bifurcate the combined department which deals with the excise and taxation in Haryana and Punjab because the combined operation of these taxes have not resulted in efficient and effective administration. Although such bifurcation will increase administrative cost yet it may be compensated through sound administration, which will yield more revenue and also check evasion.

The sales tax is administered by the Commissioner's office either on exclusive basis or in combination with other commercial taxes and state excise duties. Three tier administration is in practice in the states under study. The first tier consisting of the Commissioner at Headquarters level is almost uniform in all the states. He is assisted by Additional/Joint Commissioners. The second tier consists of Deputy Assistant Commissioners at Zonal level. In Haryana it is at District level. The last tier consists of district/ward/circle administration. It is headed by an assessing authority who has multifarious duties *i.e.* assessments, survey, recovery etc. In Uttar Pradesh the Assistant Commissioner is also assessing authority. Normally the assessment work is done by CTO/STO/ETO/AETO/ACTO.

At the grass root level, there are inspectors who assist the assessing authorities but they do not discharge their duty effectively and also harass the dealers. It is suggested that the work of inspectors should be regularly checked by superior authorities because it is the question not only of the state's revenue but also the reputation of the department concerned.

The headquarters organisation in the states under study needs two more wings *viz.*, a separate audit cell and a recovery or collection branch. At present, the audit work is done by Accounts Cell, but it is not effective and the follow up of the internal audit programmes is quite unsatisfactory. Collection of demand work is done by the assessing authorities who are burdened with multifarious duties. It is very difficult for them to take deterrent action regarding hard recovery cases for they do not have any control over recoveries. Rajasthan, Haryana and Punjab should form separate collection cell as in Uttar Pradesh and in Uttar Pradesh too the separate collection cell should further be strengthened.

A separate research and statistics cell is also in existence but in Haryana and Punjab reports are not published in a systematic manner. They should follow the working of Rajasthan and Uttar Pradesh. It is pity that no state is in a position to maintain commodity-wise revenue receipts in all cases, however, a few exercises have been made in these states in this regard.

The check posts and enforcement anti-evasion staff do the anti-evasion work. In all the states under study, check posts and enforcement wings are working whatever their nomenclature may be but the goal is the same, *i.e.* to prevent evasion of tax. Sales tax check posts/barriers have been set up at all the significant points of contact with territories of the states. It plays a vital role in preventing new area of evasion. The check posts are headed by Assistant Commissioner, Excise and Taxation Officer (grade I, II) and Inspectors in Punjab and by the Deputy Commissioner, Sales Tax Officers (grade I, II) and Inspectors in Uttar Pradesh. In Punjab, Haryana and Uttar Pradesh the important check posts are manned by higher authorities with police guards. But it is strange that in Rajasthan some of the check posts are also headed by lower division clerks as incharge of check posts. Hence, the administration of these check posts is rather poor in Rajasthan. It is pity on the part of the state government to expect curbing of evasion from lower division clerks who do not understand even the basic tenets of sales tax law. Hence it is suggested that the border check posts should be headed at least by assistant commercial taxes officer with armed police guard. Weighing machines are not provided in any state check posts which should be provided to minimise the chances of evasion. The object of establishing check posts is to transmit the information to the assessing authorities which is useful for cross verification of dealer's accounts at the time of assessment but no regular and systematic verification of these documents received from check posts is done in the circles of the states under study. This defeats the very purpose of establishment of check posts. Immediate remedial measures should be adopted in this regard.

The present appeals organisation is not a judicial organisation. First appeal is made to the Deputy Commissioner (Appeals) in Rajasthan, Haryana and Punjab while in Uttar Pradesh, the appellate authority is the Assistant Commissioner (Judicial). Assessment work done by Assistant Commissioner can be appealed to the Deputy Commissioner (Appeals). In Haryana and Punjab the Commissioner is also the appellate authority. This is not desirable. Such appellate organisation is superfluous. The second appeal is made to the Tribunal or the Board of Revenue. Tribunal is an independent body and final authority to decide cases on question of fact. If in any case the question of law arises then reference can be made to the High Court. The Commissioner and any authority having the power to revise cases, may file *suo-moto* revision, for the purpose of satisfying himself as to the legality or propriety of any cases but he cannot revise the orders passed by the tribunal. The appellate work should be separated from general organisation. This would help in inspiring confidence in the minds of people. Appellate authorities are not given any training in judicial work which they are required to perform. Therefore, they should be duly trained by judiciary before their placement on job. In Rajasthan, the appellate authorities are appointed from state civil service which is highly undersirable because officers without any background of sales tax work can do justice neither to the dealer nor to the state. Therefore, it is suggested that the appellate authorities should be appointed from state taxation service.

The cost of training is an investment on tax administration. Regular training programme should therefore, be organised through seminars, workshops, group discussions and lectures by the seniors/retired officers, eminent economists and members of the bar so that the officers may be well equipped with latest judgements and other relevant particulars, otherwise the demand they create at the time of assessment would be quashed in further appeals or in higher hearing. Punjab sales tax department organises regular training programmes, other states should also follow on the footing of Punjab.

The most neglected part of the organisation structure is the public relations. In this regard, advisory committee should be formed to eliminate the gap between the administrative authorities and the traders, all the states should organise a separate Sales Tax Advisory Committee which may include members of the trade organisations, advocates and retired seniors of the Department. Recently in Rajasthan, the Commissioner Shri P.N. Bhandri has made a good beginning by forming Vigilance Committee at Zonal and District headquarters. Other states should also follow the pattern of Rajasthan, so that grievances may be dealt with immediately.

Operational Analysis of Sales Tax

To tone up the tax machinery it is important to concentrate on the operational aspects of sales tax. It is particularly significant because, the failure of proper administration of the tax law would threaten the canon of equity and may break the moral of honest tax payers. Tax dodgers must be dealt with deterrent action and honest tax payers must be encouraged by pecuniary concessions.

The registration of dealers is a pre-condition for implementation of sales tax law. The registration fee is Rs. 10 in Rajasthan and Rs. 5 in Haryana and Punjab while in Uttar Pradesh it is Rs. 75 for the first assessment year and Rs. 50 for each subsequent year. In Rajasthan, Haryana and Punjab the present registration fees are in vogue for a long time and do not reflect the changes in the price level or in the cost of administration. Therefore, it needs revision and may be fixed at Rs. 50 to cover registration cost but it cannot be considered merely as a source of revenue.

The registration certificate must be issued without any delay and harassment. Any delay in issuing such certificate should be viewed seriously and deterrent action be taken in this regard.

It has been found that the number of registration is increasing continuously. In state sales tax law it increased by 44 per cent in Rajasthan, 80 per cent in Haryana, and 62 per cent in Punjab while under Central Sales Tax Act it increased by 80 per cent in Rajasthan, 102 per cent in Haryana and 77 per cent in Punjab. The increasing number under Central Sales Tax indicates the growing importance of inter-state trade and commerce in these states. While in Uttar Pradesh the number of registration under Central Sales Tax has declined by 8.97 per cent during the same period which is an example of cancellation of forged registration certificates. Other states should also follow the pioneering efforts of Uttar Pradesh.

The provision of quarterly submission of returns exists in all the states under study. It is useful for regular flow of revenue to the state exchequer.

The assessment proceedings are necessary in consequence of the imposition of tax. If a dealer fails to file return within the prescribed period and the authority has reason to believe that the dealer has evaded tax then he can make assessment to the best of his judgement. But making best judgement assessment the assessing authority must be guided by judicial considerations and by rules of justice, equity and conscience. Delay in assessment is common complaint. It is caused either due to submission of incomplete and defective returns or adjournments sought by dealers during the course of assessment. Therefore, in order to avoid delay in the assessment of sales tax the dealer should be exhorted to file returns with greater care.

The benefit to small dealers under self assessment scheme has been provided in almost all the states under study but in practice all the dealers are called in the office of the assessing authorities with their documents which is clear cut violation of the policy of the department. Hence, it is suggested that inspecting authorities should regularly watch the performance of the policy so that the real benefits of the scheme can reach the small traders and after the finalisation of assessment, 10 to 20 per cent cases must be scrutinised by the inspecting authorities.

Pendency of assessment cases is a great problem faced by all the states under study. In Rajasthan the number of pending cases increased from 1,37,665 in 1976-77 to 1,61,824 in 1983-84 while in Uttar Pradesh it decreased from 4,24,586 to 4,16,743, in Haryana from 44,940 to 40,310 and in Punjab it increased from 83,577 to 2,54,223 during the same period. In Punjab the pending cases increased more rapidly. Therefore, it is suggested that the number of assessing authorities should be increased to settle pending cases. Normally, old cases for assessment remain unassessed for a long time. It has been observed that the assessing authorities are tempted to tackle new cases in order to show larger number of cases assessed. Therefore, incentives for the disposal of complicated cases should also be given. And also the work of assessing authorities should be evaluated on the basis of performance keeping in view that the demand they create at the time of assessment whether maintained or not by the appellate authorities. The Commissioner must ensure that case of legal and procedural mistake by the assessing authorities does not escape punishment.

The arrears of sales tax is also a big problem. It has been observed that the administration of sales tax in the states has not been able to tackle perfectly the problem of tax delinquency. Arrears had increased by 7.27 times in Rajasthan, 3.97 times in Uttar Pradesh, 7.28 times in Haryana and 5.29 times in Punjab during 1976-77 to 1983-84. In fact the growth of arrears is low in Uttar Pradesh but this is the only state where arrears highly affect the revenue and administration of sales tax. The total arrears to the sales tax revenue, in Uttar Pradesh is in the range of 30.09 to 61.81 per cent during the same period, which is an alarming situation. The major cause is that the old arrears generate further new arrears and these create a cumulative effect on the revenue of sales tax. The main reasons of mounting arrears are as under :—

(i) The number of institution of appeals has been increasing;

(ii) there has been delay in compliance of appeals effect;

(iii) sometimes dealers disappear from the scene and become untraceable;

(iv) the assessing authorities lack powers for the collection of arrears which are recoverable as land revenue.

It is, therefore, suggested that strict measure should be adopted to check the increasing arrears. Extension of time may be given on justifiable reasons. The old arrears should be cleared through attachment or any other procedure. Special campaigns must be started to clear the arrears, separate recovery cell at Zonal/District level would help to solve this problem and timely disposal of assessment cases would not increase further arrears. Closed business should be assessed immediately.

To check the evasion of sales tax, rate differentiation among the states should be avoided. Inter-state coordination regarding information and transaction will be helpful to prevent the misuse of 'C' forms and co-operation between neighbouring states will help to check cross entries and checking of under-estimation of imported goods. Regular system of cross verification of the bilties, challans, books and other documents should be developed in circle offices. Incentives to the honest authority who detects the evasion, surprising and specific complaint raids, regular inspection of inspectors' work, punishing the personnel found guilty of collusion with the dealers in evasion of tax are such methods which would help in reducing the evasion. Moreover, incentive schemes to full tax payers must be introduced and tax dodgers must be prosecuted.

The trend of disposal of appeals is normal but the number of institution of appeals cases in relation to assessed cases has been mounting. The percentage of appeals institution to cases assessed varies in the range of 5.17 to 7.85 in Rajasthan, 19.36 to 30.04 in Uttar Pradesh, 2.97 to 4.01 in Haryana and 2.01 to 4.97 in Punjab during the period of study. Conclusively Rajasthan, Haryana and Punjab are in a better position than Uttar Pradesh. The main causes responsible for the increase in appeals are the following :—

(i) Unwarranted penalties by assessing authorities;

(ii) Non-acceptance of the best judgement assessment in most cases by the dealers;

(iii) Procedural mistakes committed by the assessing authorities; and

(iv) The meagre fee for the institution of appeal.

It is, therefore, suggested that in case of non-submission of any information required by the assessing authority, appeal made by the dealer should not be considered. Fee should be increased considering the price spiral. The Commissioner must ensure that the case of wilful legal and procedural mistakes committed by the assessing authorities are properly punished. To reduce the number of appeals the idea of "Lok Adalats" may be introduced in the sales tax cases. Cases of unwarranted and petty penalties may be settled by both the parties without filing further appeals. This will reduce the burden of appellate authorities and the Government will not be put to loss by making expenditure in appellate work.

The number of appeals disposed has shown a fluctuating trend in the states under study. The number of pending appeals increased by 59.5 per cent in Rajasthan, by 162 per cent in Haryana while in Uttar Pradesh and Punjab it showed a decrease of 25.8 per cent and 14.9 per cent during the period of study. Therefore, the administration of Rajasthan and Haryana needs to take quick steps to increase the disposal of appeals.

In Rajasthan and Uttar Pradesh the number of revision cases disposed of was declining while the number of pending cases was increasing, the tribunal is the only solution in case of Rajasthan which has been constituted in 1985 while in case of Uttar Pradesh it is suggested that more tribunal benches should be constituted. In Punjab, the tribunal has worked more efficiently and effectively. It disposed 173.39 per cent more cases during 1982-83. To solve the problem of increasing number of revision cases, in Rajasthan, it is suggested that the additional members should be included in the tribunal to clear pending work and the tribunal should make camp-courts at the district headquarters to impart quick justice to the assessees.

The cost of collection of sales tax is not increasing in comparison to the increase in revenue of sales tax. In Punjab, it was less than 2 per cent while in Rajasthan it was also less than 2 per cent except in 1978-79. In Haryana it varied between 1.97 to 2.30 per cent throughout the period of study. The collection cost was the highest in Uttar Pradesh varying between 2.57 to 3.10 per cent during 1978-79 to 1983-84. The cost elasticity of sales tax revenue indicates that one per cent increase in sales tax revenue leads to .91 per cent increase in cost of collection in Rajasthan, 1.08 per cent in Uttar Pradesh, .85 per cent in Haryana and .90 per cent in Punjab. The increase is less than one in case of Haryana, Punjab and Rajasthan which is a welcome indication from the point of improving its administration. In Uttar Pradesh it is too high and, therefore, efforts are needed to effect a cut in collection cost. Therefore, the Department should pay greater attention to improvement of its operational efficiency which gives more revenue to minimisation of cost of collection. Another thing is that in the collection cost, there is no provision of depreciation on building, furniture, vehicles and other fixed assets. Therefore, the collection cost figures are not showing actual position. It is, therefore, suggested that all the states should make a provision for depreciation on departmental assets.

Incidence of Sales Tax

The per capita incidence of sales tax is higher in Haryana followed by Punjab, Rajasthan and Uttar Pradesh, but the share of sales tax in state's net domestic products is negligible. The per capita incidence in a rupee varied between 2.697 to 4.018 paisa in Rajasthan, 2.599 to 3.073 paisa in Uttar Pradesh, 3.062 to 4.391 paisa in Haryana and 2.815 to 3.706 paisa in Punjab. It is higher in the industrially developed states where per capita income is also higher. In Uttar Pradesh it is very meagre. The commodity-wise importance of sales tax shows that foodgrains and other food items generate highest revenue in sales tax. The percentages of revenue from food items tosales tax was 18.02 in Rajasthan, 19.00 in Uttar Pradesh, and 18.00 in Haryana in 1983-84. Other items which contribute sizeable share in sales tax revenue are building materials, motor vehicles and their parts, scientific equipments and fuel items. These five items contribute more than half of the sales tax revenue in Rajasthan while in Uttar Pradesh and Haryana these items contribute 40 per cent in sales tax revenue. The per capita incidence is also higher on food items. It was Rs. 12.21 in Rajasthan, Rs. 7.26 in Uttar Pradesh and Rs. 23.79 in Haryana in 1983-84.

Finally, it is hoped that the implementation of the above suggestions would go a long way towards toning up the administration of sales tax in the states under study. Besides this, it would also well up the volume of the revenue obtained through sales tax due to the removal of the legal and procedural flaws.

APPENDIX I

List of Goods Which are Taxable at Last Point in Rajasthan during 1983-84

S. No.	*Class of goods*	*Rate of Tax (per cent)*	*In force with effect from*
1.	Ajwain	8	12-11-56
2.	All articles made of gold and silver	5	1-5-56
3.	Cotton	4	6-5-57
4.	Cotton yarn excluding cotton waste	2	5-5-57
5.	Cotton yarn waste	2	24-10-57
6.	Coal other than charcoal including coke in all its forms	4	6-5-55
7.	Dhania	8	14-4-55
8.	Gond & Karthilar	8	14-4-55
9.	Iron ore	3	24-10-57
10.	Iron Steel	4	6-5-57
11.	Iron dust and Iron steel defectives	4	24-10-57
12.	Jute	4	6-5-57
13.	Jewellery	10	1-5-56
14.	Poppy seeds	4	14-4-55
15.	Maithidana	8	14-4-56
16.	Mirchi	8	14-4-56
17.	Mica	4	29-8-62
18.	Oil seeds	4	6-5-52
19.	Ornaments made of real gold and silver	4	1-5-56
20.	Pearls real and cultured A	—	1-5-56
21.	Raw Wool	4	20-10-57
22.	Raw and dressed hides and skins	4	6-5-57

23.	Suwa	—	11-12-56
24.	Zeera	8	14-4-55
25.	Indian made foreign liquors B	—	6-3-64
26.	Sheep, goat and Camel	per head	16-3-63
27.	Peacock feathers	—	22-10-62
28.	Gems and stones C	—	16-3-66
29.	Oil Cakes D	1%	1-4-66
30.	Poppy heads	20	26-3-69
31.	Tender leaves	—	21-2-69
32.	Galvanised plain sheets	8	9-3-70
33.	Galvanised corrugated sheets	8	9-3-70
34.	Non-ferrous metal scrap including untensil scrap	—	9-3-70

Source : (*i*) *Department of Commercial Taxes*, Government of Rajasthan, Jaipur.
(*ii*) R.S. Sharma : "Rate structure and its execution", *Tax Guide*, August, 1981, pp. 28-29.

A=withdrawn with effect from 8-3-68 after introduction of multiple point of taxation.

B=withdrawn with effect form 7-4-76 after introducing first point of Taxation.

C, D=withdrawn with effect from 8-3-68 after introducing first point of Taxation.

Goods are Taxable at the Point of Sales to Consumer (Last Point Sales) in Uttar Pradesh during 1983-84

S. No.	*Description of goods*	*Rate of Tax (per cent)*	*Notification No. and date*
1.	Bhang, Ganja and Charas	14	ST-2-5484/X-10 (i) 80 U.P. Sales Tax Act 15-48 order B, 7-9-81
2.	Motor vehicles including Motor cars, Motor cycle combinations, Motor Scooter, Moped, Motor vans, Lorries, Trucks, including Tractors	10	,, ,,
3.	Articles of gold or silver with or without any other metal or alloy	8	ST-2-5785/X-10 (i) 80, dt. 7-9-81
4.	Footwear of all kinds	8	,, ,,
5.	Gota, lachka, thappa, salma, sitara, gokhru, including their cutting waste or garlands of Zari	6	,, ,,
6.	Lassi and hot drinks such as tea and coffee	4	,, ,,
7.	Old discarded, obsolete Machinery stores & Vehicle including waste product except cinder, coal ash	8	,, ,,
8.	Old newspapers (raddi) including paper bags paper buntings, paper flags, posters, banners	6	,, ,,
9.	Ornaments made of gold or silver with or without any other alloy and jewellery	6	,, ,,
10.	Prepared pan	4	,, ,,
11.	Ramraj, geru, surkhi, sand, lime, bajri, marble, chips,		

	moram, gitti, stone ballast, stone and articles of stone except of glazed stone	6	ST-2-5785/X-10
12.	Raw wool	4	(i) 80, 7-9-81
13.	Saw dust, charcoal and coke briqueties	4	,, ,,
14.	Sweetmeats, namkins, cooked foods, revari, gajak, biscuits, bread, cakes, pastries, buns, rusk and sugar products, such as sugar candy, batasha, gatta, sugar toys and ileachi-dana	4	,, ,,
15.	Tapes, niwar, and laces, including cord string or line used for typing purpose or drying clothes	4	,, ,,
16.	Wire and Wire mesh made of brass, copper, German silver or any other alloys but excluding wire required for distribution and transmission of electrical energy.	4	ST-2-5786/X-10 (i) 80, dated 7th Sept. 1981

Source : *Sales Tax Rate list*, Government of Uttar Pradesh, with effect from. Ist April, 1983, pp. 3-12.

List of Goods Which are Taxable at Last Point in Haryana during 1983-84

S. No.	*Class of goods*	*Rate of Tax (per cent)*	*In force with effect from*
1.	Bullion and species	1/2	11-1-57
2.	Cotton sewing thread	2	5-3-80
3.	Ornaments and Jewellery (other than jewellery) containing precious stones)	2	1-7-66
4.	Pesticides	2	1-2-68
5.	Raw wool	2	1-2-67
6.	All type of yarn and all type of thread other than carpet, woollen yarn and knitting wool	2	1-4-68
7.	Rate of tax on the sale of readymade garments made out of handloom, or mill made cloth (excluding fur coats and pure silk) if value of per piece does not exceed Rs. 30	2	1-6-68
8.	Sales made to any state government of India	4	1-7-76
9.	Cotton waste and cotton yarn waste	4	1-10-75
10.	Leather	4	21-9-76
11.	Wheat flour including maida, suji, maize, barley, ghat, gram, churi, jowar, guar, giri, and its dal and flour and chilka of all foodgrain cereals and pulses and vegetable seeds	4	27-3-80
12.	Tractors (manufactured in India)	4	1-10-76
13.	All furniture (including Iron and steel)	12	—

14.	Sanitary goods and fittings	12
15.	Leather goods but not including footwear	12
16.	Glassware, Glazedware, Chinaware and crockery	12
17.	Refrigerators and air conditioners plants and components	12
18.	Wireless reception instruments and apparatus, radio and radio valves, accumulators, amplifiers and loud-speakers and spare parts	12
19.	Cinematographic and Photographic equipments	12
20.	Dictaphone, sound transmitting equipment, telephone and spare parts	12
21.	Typewriter, Tabulating, Calculating Duplicating Machine, Binoculars, Telescopes, Gramophones and their parts	12
22.	Cosmetics, perfumery and toilet goods (excluding tooth paste, powder, kumkum, dhoop agarbati)	12
23.	All clocks and time pieces & parts	12
24.	Cigarette cases and lighters	12
25.	Electrical appliances (including bulb, motor, motor starter monoblock pumping set etc.)	12
26.	Pile carpets	12
27.	Cutlery	12
28.	Vaccum flask	12
29.	Picnic set, foam rubber product	12
30.	Articles made wholly or principally of stainless steel (excluding surgical equipment)	12

31.	Perambulators	12	
32.	Fur and articles of personal or domestic use made from fur	12	
33.	All tiles including mosaic tiles (excluding roofing tiles laminating sheets and sunmica sheets)	12	
34.	Generators and Transformers	12	
35.	Plastic Celluloid, bakelite goods and goods of similar substance	10	18-3-80
36.	Liquor (Foreign and Indian made foreign liquors)	20	w.e.f. 30-3-78 31-3-81 and 1-4-81 at last sale.

Source : *Administrative Report*, Excise and Taxation Department, Government of Haryana, Rate list pp. 1-5.

Note: Item Nos. 14 to 34: vide/Haryana Govt. Notification No. So/25HA/20/73/S/15/83 with effect from 31-3-1983.

List of Goods Taxable at Last Point in Punjab during 1983-84

S. No.	*Class of goods*	*Rate of Tax (per cent)*	*In force with effect from*
1.	Bullion and its species	1/2	
2.	Silver ornaments	1	
3.	All types of yarn with cotton thread, other than knitting wool and cotton yarn	1	
4.	Readymade garments except fur coats, pure silk cloth, ready made hosiery	1	
5.	Readymade umbrella except silk covers	1	
6.	Gobar gas plants and its accessories	1	11-7-77
7.	Cotton yarn	2	13-10-76
8.	Hides and skins whether in raw or dressed in state	2	13-10-76
9.	Pesticides	2	
10.	Ornaments except silver and jewellery containing semi-precious, and artificial semi-precious stones	2	
11.	Cotton waste and cotton yarn waste, and pillow covers except silk pillow covers	2	
12.	Raw wool	2	
13.	Pure silk fabrics	3	
14.	Tractors imported from abroad	4	
15.	Condensed milk, butter, milk powder, ice-cream, cheese	4	
16.	Foodgrains and pulses (maida, suji, wheat flour, maize, bajra, barely, gram dal, chura, mung, dal mung, mash, dal mash, moth, dal moth, masoor, arhar, jowar, gowar dried, peas and its dal and flour	4	

17.	Bodies of motor vehicles excluding chassis	5
18.	Motor vehicles including chassis, accessories, motor cycles, scooters and accessories with tyres and tubes	10
19.	Refrigerators and air conditioning plant and their parts	10
20.	Wireless instruments with television, radio, radiogramophone with spare parts and electrical valves, accumulators, amplifiers etc.	10
21.	Cinematographic equipment and Photographic and other cameras and enlargers	10
22.	Clocks, time pieces and watches and parts thereof	10
23.	All furniture of iron and steel and other furniture other than of iron & steel	10
24.	All arms excluding kirpans	10
25.	Cigarette cases and lighters	10
26.	Recording sound and transmitting equipment apparatus with dictaphones, telephones and loudspeakers	10
27.	Typewriters, tabulating machines, calculating machines and duplicating machines and parts	10
28.	Binoculars, telescopes and opera glasses	10
29.	Cosmetics excluding tooth paste, powder, kumkum and soap	10
30.	Pile carpets	10
31.	Cutlery, vaccum flask and picnic sets	10
32.	Sanitary goods and fittings	10
33.	Leather goods except footwear	10

34.	Glassware, glazedware and Chinaware	8
35.	Foreign liquor	10
36.	Articles of stainless steel except razors, blades, surgical instruments	10
37.	Tiles excluding roofing tiles	10
38.	Perambulators	10
39.	Plastic cellouloid except toys for children and footwear	10
40.	Foam rubber products and fur products	10

Sources : *Rate of Sales Tax in the Northern States*, All India Manufacturer's Organisation, Delhi, 1982, pp. 32-5.

APPENDIX II

Comparative Rate Chart of Sales Tax in Northern States Under Study During 1983-84

(In per cent)

S. No.	*Commodities*	*Rajasthan*	*Uttar Pradesh*	*Haryana*	*Punjab*
	Foodgrains and other eatable products				
1.	Oil cakes	1	4	6	—
2.	Bajra, Barley, Jowar or Millo, Maize, Ragi, Kodan, Kutki and Moth in all their forms. Dal & Bran excluding corn flakes	2	4	4	4
3.	Paddy, Rice and Wheat in all their form and Bran excluding Maida	3	4	4	4
4.	Maida, Suji and Sewiayan	4	4	4	4
5.	Gram or gulab gram, tur or arhar, moong, masoor or black gram, chaula, lakh or kesari, gowar and kulthi in all their forms	4	4	4	4
6.	Matira and Tumba seeds, Posta dana	4	—	—	—
7.	Oil seeds	4	4	4	4
8.	All edible oils except Hydrogenated oil, Palm oil, Solvent oil	5	4	8	7
9.	Palm oil refined or not	8	12	—	—
10.	Solvent oil	8	—	—	7
11.	Hydrogenated oils including vanaspati	10	10	8	7
12.	All types of baby foods sold in sealed containers	5	6	—	4

13.	All kinds of eatables and non-alcoholic liquids such as fruits syrups, ark, chatni, murabbas, packed in tins and other kinds of packing	10	12	8	7
14.	Cornflakes and wheat flakes	10	8	8	7
15.	Custard baking powder and ice cream powder	10	8	8	7
16.	Dry fruits	10	6	8	7
17.	Margarine	10	10	8	7
18.	Refined coconut oil	10	10	N.A.	N.A.
	Jewellery Products				
19.	Bullion (gold & silver)	1	1	1/2	2
20.	Ornaments made of silver excluding jewellery consisting of gems, stones, and pearls	2	4	2	2
21.	All types of gota, gota kinari salma, sitara and badla made of gold, silver or stainless steel and all articles of gold and silver other than ornaments and jewellery	5	6	8	7
22.	All articles made of ivory or inlaid therewith	5	8	8	7
23.	Jewellery consisting wholly or partly of gems or stones or pearls	10	10	2	7
	Cotton Products				
24.	Cotton yarn and cotton yarn waste	2	2	4 Cyw 2 cy	2
25.	Worsted and semi-worsted woollen yarn including woollen carpets yarn but except woollen knitting yarn	2	2	N.A.	N.A.
26.	Tyre cord fabrics or warp-sheets	1	—	7	7

27. Readymade garments	3	6	2	2
28. All kinds of hosiery products excluding products of wool, synthetic wool and pure silk	3.5	4	8	7
29. Cotton (indigenous or imported)	4	4	4	4
30. Cotton waste	4	4	4	2
31. Raw wool and wool tops	4	4	2	2
32. Sewing thread	4	2	2	2
33. Silk fabrics, silk tie, and dye sarees, chunnies and odhanies excluding garments of silk and khadi silk	3	8	N.A.	N.A.
34. All kinds of yarns or waste thereof whether spun or filament, made from man	3	2	2	1
35. Acrylic yarn *i.e.* yarn made of non-cellulose acrylic fibre or waste thereof	1	2	N.A.	N.A.
36. Jute	4	4	4	4
Iron and steel & their products				
37. Iron ore	3	—	—	—
38. Iron and steel (defined in clause (iv) of section 14 of the C.S.T. Act 1956)	4	4	4	4
39. Iron Dust	4	—	—	—
40. Iron and steel safes, almirahs and treasure chests	12	10	12	10
41. Article and wares made of stainless steel except safety razors	12	10	12	10
Construction Materials				
42. All types of sanitary and fitting and pipes and pipe fitting except cement and cement articles	10	12	12	10

43. Marble in all its forms	12	6	--	7
44. Plywood, strawboard, card-boards, including fibre sheets, batten board, black board, leather board, insulating board, veneered penels and cellulaı wood panels	10	8	8	7
45. Cement and articles made of cement including pipes and pipe fittings	12	8	12	7
46. Paints, pigments, distempers, varnishes, paint brush, sand paper, turpentine oil, thin-ners etc.	12	12	12	10
47. Dyes and dry colours	9	8	8	6
48. Glazed tiles, vitreous tiles, vitrum tiles, mosaic tiles, linoleum & laminated sheets like sunmica etc.	12	12	12	10
49. Asbestos including flat and corrugated sheets	12	N.A.	N.A.	N.A.
Packing material				
50. Gunny bags, Jute twine, craft paper, empty tins, empty bottles, wooden and tin box, plastic packing material, paper and cotton cloth bags	4	4 to 6	8 Paper card-boards Straw boards & Products	7
51. Cartones, boxes, cones and cylinders made of paper or card-board	4	8	8	7
Power sources				
52. Coal including coke in all its forms but excluding char-coal	4	4	4	4
53. Fire works including colour-ed matches and crackers	12	12	8	6

Photographic goods				
54. Binoculars, telescopes and opera glasses	10	12	12	10
55. Cinematographic equipments including cameras, projections, and sound recording and reproducing equipments, lenses, film and parts and accessories	12	12	12	10
56. Photographic chemicals and albums	12	12	12	10
57. Cameras, enlargers, lenses, film, plates, paper cloth and other parts required. X-Ray apparatus and film	12	8 to 12	12	10
Electrical goods				
58. All plants and equipment and their accessories required for generation, transmission or distribution of electric power	5	12	12	10
59. Electroplated, nickle plated German silver goods	8	—	—	—
60. All kinds of electrical goods including torches, cells, casing, electric fans, lighting bulbs, electrical earthware, porcelainware and other accessories	10	12 (8 Cells)	12	10
61. Copper wire	10	4	—	—
62. Gramophones, records and needles and accessories	10	12	12	10
63. Refrigerators, air conditioning and other cooling plants and apparatus and components, and parts thereof	10	12	12	10
64. Dictaphones and tape recorders and their accessories thereof	12	12	12	10

65. Sound transmitting equipments including telephones, intercoms, loudspeakers, microphones, and spare parts and accessories	12	12	12	10
66. Wireless reception instruments and apparatus, radio, gramophones, electrical valves, accumulators, amplifiers, and their spare parts	12	12	12	10
67. Radio transistors, except their parts	8	12	12	10
68. Closed circuit TVS Cameras, video T.V. cassettes, video players	15	12	12	10
Office equipments				
69. All kinds of furniture and office equipment other than metal furniture or equipment	10	12	12	10
70. Teleprinters, cash register machine, Index machine, franking duplicating machines and parts and accessories thereof	10	12	12	10
71. Metal furniture, cabinet wares and office equipment	12	12	12	10
72. Computers of analogy and digital varieties and their part thereof	10	—	—	10
73. Pile carpets	12	10	12	10
Mineral oils including lubricants				
74. Petrol	15	—	8	7
75. Aviation spirit	12	—	8	7
76. High speed diesel oil	12	—	8	7
77. Light diesel oil	12	—	8	7
78. Crude oil	4	4	4	4

	Steelware, cutlery, glass goods and watches etc.				
79.	Picnic sets	12	12	12	10
80.	Table cutlery knives, forks and spoons	12	10	12	10
81.	Glass (except glass for spectacles, bangles, chimneys of lamps etc.)	12	10	8	8
82.	All kinds of clocks, electric times swithes, mechanical timer	10	10	12	10
83.	Crockery	10	10	12	8
84.	Chinawares and glazed earthenwares	10	10	12	8
85.	Vaccum flasks of every description including hot water, ice and food jars	10	12	12	10
86.	Glass bangles, glass phials	4	N.A.	N.A.	N.A.
	Narcotic products				
87.	Bhang	20	14	—	—
88.	Denatured spirit	20	—	—	—
89.	Poppy heads	20	—	—	—
90.	Opium	20	20	—	—
91.	Tobacco pipes, cheroot pipes and cigar and cigarettes	12	—	7	—
92.	Beer and other kinds of foreign and Indian made foreign liquors excluding denatured spirits	10	—	12	10
93.	Cigarette Cases and lighters	15	12	8	10
	Heavy Machinery and Parts				
94.	Tractors and spare parts worked or operated by tractors	4	6	8 Imported 4 Indigenous	4 Imported 2 Imdigenous

95. All kinds of welding electric-rod and welding rods	10	8	—	7
96. Ball bearings, Fuel injection equipments and pistons	10	—	—	N.A.
97. Motor vehicles, chassis of motor vehicles, and motor bodies	10	10	12	10
98. Motor cycles and scooters, three wheelers, tyres and tubes of motor vehicles and accessories (Tyre, tubes) thereof	10	10	12	10
99. Perambulators and parts thereof	10	10	12	10
Other				
100. Arms and weapons (rifles, revolvers, pistols etc.)	15	14	12	10
101. Aerated waters	12	—	8	10
102. Sheets, cushions, pillows, mattress and other made from foam rubber or plastic foam	10	12	12	10
103. Potash explosives	10	—	—	—
104. Perfumery (excluding agar-batties dhoop and loban), cosmetics, toilet soaps, tooth-paste, manjan, comb, brush, hair oil, safety razors, blades, and other shaving articles	10	12	12	10
105. All kinds of leather goods except footwear	10	—	12	10
106. Medicines and drugs except chlorequines	5	6	8	7
107. Chemical fertilizers	5	5	—	—
108. Kattha	4	N.A.	N.A.	N.A.
109. Mica	4	N.A.	N.A.	N.A.
110. Hides and skins, whether in a raw or dressed	4	4	4	2

Note : Surcharge at the rate of 2 per cent and 20 per cent on the amount of sales tax is also levied except on the amount of sales tax on declared goods in Haryana and Rajasthan respectively.

Source : *Statistical Abstract*, Commercial Taxes Department, Rajasthan, 1983-84, pp. 213-27.

APPENDIX III

Selective Exempted Commodities in Northern States Under Study During 1983-84

S. No.	*Commodities*	*Rajasthan*	*Uttar Pradesh*	*Haryana*	*Punjab*
1	2	3	4	5	6
1.	Husk of all foodgrains and pulses	Ex.	—	—	Ex.
2.	Vegetables (fresh)	Ex.	Ex.	C.E. 1	C.E.
3.	Milk	Ex. 1	Ex. 1	Ex. 1	Ex. 1
4.	Meat	Ex.	C.E.	C.E.	C.E.
5.	Fish	—	C.E.	C.E.	C.E.
6.	Eggs	Ex.	—	C.E.	Ex.
7.	Fresh fruits	C.E.	Ex.	Ex.	Ex.
8.	Common salt	Ex.	Ex.	C.E.	Ex.
9.	Flowers	C.E.	Ex.	Ex.	Ex.
10.	Pan (prepared pan)	Ex.	Ex. 9	Ex.	Ex.
11.	Books	Ex.	Ex.	Ex.	Ex.
12.	Periodicals (Not Raddi of periodicals)	Ex.	Ex.	Ex.	Ex.
13.	Exercise and drawing books	Ex.	—	Ex.	Ex.
14.	Writing slates and slate pencils and chalks	Ex.	Ex.	Ex.	Ex.
15.	Spinning wheel (charkha and its parts)	Ex.	Ex.	Ex.	Ex.
16.	Hand spun yarn	Ex.	Ex.	Ex. 2	Ex. 2
17.	Articles ordinarily prepared by Halwais	—	—	Ex. 3	Ex. 3
18.	Artificial hearing aids and their accessories	Ex.	Ex.	Ex.	Ex.
19.	Vegetable seeds and saplings	Ex.	Ex.	Ex.	Ex.

20.	Sugar	—	—	Ex. 4	Ex. 4
21.	Bakery goods	—	—	Ex. 4	Ex. 4
22.	Edible oils	Ex. 5	Ex. 5	Ex. 5	Ex. 5
23.	Poultry feed (except gowar, oil cakes, cotton seed)	Ex.	Ex.	Ex.	Ex.
24.	Condoms	Ex.	Ex.	Ex.	Ex.
25.	Curd	Ex.	Ex.	Ex.	Ex.
26.	Deshi Ghee	—	—	Ex. 7	—
27.	Sugarcane	Ex.	—	—	—
28.	Water (excluding distilled or aerated water)	Ex.	Ex.	Ex.	Ex.
29.	Handloom clothes—All varieties of cotton, woollen or silken textiles including rayon, artificial silk whether manufactured by handloom or powerloom	Ex. 6	Ex. 6	Ex. 6	Ex. 6
30.	Kikar bark	—	—	Ex.	Ex.
31.	Country made shoes (Deshi Jootis)	Ex. 11	Ex. 11	Ex. 11	Ex. 11
32.	Kuth and Ramdana	—	Ex.	Ex.	Ex.
33.	Medicines	—	Ex. 12	Ex. 12	Ex. 12
34.	Artificial limbs, surgical appliances and other rehabilitation equipments or aids	Ex.	Ex. 13	Ex.	Ex.
35.	All goods sold to the Indian Red Cross Society	Ex.	Ex.	Ex.	Ex.
36.	Photographs including X-Ray photographs	—	—	Ex. 14	Ex. 14
37.	Varieties of canvas cloth, tarpaulines and similar other products, manufactured with the cloth as base as are manufactured in textile mills, powerloom and processing factories	—	Ex.	Ex.	Ex.

38. Leather cloth and inferior or limitation leather cloth ordinarily used in book binding tissue or synthetic water proof fabrics whether single textured or double textured, and book-binding cotton fabrics	Ex.	Ex. 18	Ex.	Ex.
39. Crudely tanned leather usually tanned by villagers in villages (except factory tanned)	Ex.	Ex.	Ex.	Ex.
40. Reori, Batashas, Gajjakas Misri, Golies, Makhans, Marunda, Phullian	Ex.	Ex.	Ex.	Ex.
41. Tobacco whether cured, uncured or manufactured and all its products including biris, cigars and cigarettes	Ex. 22	Ex.	Ex.	Ex.
42. Fodder of every type (except oil cakes)	Ex.	Ex. 19	Ex. 17	Ex.
43. Bardana (Packing material and containers)	Ex. 15	Ex. 15	Ex. 15	Ex. 15
44. Straw covers	—	—	Ex. 16	Ex. 16
45. Water pumping set (in complete form)	Ex. 23	—	—	—
46. Gobar gas plants and Machinery	Ex.	—	Ex.	Ex.
47. Bristles	—	Ex.	—	—
48. Honey	—	Ex.	—	—
49. Lottery-tickets	—	—	Ex.	—
50. Kum Kum, Sindur, Mehandi	Ex.	—	—	—
51. Bangles made of lac and products of lac	Ex.	Ex.	—	—
52. Firewood	Ex.	Ex.	—	—

53. Agricultural implements (non-mechanised)	Ex.	Ex.	Ex.	Ex.
54. Fertilizer and manures (not including bonemeal and crushed bones and chemical fertilizers)	Ex.	Ex.	Ex.	Ex.
55. Hand spun and Hand woven Khadi and yarn produced by the All India Khadi and Village industries or by any other commission or person certified by it and sold exclusively by class dealer	Ex.	Ex.	Ex.	Ex.
56. Handloom clothes excluding pure silk handloom cloth	Ex.	Ex.	Ex.	Ex.
57. Articles made of minakari hand painting	Ex. 20	—	—	—
58. Sirkee made and sold by the same person	Ex.	—	—	—
59. Indian style seats of flush latrines	Ex.	—	—	—
60. Handmade soap	Ex. 20	—	—	—
61. Products of Marble	Ex. 20	Ex. 20	—	—
62. Kites	Ex. 20	—	—	—
63. Products of elephant teeth	Ex. 20	—	—	—
64. Ambulance vans	—	Ex. 21	—	—
65. Fertilizers	—	—	Ex.	Ex.
66. Deshi sweetmeats and Namkins	—	—	Ex.	Ex.
67. Indian made foreign liquors of 60 degrees	—	—	Ex.	Ex.
68. Beer when sold by country liquor licences	—	—	Ex.	Ex.
69. Students instruments	—	Ex.	—	—

70.	Products of cottage and industries (as provided Schedule of Khadi and Gram Udyog Commission)	Ex.	Ex.	Ex.	Ex.
71.	Live stock	—	Ex.	—	—

Source : (1) All India Manufacturer Organisation, *Rate of Sales Tax in Northern States*, Regional Board, New Delhi, 1982, pp. 5 to 7, 35 to 38.

(2) *Rate List*, Government of Uttar Pradesh Publications, 1983, pp. 15 to 38.

Indications

Ex. Exempted to levy tax.

C.E. Conditional exempted, that when goods are sold except sealed container.

Ex. 1 Except condensed and dried milk, or when purchased for use in the manufacture of any goods other than tax free goods for sale.

Ex. 2 Goods sold by person, who deals in hand spun yarn exclusively.

Ex. 3 Exempted when sold by halwais exclusively.

Ex. 4 Goods prepared without using power, or mechanical devices at any stage and sold otherwise than containers, packets and bakers dealing exclusively in such goods.

Ex. 5 Oil produced by indigenous kohlus whether worked by animal or human beings sold by owners or such kohlus only.

Ex. 6 But not including carpets, druggets, woollen duries and purses.

C.E. 1 Vegetables except red chillies dry and except sold in bottles or cartons.

Ex. 7 If manufactured without aid of any electric power at any stage.

Ex. 9 Pan orher than prepared pan.

Ex. 10 Sugar containing more than 90 per cent sucrose, but excluding khandsari sugar, cooked food, confectionery, sweetmeat and other sugar products such as batasha, sugar candy, sugar toys etc.

Ex. 11 When sold by the maker of such shoes himself and does not employ any outside labour or power at any stage of shoes.

Ex. 12 When sold by registered medical practitioners who dispense medicines exclusively to their own patients.

Ex. 13 Sales of artificial limbs and rehabilitation aid by artificial limbs co-operations of India, KANPUR.

Ex. 14 When sold by photographers and radiologists, prepared by himself.

Ex. 15 When sold by a person who deals exclusively in goods declared tax free under Act. And sells packing material and containers only as incidential to his main business.

Ex. 16 When sold by manufactruers themselves or through their labour union.

Ex. 17 But not including oil, cakes, gurguri and husk of food-grains, pulses and cotton seeds.

Ex. 18 Exemption is allowed if the additional central excise duties leviable thereon have been paid and the dealer furnished proof to the satisfaction of the assessing authority.

Ex. 19 Cattle fodder except khali, rice bran and rice husk.

Ex. 20 When sold by a person engraving these articles himself or by any member of his family but does not employ any outside labour or power at any stage of process.

Ex. 21 Provided that the Vans are sold to hospitals run for public welfare and having at least 50 beds for indoor patients and dealers making the sales, furnishes the evidence to the assessing authority of such sales.

Ex. 22 Exemption is allowed if additional excise duty is levied.

Ex. 23 During budgetary provision 1987-88, exemption with-drawn.

APPENDIX IV

Commodity-Wise Collection during 1983-84

Commodity	*Rajasthan (Rs. in lakhs)*	*Uttar Pradesh (Rs. in lakhs)*	*Haryana (Rs. in lakhs)*
1. **Food items**			
Foodgrains including cereals and pulses	1164.94	2640.98	1737.78
Atta, Maida, Suji	—	229.95	—
Aerated water and soft beverages	22.79	56.96	52.52
Cooked food including Dhaba and Restaurant	10.79	81.93	—
Deshi ghee and milk products	69.52	130.84	43.39
Ground-nut oil	—	12.72	—
Gur and shakar powder	384.75	1186.10	156.20
Ice candy and Ice	—	29.08	—
Khandsari molasses and sugar	1.17	67.38	
Kirana	.39 (Zeera)	801.09	277.04
Molasses other than Khandsari		42.98	
Oil of all kinds	854.48	474.12	51.73
Oil seeds	1018.70	325.98	235.64
Rice bran, rice polish, and husk		22.61	
Tea and Coffee	356.40	489.89	141.50
Vanaspati ghee and cocount oil	432.00	1947.68	529.71
Oil cakes	34.17	—	50.88

Biscuits, Bread, Toffee, Cakes, Ice cream, Fish and Deshi Namkins	109.04	—	—
Chillies and Dry fruits	8.83	—	—
	4467.97	8540.29	3276.39
2. **All kinds of Cotton, yarn, Hosiery, Silk, Carpets, Jute and their Products**			
Carpets except cotton, carpets and durries		31.12	
Cotton carpets and durries		9.28	
Cotton yarns, cotton, cotton waste	61.40	420.68	79.60
Cotton hosiery	35.34	75.98	154.76
Jute and jute goods	—	173.38	—
Pure silk cloth including silk dhoties		1.72	
Raw and ginned cotton	347.41	9.95	312.48
Readymade garments	13.17	95.19	13.35
Silk yarn (Synthetic yarn)	175.08	25.01	
Wollen goods including knitting wool		41.48	
Raw Wool	29.05	—	24.87
All kinds of yarn other than knitting wool	4.81		46.28
	666.26	883.79	631.34
3. **Timber, Furniture and their Products**			
Furniture other than Iron and Steel	54.68	70.89	46.91

Woods and timber of all kinds		492.61	
Timber	34.36		213.42
Timber Products			122.54
	89.04	563.50	382.87
4. **Building Materials**			
Bricks		639.50	168.76
Cement	1805.65	1275.42	651.49
Mill stores and hardware		143.13	100.06 (hardware)
Pipes and fittings		305.52	
Sanitary goods		56.06	124.30
Tiles of all kinds		37.38	
Hard-board including fibre-sheets, leather-board, plywood, and laminates		84.80	
Lime stones, bricks	381.58		
Cement Products	14.90		
Marble	12.64		
Chipps Powder	2.72		
	2217.49	2541.81	1044.61
5. **Medicines**			
Medicine drugs	415.32	1311.91 (with pesticides)	282.84
	415.32	1311.91	282.84
6. **Motor and Motor Parts**			
Bicycles, tricycles, rickshaws, perambulators and others	31.54	592.24	190.32

Motorcycles and their combination, Motor, Scootors, Motor parts, tyres, tubes & others	—	504.50	126.13
Motor vehicles with chassis of Motor vehicles and Motor bodies and Motor tyres and tubes	749.07	1280.61	462.76
Tractors and their parts	—	637.86	1195.80 (Indigenous 3.61 Imported)
Motor, Motor cycles, Tractors & their parts	923.80		
Cells and Batteries & Rediators	56.96		
	1761.37	3019.02	1978.62
7. Scientific Equipment and Machinery			
All clocks, time pieces and watches	13.52	42.62	
Machinery and spare parts	613.29	1046.86	
Sewing Machines & their parts	3.19	54.03	
Typewriters, tabulating machines, duplicating etc.	9.20	22.53	
All scientific goods			73.49
Sound transmitting equipment with tele-phones, loud-speakers and spare parts		269.83	
Tape recorders, Dicta-phones other parts		139.93	
Cylinders	12.64		
Bal l bearings	173.83		
	825.67	1575.80	73.49

8. **Electrical goods**			
Electrical goods		564.64	88.59
Refrigerators		251.60	49.95
Radio, T.V. and its parts	13.33 (T.V.)	210.47	107.85
Brasswares	17.91	121.07	
All electrical goods, appliances, fans	18.13		
Bulbs	350.13	612.32	
	399.50	1760.50	246.39
9. **Photographic goods**			
Cameras, Projectors, Lenses, Photo goods films etc.	19.41	9.83	8.25
	19.41	9.83	8.25
10. **Iron and Steel**			
Articles made of stainless steel		47.01	
Iron and steel	240.57	1471.60	716.33
Iron and steel furniture	262.59	111.41	
Stainless steel	43.95	—	139.70
Tin	9.58		
	556.69	1630.02	856.03
11. **Bullion and Jewellery items**			
Bullions	1.36	34.03	2.06
Jewellery	1.21	—	7.96
Artificial Jewellery		7.22	—
Gold and Silver ornaments	8.62	111.21	—
	11.19	152.46	10.02

12. **Fuel Items**			
Coal	9.66	637.38	73.27
Petroleum Products	—	—	722.55
All kinds of lubricants		833.16	—
Fire wood	—	26.42	—
Kerosene oil	—	10005.39	—
Petrol and diesel and products	3917.51		
Cooking gas	12.24		
	3939.41	2502.35	795.82
13. **Crokery, Cutlery and Cosmetics**			
Crockery and cutlery	26.39 (.36)	62.14	149.98
Plastic goods		—	36.38
Cosmetics	31.05	259.05	25.69
Pesticides	33.85		24.16
	91.65	321.19	236.21

Source: Material furnished by the state Governments Sales Tax Departments.

BIBLIOGRAPHY

Books :

Agarwal, A.K., *Commodity Taxes in India*, Chugh Publications, Allahabad, 1981.

Agarwala, S.K., *All India Sales Tax Manual,* Central Law Agency, Allahabad, 1952.

Andley, K.K. and Sundharam, K.P.M., *Public Economic and Public Finance*, Ratan Prakashan, Agra, 1979.

Bhargava, R.N., *Public Finance*, George Allen and Unwin Ltd., London, 1954.

Bhatia, H.L., *Centre-State Financial Relations in India*, Abhinav Publications, New Delhi, 1979.

——— *Public Finance*, Vikas Publishing House (P) Ltd., New Delhi, 1983.

Bhoothalingam, S., *Review of Sales Tax in Andhra Pradesh*, NCAER, New Delhi, 1971.

Browning, Edger K. and Browning, Jacquenleme M., *Public Finance and Price System*, Macmillan Publishing Company, New York, 1979.

Buehler, A.G., *General Sales Taxation*, Business Course, New York, 1932.

Burton, J.H., *How to Appeal Against Tax Assessments*, A. Jordan Publications, London, 1950.

Chaturvedi, K.R., *The Central Sales Tax Law*, Eastern Law House (P) Ltd., Calcutta, 1965.

——— *The Principles of Sales Tax Laws*, Eastern Law House (P) Ltd., Calcutta, 1967.

Chelliah, Raja, J., *Fiscal Policy in Underdeveloped Countries* (with special reference to India), 1960.

Cnossen, Sijbren, *Excise System—A Global Study of the Selective Taxation of Goods and Services*, The John Hopkins University Press, Baltimore and London, 1977.

Dalton Hug, *Principles of Public Finance*, Allied Publishers (P) Ltd., New Delhi, 1978.

De Marco, De viti Antonio, *First Principles of Public Finance*, Jonathan Cape, London, 1950.

Due, John F., *Indirect Taxation in Developing Economies*, The John Hopkins Press, Baltimore and London, 1970.

———, *Provincial Retail Sales Taxes in Canada*, Canadian Tax Foundation, Toronto, 1953.

———, *Sales Taxation*, Routledge and Kegan Paul, London, 1957.

———, *State Sales Tax Administration*, Public Administration Service, Illinois, 1963.

———, *The General Manufacturer Sales Tax in Canada*, Canadian Tax Foundation, Toronto, 1951.

Elliot, H.M., *History of India*, Rubner and Company, London, 1875.

Framption, George T. and Smith, Numa R., *Law and Contemporary Problems*, Duke University School of Law, 1941.

Gandhi, V.P., *Tax Burden in Indian Agriculture*, The Law School of Harvard University, Cambridge, 1965.

Ghosh, A.B., *Sales Tax in India*, Ranjit Printers, Delhi School of Economics, Delhi, 1954.

Groves, H.M., *Financing Government*, Henry Holt and Rinehart Company, New York, 1968.

Gupta, B.N., *Indian Federal Finance and Budgetary Policy*, Chaitanya Publishing House, Allahabad, 1970.

Gupta, Das B., *Provincial Taxation Under Autonomy*, Oxford University Press, London, 1948.

Hanson, J.L., *A Dictionary of Economic and Commerce*, London 1977.

Hicks, Ursula K., *Development Finances—Planning and Control Public Finance*, Cambridge University Press, London, 1965.

Hornby, Gatenby and Wakefield, *The Advance Learners' Dictionary of Current English*, Oxford University Press, 1974.

Hultzsch, E., *South Indian Inscriptions*, Government Press, Madras, 1891, Vol. II.

Indian Law Institute, *Inter-State Trade Barriers and Sales Tax Laws in India*, N.M. Tripathi Private Ltd., Bombay 1962.

Jacoby, N.H., *Retail Sales Taxation*, Commerce Clearing House, Chicago, 1938.

Jain, J.K., *Law of Sales and Purchase Tax in Rajasthan*, Anand Prakashan, Jaipur, 1980.

Jain, M.L., *Rajasthan Sales Tax Act, 1954*, P.K. Prakashan, Jaipur, 1982.

Jain, Rajendra, *State Taxation in India*, Progress Publishers, Bhopal, 1972.

Kangle, R.P., *The Kautilya Arthasastra—A Study*—Part III, University of Bombay, Bombay, 1965.

Khaitan, B.P., *Evolution of Sales Tax in India*, National Law Publications, Indore, 1963.

Kumar, D., *Search and Seizure*, Jaipur Printers, Jaipur, 1971.

Lakdawala, D.T., and Nambiar, K.V., *Commodity Taxation in India*, Sardar Patel Institute of Economics and Research, Ahmedabad, 1972.

Lokanathan, P.S., *Sales Tax System in Andhra Pradesh*—A Review NCAER, New Delhi, 1963.

Mahler, Jr. Walter W., *Sales and Excise Taxation in India*, Orient Longman Ltd., New Delhi, 1970.

Malik, P.L., *Uttar Pradesh Sales Tax Act, 1948*, Eastern Book Company, Lucknow, 1982.

Mathur, Saxena, *Public Economics*, Jai Prakashnath and Co., Meerut, 1958.

Moak, L.L. and Cown, F., *Administration of Local Sales and Use Taxes*, Municipal Finance Officers Association, Chicago, 1961.

Mookerje, Radha Kumud, *Chandra Gupta Maurya and His Times*, Motilal Banarsi Das, Delhi, 1966.

Musgrave, R.A., *The Theory of Public Finance*, Mcgraw Hill, New York, 1959.

National Industrial Conference Board, *General Sales or Turnover Taxation*, N.I.C.B. New York, 1932.

National Institute of Public Finance and Policy, *Sales Tax System in Bihar*, Somaiya Publications Pvt. Ltd., Bombay, 1981.

N.C A.E.R., *Incidence of Taxation in Gujarat*, New Delhi, 1970.

——, *Incidence of Taxation in Mysore State*, New Delhi, 1972.

Oster, C.V., *State Retail Sales Taxation*, Bureau of Business Research, Ohio State University, Columbus, Ohio, 1957.

Plank, E.H., *Public Finance*, Richard D. Irwin, Illinois, 1953.

Pokharana, N.L., *Current Rajasthan Taxation Manual*, Asha Publishers, Ajmer, 1982.

Poole Kenyon E., *Public Finance and Economic Welfare*, Rinehart & Company, New York, III Edition.

Pullani, M L., *Haryana General Sales Tax Act with Rules*, Legal Book House, Chandigarh, 1984.

Purorbit, M C., *Sales Taxation in India*, S. Chand and Co. Pvt. Ltd., New Delhi, 1975.

Rai, Champat, *Law and Practice of Sales Tax in India*, K. Rai and Company, Delhi, 1953.

Rao, Hemalata, *Centre.-State Financial Relations*, Allied Publishers (P) Ltd., New Delhi, 1981.

Rate of Sales Tax in the Northern States, All India Manufacturers' Organisation, Delhi, 1982.

Rayudu, Venkata A., *Taxation and Economic Development in India*, Chugh Publications, Allahabad, 1985.

Sastri, K.V.S., *Federal-State Fiscal Relations in India*, Oxford University Press, London, 1966.

Seligman, E.R.A., *The Shifting and Incidence of Taxation*, Columbia University Press, New York, 1932.

Sharp, L.S., *Federal Finance in the Coming Decade*, New York, 1941.

Shoup and Haig, *The Sales Tax in American States*, Columbia University Press, New York, 1934.

Singh, S.D., *Principles and Law of Sales Tax*, Eastern Book Co. Lucknow, 1973.

Singh, Shiv Kumar, *Central Excise Duties and Economic Development of India*, S. Chand and Co. Ltd., New Delhi, 1977.

Smith Adam, *Wealth of Nations*, The Modern Library, Random House, New York, 1937.

Srivastava, G.K , *Commercial Taxes in India*, Pitaliya Publications, Jaipur, 1975.

Thimmaiah, G., *Perspectives on Tax Design and Tax Reform*, Ashish Publishing House, New Delhi, 1984.

Tikka, T.R., *A Study of Punjab Sales Tax Act and Central Sales Tax*, Pradeep Publications, Jalandhar, 1985.

The Constitution of India, Eastern Book Company, Lucknow, 1977.

Tripathy, R.N., *Public Finance in Underdeveloped Countries*,

Sterling Publishers Pvt. Ltd., New Delhi, 1985.

Vasisht, W.C. *A Chrono Legal Study of the Punjab General Sales Tax Act*, Neelam Publishers, Jullundur, 1981.

Verma, S.R. and Suri, A.M., *East Punjab General Sales Tax Act*, Law Reporter Press, Simla, 1949.

Wheare, K.C., *Federal Government*, Oxford University Press, London, 1968.

Articles

Agarwal, A.K., "Replacement of Sales Tax by Additional Duties of Excise", *Southern Economist*, May 15, 1982.

Ahmed Mahfooz, "A Cost of Tax Collection in India", *Economic and Political Weekly*, Vol. III, No. 7, February 17, 1968.

Ansari, M.M., "Resources Mobilisation and Cost Efficiency of the States Taxes", *Margin*, Vol. 15, No. 2, January, 1983.

Bhargava, P.K., "Additional Resources for Development of Uttar Pradesh", in Sinha and Mishra : *Financing of State Plans*, Sterling Publishers (P) Ltd., New Delhi, 1984.

———, "Sales Tax : The State Milch Cow", *Eastern Economist*, October 20, 1967.

———, "Tax Policy in a Developing Economy—Need for Greater Incentives", *Capital*, Sept. 1968.

Bhargava, R.N., "The Theory of Federal Finance", *The Economic Journal*, March 1953.

Chandrasekhar, S., "Inter-State Disparities of Tax Incidence in India", *Economic and Political Weekly*, June, 1968.

———, "Sales Tax in Andhra Pradesh", *Southern Economic Review*, Vol. III, No. 3, 1974.

Chelliah, Raja. J. "Reform of Sales Tax", *The Economic Times*, Sept., 11, 12, 1983.

Cnossen Sijbren, "The Role and Structure of Sales Tax and Excise Systems", *Finance and Development*, I.M.F., March 1975.

Due, J.F., "Incidence of General Sales Tax" *Public Finance*, Vol. 5, 1950.

Friedlander, A.F., "Indirect Taxes and Relative Prices", *Quarterly Journal of Economics*, Vol. 31, Feb. 1967.

"Formulae to Allay Fear over ST Replacement" *Hindustan*

Times, Delhi, May 24, 1983.

Gopal, M.H., "Tax Administration as a Factor in Economic Growth in India", *Southern Economic Review*, Vol. I, April 1972.

Goswami, B.P., "Expanding Scope of General Sales Taxes", *Southern Economist*, Jan. 26, 1972.

———, "The Role of Sales Tax in State Finances", *Southern Economists*, April 15, 1972.

Kaushik Basu, "Inflation and Evasion", *Economic and Political Weekly*, March 24, 1984.

Lakdawala, D.T., "Plan Finance in Federal Eeonomy", *Yogana*, May 16, 1979.

———, "Value Added Tax", *The Indian Economic Journal*, No. 2, October-December 1976.

Mcgrew, J.W., "Effect of a food Exemption on the Incidence of Retail Sales Tax", *National Tax Journal*, Vol. II, 1949.

Menon Ramesh, "Sales Tax—The New Haven", *India Today*, October 31, 1983.

"MODVAT will benefit consumers", *The Economic Times*, March 2, 1986.

Nath Shyam, "Incidence of Indirect Taxation in Rajasthan", *Margin*, Vo. 12, No. 3, April 1980.

———, "Level Growth and Composition of the Tax System in Rajasthan", *Rajasthan Economic Journal*, Vo. 1, January, 1977.

Oster, C.V. and D. Lynn Arther, "Compliance Costs and the Ohio Axle Mile Tax—A case study", *National Tax Journal*, June 1955.

Pahariya, B.L., "Inter-State Financial Relation and Dependence in India", *Manthan*, April 1980.

Purohit, M.C., "Incidence of Sales Tax : An Empirical Analysis", *Indian Journal of Economics*, Vol. II, October, 1971.

———, "Structure of Sales Taxes in India", *Economic and Political Weekly*, Vol. No. XVII, No. 34, August 21, 1982.

Rao, V.K.R.V., "Centre-State Financial Relations in India", *Institute for Social and Economic Changes, Staff Paper*, No. 7, 1953.

Sarkar, Sunil Rajan, "Sales Tax Has a History in India", *Indian Journal of Economics*, Vol. 34, October 1953.

Sarvane, M., "Tax on Value Added for India : Issues and

Alternatives", *Reserve Bank of India Bulletin*, March 1976.

Sharma, R.S , "Rajasthan ST—A case study", *Financial Express* Sept. 13, 1981.

——, "Rate Structure and Its Executions Under Rajasthan Sales Tax Act", *Tax Guide*, Ganga Nagar, August 1981.

Singh Balgit, "An Approach to States Taxes", in Joshi M. *Mobilisation of States Resources*, Impex India, New Delhi, 1967.

Srivastava, G.K., "Incidence of Commercial Taxes in Rajasthan", *Eastern Economist*, June 7, 1974.

Toye, J.F.J., "How Progressive are Indian Consumption Taxes" *Economic and Political Weekly*, March 20, 1976.

"Traders Protest Against Sales Tax Ordinance", *Capital*, April 12, 1956.

Tress, R.C., "Trend in Public Finance", *Lloyd Bank Review*, No. 29, July 1953.

"U.P. Tax Relief on Farm Equipment", *Hindustan Times*, January 9, 1985.

Government Publications

—— *Annual Administrative Report*, Excise and Taxation Department, Haryana (1976 to 1984).

—— *Aunual Administrative Report*, of Sales Tax Department, Uttar Pradesh, Lucknow, (1982-83).

—— *Budget Estimates of Different States* (1978 to 1984).

—— *Census of India*, 1971 and 1981.

—— *Estimated Net Domestic Products*, Central Statistical Organisation, 1984.

Government of Bombay, *Report of Sales Tax Enquiry Committee*, Central Press, Bombay, 1958.

Government of India, *Report of the Indirect Taxation and Enquiry Commission*, 1953-54.

Government of India, *Report of the Indirect Taxation Enquiry*, Part II, January, 1978.

Government of India, *Twelfth Report*, Law Commission of India, Ministry of Law, 1968.

Government of India *Tripathi Committee Report*, Ministry of Finance, 1983.

Government of Punjab, *Survey and Analysis of General Sales*

Tax in Patiala District (1960-61), Economic and Statistical Organisation, Chandigarh, 1963.

Government of Punjab, *Public Finance*, Economic'and Statistics Adviser, Chandigarh.

Government of Uttar Pradesh, *Taxation and Enquiry Committee*, Uttar Pradesh, 1974.

——— Report, *Facts and Figure at Glance* (1983-84) Punjab Excise and Taxation Department, Punjab, Patiala.

Report, The Committee for Drafting the Rajasthan Sales Tax Bill, Government of Rajasthan, 1973.

——— *Reserve Bank of India*, *Bulletins* (Monthly).

——— *Tales Tax Rate List*, Government of Uttar Pradesh, Lucknow, 1983.

——— *Sales Tax Acts and Rules* of Rajasthan, Uttar Pradesh, Haryana and Punjab.

——— *Statistical Abstract*, Commercial Taxes Department, Rajasthan (1976 to 1984).

——— *Statistical Abstracts*, Directorate of Economics and Statistics, Rajasthan (1982 to 1984).